BUDDHIST
INDIA
REDISCOVERED

BUDDHIST INDIA REDISCOVERED

ARUNA DESHPANDE

JAICO PUBLISHING HOUSE
Ahmedabad Bangalore Bhopal Bhubaneswar Chennai
Delhi Hyderabad Kolkata Lucknow Mumbai

Published by Jaico Publishing House
A-2 Jash Chambers, 7-A Sir Phirozshah Mehta Road
Fort, Mumbai - 400 001
jaicopub@jaicobooks.com
www.jaicobooks.com

© Aruna Deshpande

BUDDHIST INDIA REDISCOVERED
ISBN 978-81-8495-247-6

First Jaico Impression: 2013

No part of this book may be reproduced or utilized in
any form or by any means, electronic or
mechanical including photocopying, recording or by any
information storage and retrieval system,
without permission in writing from the publishers.

Printed by

TERRORISM DIVIDES THE WORLD
TOURISM UNITES THE WORLD

Buddhism

The path of blissful living . . .

The path of eternal love . . .

The path of profound truth . . .

and above all

*The path showing how
to live life in TOTALITY*

Bhagwan Buddha is more relevant today than ever.

"Go monks, and travel for the welfare and happiness of the people, out of compassion for the world, for the benefit and welfare of happiness of gods and men. No two of you go the same way. Teach the doctrine, monks, which is fine in its beginning, middle and end, with its meaning and later, sheer the whole and, proclaim the pure holy life. There are beings, naturally of little passion, which are languishing for lack of hearing the Doctrine; they will understand it."

With these words, the Buddha dispatched the first 60 monks from Sarnath, he had converted and ordained after his Enlightenment at Bodh Gaya.

Therefore, sending his followers to preach his Dhamma was the start of Buddhist tourism, credited to Buddha himself.

Buddham Sharanam Gacchami

Visit India – The Holy Land of Many Gods

My efforts are dedicated to my husband,

Jagdish

Who found peace in nirvana than on this earth

CONTENTS

ACKNOWLEDGEMENTS		XIII
FOREWORD		XVII
1.	THE WONDER THAT IS INDIA	1-13
2.	SITES OF ASHOKAN EDICTS & PILLARS	15-21
3.	ATTHAMAHATHANANI – Lumbini – Bodh – Gaya – Sarnath – Kushinagar – Sravasti – Sankisa – Rajgir and Vaishali	23-83
4.	ANDHRA PRADHESH	85-115
5.	GUJARAT	117-133
6.	HARYANA	135-139
7.	HIMACHAL PRADESH	141-162
8.	JAMMU AND KASHMIR	163-196
9.	KARNATAKA	197-204
10.	KERALA	205-208
11.	MADHYA PRADESH AND CHHATTISGARH	209-222
12.	MAHARASHTRA	223-262
13.	NORTH-EASTERN STATES	263-274
14.	ORISSA	275-306

15.	PUNJAB	307-312
16.	RAJASTHAN	313-316
17.	SIKKIM	317-344
18.	TAMIL NADU	345-351
19.	WEST BENGAL	353-365
APPENDIX 1		367-368
APPENDIX 2		369-370
APPENDIX 3		371-376
GLOSSARY		377-381

ACKNOWLEDGEMENTS

Buddhist India Rediscovered is a compilation of Buddhist sites (including caves, monasteries, temples and archaeological sites) in India from a tourism point of view.

I have no regrets confessing that I am not a historian or an archaeologist, a research student, or an intellectual, but a common citizen of India who is very much in love with her country.

Having worked with travel agents and tour operators Trade Wings Limited in Mumbai for 20 years, I had several opportunities to travel and interact with many kinds of people. Over a period of time, I developed the habit of collecting and jotting down all the interesting information I gleaned from my travels and rewriting it in simple words to promote tourism.

I thank M/S Jaico Publishing House for the great success my first two books – *India: A Travel Guide* and *India: A Divine Destination* – have achieved.

My profession, tourism promotion, for which traveling was indispensable has now become my passion. What people need now is the chance to travel. Secular growth unites people across countries and continents, and what better way to make people meet and get to know each other and their cultures than to promote tourism.

Today, the entire world is looking for peace, peace through religions, amity and the brotherhood of nations and a lot of attention is focussed on Buddha Dhamma. India is the birthplace of Buddha and Buddhism. Buddha made known to us the four Noble Truths and the eightfold path of righteousness. It was he who taught us the sanctity of life and to strive for Nirvana as the ultimate goal. India is the only country to witness Buddhahood with the help of temples, monuments, caves, structural remains etc. India, where this great teacher of humanity was born, still bears witness to his holy life, and a visit to the Buddhist places of pilgrimages can uplift one's mind and soul.

Many books are available on Atthamathathanani, i.e. eight places of divine significance declared by Buddha himself, written by Indian as well as by foreign authors. But apart from known places, there are many sites which still need the attention and care of the historians and archaeologists. A few sites, neglected as they are, have fallen to ruins due to the rentless attack of nature and will be lost, if we do not take immediate action, forever. I have not yet come across any book which has the information of all Buddhist sites from all over India in a single book. Since, the purpose of the book is to provide 'the whereabouts' (which I could collect so far) of the sites which might arouse the interest of the readers, historians, researchers and archaeologists.

While traveling across the country to collect information, a few people were very helpful but some were just not ready to help. We inherit the Guru Shishya parampara, knowledge should be preserved and spread for the benefit of the mankind. Many a times, I had to stop writing due to uncertainty and non-cooperation from officials and educationalists. I must mention here my colleague Mr. Sidharth, an activist from Haryana, who is running a campaign 'Save Buddha, Save the Stupa' (refer www.thebuddhistforum.com). His continuous moral support has helped me bring this book to the final stage of print.

I must thank Mr. Shirodkar from Kolhapur for his careful reading and suggestions; Ms. Shipa Wadekar from Pune, who traveled with me and provided photos; Mr. PP Ramachandra, from Mumbai for helping me access rare books from Asiatic Society in Mumbai, and many others who I met met while traveling. And my friends and relatives can now finally take a breath of peace, because for the last five years all I could talk about was the Buddha.

The book is blessed by His Holiness the Dalai Lama who has kindly written a beautiful Foreword for this book. I will carry a debt of gratitude for the office of His Holiness, Ms. Gary Dolma from Tibetan Parliament – Dharamshala and Mr. Tenzin Gelek from the scrutiny committee of the office of His Holiness.

And finally, I would like to thank to M/S Jaico Publishing House not only for ensuring the great success of my first two books – *India: A Travel Guide* and *India: A Divine Destination* – but also for helping this book, Buddhist India Rediscovered, reach the readers.

India is not a country, but a continent. I do not claim that this book is the final word on Buddhist sites in India. There are many sites still unknown to me. I would be grateful if anyone would share with me any information that would help me update the book. Do get in touch with me at arunadesh@gmail.com

Buddham Sharanam Gacchami

THE DALAI LAMA

FOREWORD

Like every Tibetan, I grew up regarding India as a holy land, the source of the Buddhist culture and wisdom brought to Tibet centuries ago by Indian saints and seers. As a young monk studying Buddhism, I longed to make a pilgrimage there. I was first able to fulfill this ambition when I was invited to India in 1956 to participate in celebrations of the 2500th Buddha Jayanti. Finally gazing at the seat of enlightenment, beneath the Bodhi Tree, I was profoundly moved. I recalled Shakyamuni Buddha's great accomplishment in this place and reflected on his overwhelming kindness to all sentient beings. Not only had he achieved perfection himself, but he also revealed that each of us has the potential to do the same.

Many people know that the Buddha attained enlightenment and taught in India more than 2500 years ago. Not so many are aware of how widely the practice and study of his teachings flourished in India in the centuries after he lived. Evidence of this can be found today in the remains of Buddhist monuments that dot the Indian landscape, and also in the living Buddhist traditions of South-east, Central and East Asia, all of which look to India with reverence as the land of the Buddha.

In this book, Buddhist India – Rediscovered, Aruna Deshpande has compiled a remarkably thorough catalogue of India's Buddhist sites that illustrates how widespread Buddhist communities once were throughout the country. She records not only the well known places of pilgrimage, such as Bodhgaya, Sarnath and Kushinagar, but also those more obscure places where the remains of monasteries, stupas and Ashokan edicts have been excavated. Whether their interest is in history and culture or Buddhist pilgrimage, I am sure many readers will find this work of great value.

April 21, 2011

1

THE WONDER THAT IS INDIA

India is a land of stupendous dimensions — colourful, exotic, traditional, and modern. India is a land of contrasts, conundrums, mysteries, and wonders. India is kitsch and class. In India, there is a constant interplay of religion and secularism, simple living and regal splendour, devotion and patriotism, yet the people are absorbing, all-compassing, and friendly. A land steeped in spirituality where every grain of sand is sacred, India is also a pioneer in science and technology and a nuclear power to reckon with.

To the Indians themselves, their country was long known as 'Jambudvipa' (the continent of the Jamboo tree), or 'Bharat Varsha', the land of ancient king and emperor Bharata, the son of Dushyanta of Kalidasa's *Shankutala* fame. He was the great unifier of the land from north to south and east to west, in a remote antiquity.

The names 'India' and 'Hindustan' (the land of Hindus) are both of foreign origin. 'India' was the land of the Indus river, so designated by the Greeks who came with Alexander in the fourth century BC. The Greeks, dropped the hard aspirates, and called the Hindus 'Indof' or 'Ivooi'. Three centuries before the Greeks came here, the ancient Persians transformed the old Indian name 'Sindhu' into 'Hindu' over time, and the Greeks in their turn dropped the 'h' and made it plain 'Indus'. The Muslim conquerors were followers of the Persian tradition. So they preferred to rename India 'Hindustan' (the abode of Hindus).

Geography

Location: 8°4' and 37°6' north latitude; 68°7' and 97°25' east longitude

◀ Roses in the beautiful Shalimar gardens, Srinagar, Kashmir

Distance: North-South – 3,214 km; East-West – 2,933 km
Length of coastal line: 15,200 km

Climate
India has three main seasons:

Summer (April to June)
During the summer, the mountain and hilly areas are cool and pleasant. Barmar in Rajasthan remains the hottest, with the temperature shooting up to 50°C during the day time.

Rainy or Monsoon (June to October)
Mawsyanram in Assam is the wettest place in the world which receives 1,187 cm rainfall, and the driest place is Jaisalmer in Rajasthan, which receives only 10 cm rainfall in a year.

Winter (October to March)
The Himalayan regions are the coldest, particularly Drass and Kargil in Ladakh, where the temperature falls below 4°C.

Flora
India's landscape, characterised by an amazing variety of latitudes and altitudes, temperature and moisture, produces a corresponponding variety in flora and fauna. Complex physiographic, climatic and geographical conditions have given rise to as many as 30,000 species of plants in the country, ranging from thorny bushes to evergreen forests.

Fauna
India is a unique sub-continent. It has vast variations in geography, climate, and vegetation across the country. As a consequence, there is a high degree of diversity in habitat and wildlife. The numbers of species that inhabit India and its dependencies is very large, more than the number of species found through the whole of Europe.

As per Ministry of Tourism Report 2012, India has around 102 national parks and 441 sanctuaries. While some are not easily accessible, many have excellent facilities for visitors. Depending on the area and terrain, wildlife watching can be quite exciting.

Languages

India's cultural population comprises a fifth of the whole human race, including several races and people belonging to all stages and states of social evolution and civilisation. India embraces a multitude of languages, manners and customs, cults and cultures of the most diverse kinds. Many languages with varied dialects have their origins here.

Sanskrit is the language of India's soul. Sanskrit was the formative, creative, national language of India in the past. The Dravidian languages are spoken mainly in the southern part of India, which includes Tamil Nadu, Puducherry, Karnataka, Kerala, and Andhra Pradesh.

The Indian Constitution recognises 22 languages, according to each region and its special linguistic flavour. These are Assamese, Bengali, Bodo, Dongri, Gujarati, Hindi, Kannada, Kashmiri, Konkani, Maithili, Malayalam, Manipuri, Marathi, Nepali, Oriya, Punjabi, Sanskrit, Sansthali, Sindhi, Tamil, Telugu, and Urdu. Hindi is the main link language.

The Polity

India, a sovereign socialist secular democratic republic, is governed by the Constitution of India, adopted by the Constituent Assembly on November 26, 1949 and put into force on January 26, 1950. The Constitution of India provides for a single and uniform citizenship for the whole country.

The National Emblem: The state emblem of India is an adaptation of the Sarnath Lion, the Capital of Ashoka the Emperor, as preserved in the Sarnath Museum. The Government adopted the emblem on January 26, 1950 the day when India became a Republic.

The National Flag: The national flag is a horizontal tri-colour of deep saffron (representing courage and sacrifice) at the top, white (peace and truth) in the middle, and green (faith and chivalry) at the bottom, all three colours are in equal proportion. In the center is the Chakra (a wheel), in navy blue. The Chakra appears on the abacus of the Sarnath Lion. The design of the National Flag was adopted by the Constituent Assembly of India on July 22, 1947. Its use and display are regulated by a code.

The National Anthem: Rabindranath Tagore's song *Jana Gana Mana* was adopted by the Constituent Assembly as the National Anthem of India on January 24, 1950 and gave *Vande Mataram* the equal honour of being national song. It was first sung on December 27, 1911 at the Kolkata session of the Indian National Congress.

National Calendar: At the time of Independence, the Government of India followed the Gregorian calendar based on the Christian era.

The Hindu calendar used in ancient times has undergone many changes in the process of realisation, and today there are several regional Indian calendars. Most of these calendars are inherited from a system first enunciated in the scriptures called *Vedanga Jyotish of Lagadha*. The Vikrama and Shalivahana calendar is most widely used in India. The Vikrama calendar is followed in western and northern India, and the Shaliavahana or Saka is followed in Andhra Pradesh, Karnataka, Maharashtra, and Goa.

The periods in the Shalivahana or Saka calendar correspond with dates in the Gregorian calendar as below:

Chaitra	March 22/21
Vaishaka	April 21
Jyaistha	May 22
Asadha	June 22
Sravana	July 23
Bhadrapada	August 23
Asvina	September 23
Kartika	October 23

Margasirsa	November 22
Pausa	December 22
Magha	January 21
Phalguna	February 20

India's Artistic Heritage

Indian art is considered to inspire and show the way towards a fulfilling spiritual life. Art is the natural expression of one's devotion. Indian culture is filled with poetry, drama, sculpture, painting, music and dance as an integral part of worship. These art forms are filled with beauty and are inspired by life and nature. The art of India has its own distinct identity, which makes it stand apart from the art of the rest of the world, while within the country, diverse art forms reveal features common with art from faraway parts of the country. From the *Sama Veda*, we learn that there are 64 forms of art in India.

The cultural unity of India has its own distinctive expression. The three forms of visual arts (drawing, painting, sculpture), and the performing arts (music, dance and drama) are united in their common aim to fulfil the spiritual aspirations of Indian culture.

Music, dance, and drama formed one inseparable whole in ancient India. Though, through the ages, various forms and styles of these art forms have developed, they preserve their inherent unity of purpose, aspiration, and frequently even the theme. Indian music has developed within a complex interaction between people of

▲ The tradition of Bharatnatyam has been preserved for centuries

different races and cultures. Evidence of beautiful paintings and sculptures are still intact in temples and caves throughout India.

Fairs and Festivals

The colourful mosaic of Indian festival and fairs – as diverse as the land – is an expression of the spirit of community celebrations, essential in any country. Observed with enthusiasm and gaiety, Indian festivals are like gems, glittering in the crown of Indian culture. Through the year, these festivals are vibrant interludes in the mundane routine of life. Tourism Department of Government of India and tourism departments of all major Indian states organise festivals throughout the year.

How to Reach India

The time difference in India is GMT + 5 hours in winter, and 4 hours in the summer.

Throughout India, there is only one Indian Standard Time with no change in winter or summer.

The best time to visit India is between October and March. The Indian tourism ministry has adopted the ancient Sanskrit dictum – *Atithi Devo Bhava*, which is translated as, 'Treat a guest as though he were God Himself'.

Before Coming to India

Passports: All travellers to India must possess a valid passport, except nationals of Nepal, Bhutan and Bangladesh, who will need to carry identification papers.

Visas: All foreign tourists to India, except nationals of Nepal, Bhutan, and Bangladesh, must possess a valid visa. A tourist visa is valid for three to six months.

Travel Insurance: Take a travel/medical insurance policy covering theft and loss of valuables before coming to India.

Airports

The international airports in the metro cities offer a range of services ensuring that the traveller on a business trip can continue working while waiting to board an international flight or when transferring from one international flight to another.

All airports have 'left luggage' facilities, porters and metered taxis and pre-paid taxis.

Taxis: There are pre-paid taxi counters in the arrival area of all major airports.

Coaches: There are coach services for transfer to the city at most airport terminals.

Auto Rickshaws: They carry up to three passengers and are cheaper than cabs.

Duty-free items: Duty-free items one may bring to India, include personal effects, like clothing and other articles but not commercial merchandise.

India by Air

There are several airlines that fly to domestic destinations. Indian is the biggest domestic airline and offers special travel packages – Discover India fare and India Wonderfare (subject to change). Refer to www.indiatourism.com for updated information.

India by Rail

The Indian Railways, which is the second largest rail network in the world, runs a gigantic, modern and organised transportation system that connects the metros to most major and minor destinations within India.

Many reservation offices in India have a separate counter for foreign tourists aided by a Tourist Guide Counter. Indrail Passes make flexible and budgeted travel possible. Trains like the Rajdhani Express and the Shatabdi Express ensure speedy transportation within the country. Toy trains link cities to a few hill stations and it is a pleasant experience to be taken on such a picturesque journey. Travel by special tourist trains like the Palace on Wheels, which gives you the opportunity to experience the bygone era of the Indian monarchy.

Recently, the Indian Railway introduced the Mahaparinirvana

Express covering important Buddhist sites. It is a seven nights and eight days journey from New Delhi back to New Delhi, and takes you to Bodh Gaya, Nalanda, Varanasi (Sarnath), Gorakhpur (Lumbini), Sravasti, and Agra. For details refer to www.railtourismindia.com

India by Road

India is well connected from east to west and north to south by national highways, and state highways and state roads within the state. A variety of vehicles ranging from luxury coaches, cars, state transport buses, private coach operators, taxis, three-wheelers, prepaid taxis, and car rental facilities are easily available in India. Tourists who wish to travel in India in their own cars, coaches, or trailers often bring their vehicles over land, or via overseas.

Accommodation

The diversity of accommodation in India ranges from deluxe hotels comparable to the world's most luxurious hotels, to budget hotels affordable by the most modest tourist.

Conferences: With the large number of conference facilities now available in India, the country has become one of the major convention destinations in Asia. New Delhi is the major venue, with its vast facilities for holding conferences and exhibitions in major convention halls in hotels, in auditoria, special complexes, stadiums and government exhibition grounds.

Cuisines: Visitors will be amazed at the variety of Indian cuisine, so different from the popular, if erroneous, impression of all Indian food being just curry. In truth, each region has its own cuisine, and these are carefully researched and created in restaurants that offer both the cuisine in its authentic form as well as the right ambience to heighten the dining experience. In all metro cities, and most major towns, there is a wide choice of international foods available.

Tourist Offices

Government of India Tourist offices are located in major metro cities. Every State government also runs its own tourist office in almost all important cities and major tourist sites. Trained English and foreign language speaking guides are available at a fixed rate from all important tourist offices.

Tourism Packages

Adventure Tourism: One of India's greatest attractions is its outdoors — the highest mountains in the world, immense deserts, mangrove estuaries, heavy forests, riverine plains and miles and miles of beaches along a changing coastline. It is, therefore natural, that India offers the traveller diverse facilities for adventure sports like trekking, mountaineering, water sports, sailing, parasailing, snorkelling, deep sea diving etc.

Medical Tourism: India is also called the land of healing. Contemporary India is second to none when it comes to providing great health care facilities. Medical help in India is now comparable to the best in the world. India is an ideal stop for various kinds of medical packages because it offers world-class hospitals, state-of-the-art technology, competent doctors, professional management, top quality nurses, and paramedical staff.

Besides advancement in various systems of modern medicine, India also has a rich heritage in the areas of traditional or natural medicines. Alternative or traditional systems of medicine operate on the principles of holism – i.e. they consider the human body as the synthesis of its physical, mental, and spiritual dimensions.

Rural Tourism: Almost seven million villages that have built up around rivers, lakes, deserts, hills and mountains offer an experience-oriented rural tourism. Predominantly based in a natural environment, rural tourism meshes well with the best seasons and local events.

Religious Tourism: All major religions in India have their own pilgrimage sites, heroes, and legends. This pull of religion attracts rural, urban, and an international flow of devotees and pilgrims to the religious centers of India. Indian spirituality, philosophy, and thoughts have also transcended borders. From time immemorial, the West has been attracted by the beauty of Indian spirituality. Yoga, meditation, and ancient Indian philosophy are now well established in other countries. With the advent of modern and technological advances in media channels, information about our spiritual and religious places attracts tourists from the rest of the world.

▲ The palaquin ceremony in the Mahalaxmi Temple attracts crowds of devotees to Kolhapur

Museums and Art Galleries

A storehouse of history and culture, India has inherited a bounty of artefacts and monuments, symbolising its cultural and historical heritage. Its museums and art galleries offer a glimpse into its past, spanning a history of 5,000 years under one spacious roof. In addition to general museums, there are specific museums such as museums of science, natural history, ethnography, tribal art, textile and dolls, taking visitors across a journey spanning ancient civilisations to imperial dynasties.

Shopping

Shopping is an adventure of a vibrant kind in India. India's vast cultural diversity has resulted in a treasure trove of handicrafts for the discerning shopper, in a truly remarkable variety of styles and prices. Every handicraft sold in the country is made by tightly knit communities, by using zealously guarded traditional methods passed down over the centuries from father to son. Like some other aspects of India, its shopping experience is full of contrasts. Here, chaotic and irresistible medieval-era like shops in narrow lanes with a churning mass of cyclists, buses and deafening honks of fast-paced cars are situated right next to sprawling swanky modern shopping malls.

▲ Potpourri of handcrafted handicraft

India's potpourri of shopping choices include vividly coloured garments, textiles, metalwork, jewellery, furniture, brass, silver, copper, gold, silks and brocades, leather goods, carpets and an unending list of must-haves. With over a decade of liberalisation tucked under its belt, India is also home to the latest in couture.

2

SITES OF ASHOKAN EDICTS & PILLARS

Emperor Ashoka (304-232 BC) is rightly looked upon as the first great royal patron of Buddhism. Indeed, it was through his efforts that Buddhism came to occupy the prominent position it did in India and abroad.

Emperor Ashoka, the third king of the Mauryan dynasty, is one of the greatest and most interesting rulers India has ever had. He lived in the third century BC, and according to Pali chronicles, Ashoka ruled for 41 years, from 273-232 BC.

Ashoka was the grandson of Chandragupta Maurya – founder of the Mauryan dynasty. The idea of sustaining an imperial monarchy was lodged and nurtured by his grandfather and father through an ever-growing empire, which Ashoka was expected to extend. Ashoka had an empire that commanded all major trade routes in the region. However, he did not have access to the sea, the kingdom of Kalinga stood in his way. Ashoka invaded Kalinga to capture the sea trade route that would have been immensely useful for his huge empire. During that invasion, many thousands of men were killed, several thousands were carried off into captivity and thousands died from the effects of the war. It is well known that this tremendous loss of life proved to be a turning point in the life of Ashoka. He repented starting the war and decided to undertake no further military campaigns. Instead he began to think of religious conquest – of Dhammavijaya. Ashoka was converted to Buddhism by Nyagrodha Sramanera, whereas according to the text *Divyavadana* he was converted to Buddhism by the venerable Samudra. Thus, Ashoka was converted from Candasoka (cruel Ashoka) to Dhaammasoka (religious minded Ashoka).

◄ The heritage monument in Sanchi that exemplifies the magnificence and simplicity of Buddhism

Because of his efforts, and the zeal of indefatigable missionaries, Buddhism started spreading not only throughout India, but also outside India. At one time, one-third of the population of the world was Buddhist. Credit for a large extent of this achievement must be given to Emperor Ashoka.

Sites of Ashokan Edicts

India is the only country that can boast of having the only documented heritage dating back to the third century BC, when King Ashoka commissioned the erection of the pillars with edicts that spoke of the Buddhist faith. He started documenting the main teachings of Buddhism on pillars. He travelled and also built stupas over the ash and bone relics of the Buddha. His travels are called Dhammayatras. The stupas are commemorations of his having not only accepted the Dhamma, but of ruling a gigantic kingdom while adhering strictly to the code of ethics taught by Buddha.

The edicts of Ashoka were intended to convey the lofty message of an enlightened seer who believed in eternal good. The edicts show Ashoka as a patron and protector of Buddhism who utilised his sovereignty, extending from the northernmost border to the southernmost limit of India, to spread the doctrine of the Buddha all over the country.

True to the principles of the Master's teachings, Emperor Ashoka was intent on building a *dharmaraja* based on universal wellbeing. The main sources of knowledge we have about him and his activities fall into two categories – literature and archaeology. Of these, the latter, consisting of Ashoka's own inscriptions, constitutes direct sources of his history.

In an inscription, the King is styled as *Devanam priya Priyadarsi raja*, i.e. *'King Priyadarsi, beloved of the gods'*. Identifying this king as Ashoka, has been proved beyond doubt by the discovery of the Maski version of the minor rock edicts which substitutes the name of Ashoka for Priyadarsi.

Major Rock Edicts

Major rock edicts are found closer to larger towns. These larger towns seem to be located at the borders of what used to be the empire. The sites of the rock edicts belong to major settlements, with a population probably more educated than the people of the country side. Only when the folk would go to the sacred places would they encounter the texts, either on a privately chosen date, or on festive occasions.

Major rock edicts are located in Dhauli, Jaugada (Orissa), Girnar (Gujarat), Kalsi (Uttaranchal), Sopara (Maharashtra), Yerragudi (Andhra Pradesh).

Minor Rock Edicts

Minor rock edicts are found in various complete and incomplete sets from Kandahar in Afghanistan to Jaugada in Orissa, from Kalsi at the entrance of the Himalaya valley to Erragudi in Andhra Pradesh. Most of these rocks are easily found in ancient cities that are pilgrimage sites as well. The youngest set are the pillar edicts, inscriptions chiseled on pillars mainly in Uttar Pradesh and the adjoining Nepalese Terai. In some way or the other, all of them seem to be connected either with places of the Buddhist sangha, or were part of an itinerary leading to the birthplace of the Buddha himself. This may explain why some of them are to be found in rather remote areas.

▲ Walking on history: In Siddhapur, this inscription on the floor dates back hundreds of years

Minor rock edicts are found in Ahraura (Uttar Pradesh), Amar Colony (Delhi), Bairat (Rajasthan), Brahmagiri and Gayimath, Jatinga-Ramesyara, Maski, Palkigunda, Sannati, Siddapura, Nittur, Udegolam (Karnataka), Gujarra, Rupnath (Madhya

Pradesh), Rajula Mandagiri, Yerragudi (Andhra Pradesh), Sahasram (Bihar).

Major Pillar Edicts

▲ The elegant and well-proportioned Ashoka's Pillar in west Champaner, Bihar

The earliest monolithic freestanding pillars found in India are those installed by Ashoka. Some have survived in their original place, most others, however, have been shifted to other sites, sometimes repeatedly; some pillars have been deprived of their capitals, others have been demolished either by the vicissitudes of time, or on purpose. The pillars have a certain air of perfection – they are admirably polished, their tapering end gives them elegance, their proportions are well-balanced.

Major Pillar Edicts are found in Kausambi, Mirah, Topra (Uttar Pradesh), Lauriya Araraj, Lauriya Nandangarh, Methia, and Rampura (Bihar).

Minor Pillar Edicts

Minor Pillar Edicts are found in Kausambi, Sarnath (Uttar Pradesh) Sanchi (Madhya Pradesh) and other sites.

Ashokan Pillars are also found in many other sites in India

Commemorative Inscriptions

Commemorative inscriptions are found in Lumbini and Nigliva (Nepal).

Donative Inscriptions

Donative inscriptions are found at Barabar Hills (Bihar).
The inscriptions are of outstanding interest for a study of Ashoka,

one of the greatest personalities in world history, as we can trace the successive stages in the development of his mind.

The last, but historically the oldest set of edicts which has been found so far, generally far removed from habitation sites:

Sahasram	Shahabad district, Bihar
Bairat	60 km north of Jaipur (Now in Asiatic Society – Bengal, Kolkata)
Rupnath	Jabalpur district, Madhya Pradesh
Brahmagiri	Chitradurga district, Karnataka
Jaitinga Ramesvara	Chitradurga district, Karnataka
Siddapur	Chitradurga district, Karnataka
Maski	Raichur district, Karnataka
Erragudi	Kurnool district, Andhra Pradesh
Gavimath	Near Kopal in Raichur district, Karnataka
Palkigundu	Near Gavimath in Raichur district, Karnataka
Rajula Mandagiri	Kurnool district, Andhra Pradesh
Ahraura	40 km south of Varanasi, Uttar Pradesh
Bahapur	Near Srinivaspuri, New Delhi
Pangoraria	Budhani Tehsil, Sehore district, Madhya Pradesh
Nittur	Bellary district, Karnataka
Udegolam	Bellary district, Karnataka
Sannati	Gulbarga district, Karnataka, inscription now in the office of ASI, Hyderabad

3

ATTHAMAHATHANANI

ATTHAMAHATHANANI

ALONG THE FOOTSTEPS OF BUDDHA

Vaishali
Place of second buddhist council

Rajgir
Favourite resort

Sankisa
Where Buddha descended from Heaven

Sravasti
To Heaven and Back

Kushinagar
The Mahaparinirvana

Sarnath
The Wheel of Law

Bodh Gaya
Enlightenment

Lumbini
The Birthplace

In one of his last utterances before his Mahaparinirvana, the Buddha said to Ananda, his favourite attendant,

"There are these four places, Ananda, which the believing man should visit whilst feeling reverence and awe."

"Which are the four places?"

"— The place, Ananda, at which the believing man can say, *'Here the Tathagata was born'*

"— The place, Ananda, at which the believing man can say, *'Here the Tathagata attained to the supreme and perfect insight'*

"— The place, Ananda, at which the believing man can say, *'Here was the kingdom of righteousness set on foot by the Tathagata'*

"— The place, Ananda, at which the believing man can say, *'Here the Tathagata passed finally away in that utter passing away which leaves nothing whatever to remain behind'*."

These sacred sites that were described in such glowing terms by Gautama Buddha are Lumbini, Bodh Gaya, Sarnath, and Kushinagar, which constitute a Buddhist pilgrim's Dhamma or Dharma Yatra.

There are four other sacred shrines, Sravasti, Sankisa, Rajagir, and Vaishali. These places were sanctified by Buddha and were where the Blessed One is said to have performed the 'great miracles'. Together, these eight places are known as *'atthamahathanani'* in Pali, or the eight sacred places of Buddhism.

To the Buddhists, Uttar Pradesh and the Bihar region is particularly sacred, as the Divine One sanctified by His footsteps many of its villages and towns and propounded to the people of this land all His doctrines. Again, in this territory, the Three Great

Councils took place, the earliest Buddhist literature, canonising Buddha's sermons, was written down, and the early philosophical ideas were formulated. The importance of this region in the Buddhist world, even in later years had not lessened. All this was due to the exceptional high standard of learning then, the disciplined life of the residents, and the brilliant achievements of the versatile teachers in its centers of international repute like Nalanda, Uddandapura (also known as Odantapuri), and Vikramshila, from where Buddhist philosophy and religion radiated to the entire Buddhist world, till the Mughal conquest.

In conformity with the high sanctity of this holy land, there grew many Buddhist establishments dotting the entire land. The Chinese traveller, Hiuen–Tsang, travelled extensively in this region, faithfully recording details about more than 40 cherished learning centers with smaller units in the vicinity. His enlightening account of this area is particularly interesting and elaborate.

Lumbini – The Birthplace

Location: 123 km from Gorakhpur via Sonauli

About Lumbini, the Buddha had said, *"Ananda, this place is where Tathagata was born, this is the place which should be visited and seen by a person of devotion and which causes awareness and apprehension of the nature of impermanence. At this place, Ananda, who are on a pilgrimage to (this) shrine, if they should die with devotion in the heart during the course of the pilgrimage, will after (their) death and dissolution of the body be born in a good destination, a fortunate celestial real."* (Mahaparinirvana Sutta)

Situated in the foothills of the Siwalik range, in what is known as the Nepalis Terai, Lumbini – the birth place of Lord Buddha is the first stop on the pilgrimage.

The Buddha Sakyamuni was born in Lumbini on a full moon day, in the month of Vaisakha, in 623 BC or 563 BC. The birth of no other teacher, in the world, has been accompanied by so much rejoicing among the gods as that of Siddhartha who later became Buddha. Every little circumstance surrounding his birth had been foretold and planned. His mother had been his mother in previous incarnations too, as was his father. Those who were to be his companions, even his horse, had shared his fortune in previous births.

Choosing Lumbini as the birth place was no accident either. It was chosen because it was the fairest, most beautiful vale which lay between Gautama's father's small kingdom and that of his mother's father. Lumbini was full of sal trees, flowers and its lake was covered with lotus blooms. A rivulet flowed across the valley.

An unusual incident associated with the birth of Gautama is the wonderful dream which Queen Mahamaya had on the day she conceived him. In her dreams, she was carried by the guardian angels of the four quarters to the land of the Himalayas where she was received by heavenly queens – the wives of the four world guardians. Then she was taken to lake Manasarovar (also known as Anotota) where they bathed her, and robed her in a divine dress, anointed her with perfumes, and decked her with divine flowers. Thence, she was taken to a sacred hill nearby, at the top of which was a palace. Here she was laid on a golden conch facing the east. As she laid her head upon the pillow, she beheld a divine-looking looking white elephant with six tusks. In its tusks, the elephant carried a white lotus. The divine elephant touched her right side and seemed to enter her womb. Thus, knowing that she was carrying a Great Being in her womb, the pious Mahamaya spent most of her time in prayer, and meditation.

When Mahamaya related this strange dream to King Suddhodana, he consulted astrologers, who predicted that the Queen would give birth to a son who would be either a universal monarch, or Buddha.

Realising that the time for the birth of her child was coming closer, Mahamaya sought the King's permission to go to her parental home in Devadaha, as was the tradition. Seated in a golden palanquin, Mahamaya left Kapilvastu, accompanied by her sister Prajapati and a large retinue.

On her way to Devadaha, Mahamaya had to pass through the

Lumbini grove, not far from Kapilvastu, which was in full bloom and the trees all bore fruits.

Enchanted by the pleasing sight around her, the Queen desired to rest for a while, and ordered the courtiers to stop. Alighting from her palanquin, she walked up to the foot of the blooming sal tree.

Suddenly, she felt the pains of child-birth. Her lady attendants set up a curtain around her and while she held on to a branch of the sal tree, the child was born.

While Mahamaya, attended by her sister Prajapati, was bathing in the tank nearby, the infant, to the surprise of all, stood up and took seven steps in the northern direction. At each spot His foot touched the ground, a lotus bloomed. The heavens rejoiced and the gods showered flowers on Him. This day was the full moon day in the month of Vaisakha in 623 BC, or 563 BC.

For the three centuries following the Buddha's parinirvana, Buddhist places of worship received every care and attention at the hand of a succession of kings, the most illustrious of them all being King Ashoka. He sought solace in the Buddha dhamma, after witnessing the horrors of the Kalinga war, and visited Lumbini in 250 BC. He worshipped the sacred place where the Buddha was born.

About a thousand years after the birth of Buddha, Fa–hian, the first Chinese Buddhist pilgrim, visited Lumbini in AD 406 and saw the holy tree under which the Buddha was born. He also saw the bathing tank of the Sakyas where Queen Mahamaya had bathed. Then Hiuen–Tsang, the second Chinese pilgrim, who visited Lumbini in AD 637 wrote a graphic account about what he saw at the holy site. Lumbini continued to attract pilgrims up to AD 1100.

Thereafter, it was completely engulfed by the jungle and lay buried under dust and debris till 1895, when the monolith pillars set by Ashoka at Lumbini to commemorate his visit to this holy site, were discovered by Dr. Alois Anton Fuhrea, a German archaeologist. The site was further studied by famous archaeologist Sir Alexander Cunningham. The entire Buddhist world is deeply indebted to him for the accuracy of his identification of the principal sacred places and for the manifold efforts he made to restore them.

Places of Interest

The Stone Pillars of Ashoka: Discovered in 1896, the Ashoka Pillar is the first epigraphic evidence relating to the life of Lord Buddha. The inscription engraved by Ashoka in 249 BC is still intact and testifies to the authenticity of the birthplace. The engraved inscription reads:

"By his majesty King Devanam Piyadossi, consecrated 20 years, coming in person, was worshipped (this spot) in as much as here was born the Buddha Sakyamuni. A stone bearing a figure was caused to be constructed and a pillar of stone was set up to show that the Blessed One was born here."

The village Lumbini was freed from paying religious cesses and was liable to pay only one-eighth of its share of produce.

Pushkarni: Close to the Ashoka Pillars is the famous sacred pool Pushkarni believed to be the pond in which Mayadevi took a bath just before giving birth to the Lord and also where the infant Buddha was given His first purifying bath.

Mayadevi Temple and Marker Stone: The Mayadevi shrine complex is the heart of all monuments in this holy site. The complex reveals several layers of constructions carried out over the centuries.

This temple is dedicated to Buddha's mother and has been excavated and restored. The main object of worship here is the nativity sculpture that was

▲ The stone that marks the exact spot where Buddha was born

installed here in the fourth century AD. The sanctum sanctorum is the birth spot of the Lord Buddha.

The marker stone is buried 4-5 feet under the sanctum sanctorum and pinpoints the exact location of the birth of Lord Buddha. This stone is now protected under bulletproof glass.

Peace Flame: King Gyanendra Bir Bikramshah lit the Torch of Eternal Peace in Lumbini to commemorate the International Year of Peace in 1986. This Eternal Peace Flame in Lumbini is still burning as a symbol of world peace.

Peace Bell: Immediately west of the Eternal Peace Flame, is the Peace Bell donated by the Nyigma Meditation Center, USA.

▲ The Peace Bell was donated by the Nyigma Meditation Centre

Lumbini International Research Institute: According to records, Party Reiyukai, Japan Agreement (till March 15, 2015), the Japanese started this institute to facilitate studies in Buddhism. There are about 50 rooms, including the library, study and research rooms, dormitory, cafeteria, lecture rooms, etc. in the Institute. Only the main hall is open to the general public, the rest is accessible only by students of Buddhist studies.

Lumbini Museum: The museum building is made up of a central exhibition hall, surrounded by four mezzanine spaces and the ground floor. Two mezzanine spaces on the west side and the ground floor are used for housing the administration department, workshop, and laboratory for archaeological research work. Photos, manuscripts, coin fragments of Siddhartha, Yasodhara and Rahula, fragments of the Ashoka Pillar, scroll paintings, and photocopies of valuable manuscripts, are displayed here.

Important Archaeological Sites Around Lumbini

Gotihawa, Niglihawa, and Sagarhawa are villages close to Lumbini, that have associations with historically significant monuments such as Ashoka's Pillar, monasteries, and stupas. The Department of Archaeological Excavation's activities are undertaken from time to time under the aegis of the Department of Archaeology (DOA), Lumbini Department Trust (LDT), and Archaeological Survey of India, at various sites in Nepal.

Bodh Gaya

Location: 11 km from Gaya, 125 km from Patna

Bodh Gaya is to the Buddhist what Kashi and Prayag are to Hindus, Bethlehem to the Christians, and Mecca to the Muslims. This sacred place is situated in sylvan solitude, away from the din and bustle of city life, on the banks of the Niranjana river (locally known as Falgu), about 200 yards to its west, silhouetted against the Ganjas-Bhindas Jithian range of hills.

▲ Chankamana at Bodh Gaya

The great landmark in the history of Buddhism is the place where the prince of the Sakya clan attained Supreme Wisdom. This took place in Uruvela, near Gaya, where He sat in meditation under a Pipal tree. Because of this sacred association, the place came to be known as Buddha Gaya – and eventually Bodh Gaya – and the tree as the Bodhi tree. In ancient days, the place was known as Sambodhi, as stated in an inscription by Ashoka who visited this sacred site. To the Buddhists, the place was known as Mahabodhi.

On account of its connection with this single event (the achievement of Enlightenment), Bodh Gaya may be said to be the cradle of Buddhism and to the devout Buddhist, there is no place of greater interest or sanctity.

Today, a traveller who traverses the short distance of 11 km from Gaya to Bodh Gaya in the early morning hours, will be overwhelmed by the serenity of the countryside, by the cool breeze which blows across Falgu. He will not be the only pilgrim to experience these sensations, for almost through the year, there are pilgrims making their way to Bodh Gaya. A pleasant journey, and for the soul which has the gift of sensibility, feelings and imagination, every kilometre of the region proves to be full of rich divine associations. One can picture the Bodhisattva walking along this very path towards Bodh Gaya.

When he was 29, Prince Gautama renounced his wife, child, and the crown that held the promise of power and glory. In the garb of an ascetic, he retreated to the solitude of the forest in quest of the eternal verities of life. After leaving Kapilvastu, the prince-turned-mendicant trekked on foot a distance of about 400 miles and reached Rajgir which was then renowned as the abode of great philosophers and leaders of thought. There he spent some time at the ashram of Alara Kalama. Not satisfied, he went further to the ashram of Uddaka Ramaputta and trained himself in the ways of meditation as taught by that great teacher. But peace still eluded him. To find a solution to his mental unrest, therefore, the Bodhisattva marched forward towards the forest of Uruvela Vana, some 65 km away, where he saw the river Niranjana with its clear waters, and a holy spot on its banks, and a village with brick-built houses, trees, herbs, and pastures. The mind of the Bodhisattva was greatly delighted and he decided to stay here. The five parivajrakas (companions) whom he had met at Rajgir also joined him there. Together, they started practising asceticism.

Believing that purification and final deliverance from suffering could be achieved by rigorous self-mortification, the ascetic Gautama went on testing its truth. He stayed at Uruvela (another name for Bodh Gaya) for six years, until he became the Buddha.

Self-mortification could not lead to the desired goal. He came to death's door and realised the utter futility of self-mortification. He gave up self-torture, extreme fasting, and accepted a bowl of rice pudding offered by Sujata, daughter of the chief of the neighbouring village Senani. Annoyed that Gautama was accepting food, his five companions, Kondana, Bhaddiya, Vappa, Mahanama, and Assiji left him behind for they thought that as an ascetic, Gautama had failed and taken to a life of abundance.

Because of the nourishing food, Gautama gradually regained his strength and his original appearance. He regained perfect physical and mental health.

With firm determination and complete faith in the purity of the body, mind, and strength, unaided by any teacher, accompanied by none, he resolved to make his final quest in complete solitude. The story of his acts and doings, of his penance and patience, of his sufferings and selflessness which Bodh Gaya witnessed has been recounted and depicted at great length and in detail in art and literature, in many lands, and in many languages.

Gautama, the Bodhisattva, determined to achieve enlightenment to know the ultimate truth, came to the Bo tree on the western bank of the river Niranjana, 10 km south of the present day city of Gaya in Bihar. With the golden bowl in his hand, Gautama entered the water and bathed himself and consumed the milk rice. After washing his hands and the bowl and releasing it into the water, he said, "If today I shall attain full Enlightenment, may this golden bowl swim upstream." And, the golden bowl sped upstream.

When evening came, he went to the Bodhi Mandala, the site of the tree of Enlightenment with a bundle of kusa grass offered to him by Sotthiya, a grass cutter, and after spreading the grass at the foot of the tree, he sat cross-legged comfortably, facing the east.

When the Bodhisattva sat under the Bodhi tree with the firm decision to arrive at perfect Enlightenment, Mara, the god of evil nature, was unhappy. Mara is the personification of evil in Buddhist mythology.

Gathering his host of demons and summoning his three alluring daughters – Tanha, Raga and Rati – to accompany him, Mara repaired to the spot, where, bathed in golden light emanating from his body and illuminating all the quarters of the globe, sat the Sakya Muni in profound meditation. Mara employed all wiles and weapons, used both affection and affliction, and pleasure and terror, and virtue and violence, to make the Boddhisattva desist from his pursuit. But nothing succeeded, everything was in vain.

Then, after Mara had been thus vanquished, the Bodhisattva entered, at nightfall, into the meditation which enlightens understanding, and, before the day began to break, attained the highest and most perfect wisdom.

The tree became known as the 'Bodhi Tree', 'Tree of Enlightenment', or 'Tree of Wisdom'. It is a type of fig tree with light green leaves of a very distinctive shape, known to botanical science as the *ficus religiosa,* and its descendent still stands alive and well, on that very spot. The sacred tree has passed through many vicissitudes and the present tree is one of the many successors of the original Bodhi tree.

After his Enlightenment, the Buddha fasted for seven weeks.

Throughout the first week, he sat under the Bodhi tree in utter solitude, and calmly maintained one posture, he then experienced the bliss of emancipation *(Vimutti Sukha).*

In the second week, as a mark of gratitude to the inanimate Bodhi tree that sheltered him during his struggle for Enlightenment, he stood at a certain distance, gazing at the tree with motionless eyes. This event is known as *animeshlochana.*

Buddha spent the third week walking to and fro, from east to west. This incessant walking is known as *dirghachankamana.* It is said that beautiful flowers blossomed wherever his feet touched the ground.

The fourth week he spent in a bejewelled chamber created by his psychic powers, and he contemplated the intricacies of the *Abhidhamma* (higher teaching). He sat in deep contemplation of the six rays of blue, yellow, red, white, orange, and a combination of all these colours emanated from his body. The Buddhist prayer flag used in all Buddhist countries incorporates these colours.

During the fifth week, the Buddha sat in one posture and enjoyed the bliss of *Vimuttisukha* (emancipation), under the famous Ajapala banyan tree in the vicinity of the Bodhi tree. According to the *Jatakas* it was during this week that the daughters of Mara tried to tempt Buddha away from his self-chosen path.

From the Ajapala banyan tree, the Buddha proceeded to the Mucalinda where he spent the sixth week, again enjoying the bliss of emancipation. Unexpectedly, the region was shrouded by heavy rain clouds, and the combination of heavy rains, gloomy weather, and cold winds prevailed for seven days. Then Mucalinda, the serpent king, came out of his abode, and coiling around the body of the Buddha seven times, remained there, his large hood swaying gracefully over the Buddha's head, and protecting him from the rains.

In the seventh week, Buddha passed a place south of the temple where the merchants, Tapassu and Bhallika took refuge in Buddha and Dhamma. The place is called 'Rajbejata'. At the end of the seventh week, two merchants, Tapassu and Bhallika, offered Buddha rice cakes and honey, and became the first disciples to join his order after uttering the immortal words – *'Buddham saranam gacchami, Dhammam saranam gacchami'*, which means, 'I take refuge in Buddha, I take refuge in the doctrine of Buddhism'.

Places of Interest

Numerous shrines and monuments were constructed here, through the centuries.

The Mahabodhi Temple: The Mahabodhi Temple is a unique living memorial in the history of the world and the most venerable of its kind. Many temples in neighbouring countries have been modelled on this temple. Ashoka is said to have erected a shrine exactly where Buddha received Enlightenment and perhaps it is this shrine that is

▲ The Buddha's serene eyes inspire the devotees who come to the Mahabodhi Temple

represented in early Buddhist art. Beginning with the visit of Ashoka the Great in 259 BC, streams of pilgrims flowed towards this place, without ceasing, and this journey continues till date.

This temple has a balustraded gallery surrounding the sacred Bodhi tree. The temple enshrines the great gilded figure of the Blessed One in the *bhumisparsha-mudra* that symbolises the supreme event of Enlightenment.

The outer side of the Mahabodhi temple has innumerable niches, carvings, creepers, and images. The main niches on the wall contain an unusually fine image of Buddha which has been gilded by the Tibetans.

The Bodhi Tree: The Bodhi tree is situated in the west of the temple. The present Bodhi tree belongs to the fourth generation of the original Bodhi tree. It is said that the original Bodhi tree was destroyed by Ashoka's wife Queen Tissarakshita (third century BC), because she disapproved of his strong support of Buddhism. The present tree was grown from a sapling grafted from one of the original tree's branches that was saved during the reign of King Harshavardhana of Kannauj (seventh century AD). The tree was cut down by Shashanka, the Shaivite king of Bengal. King Harshavardhana planted a new sapling again, using a graft brought from Sri Lanka where a sapling was sent by Ashoka, through his son Mahendra and daughter Sanghamitra. This tree is still surviving and the descendant of that tree also thrives at Anuradhapur in the center of the island. This tree was seen by Hiuen-Tsang in AD 637.

During excavations in 1870, the Bodhi tree fell down and a sapling was planted by archaeologist A Cunningham in its original place. This is the Bodhi tree which we see today.

Vajrasana: Vajrasana or the Diamond Throne is the seat which sprung up at the foot of the Bodhi tree where the Bodhisattva sat to attain Supreme Enlightenment. The holy seat is now marked by a real sandstone slab, which is 7 feet 6 inches long and 4 feet 3 inches broad, and 3 feet high.

Mucalinda Lake: This is a small pond filled with rainwater from when Buddha spent his sixth week under the tree.

Stone Railing Round the Vihara: Around the temple lie innumerable relics, of which the most important are the portions of stone railing which probably surround the original shrine. These stone railings represent two different periods of construction, the former going back to about second century BC and the latter the early Gupta period. The entire railing is made of sandstone and is very well designed. The pillars, coping stones, and the railings are adorned with fascinating sculptures, depicting Buddhist *Jataka* stories, animals, birds, and scenes from everyday life.

Votive Stupas: Richly decorated votive stupas, scattered everywhere still attract the admiring gaze of the pilgrims and visitors who flock to this venerable shrine.

Niranjana River: The river flows about 200 yards in front of the Mahabodhi vihara. There is very little water during most of the year, but is full to the brim during the rains. It was in this river that the Lord bathed and solemnly declared that were he to become the Buddha, the bowl would go upstream and join those of the previous Buddhas. According to *Jataka Tales,* it is said that the Buddha's soul has come on the earth 25 or 26 times in human form before he could get Bodhisattava.

Sujatakuti: At a distance of 2 km across the Niranjana river, there is a high mound overgrown with trees and shrubs. Some believe that this is where Sujata lived.

There are a number of modern temples and monasteries built at Bodh Gaya by Buddhists from other countries. The important ones are Tibetan, Chinese, Thai, Japanese, New Japanese, and Burmese monasteries.

At Bodh Gaya's Mahabodhi temple, what lies around and about, or even within the holy shrine, is something greater than the brick and mortar spire and sculpture. It is the serene air and a sense of deep spirituality with which the place vibrates; it is the sacred memory of great efforts and the stupendous realisation that a holy being felt here 2,550 years ago. Back then, a man like any one of us, made of flesh and bone, sought a truth on behalf of all mankind and found a way out of all of life's allurements. It is these facts which Bodh Gaya enshrines. Such an atmosphere might be similar to that of any other holy place, of any other religion, but someone who can feel subtle sensations will experience a strong presence, that is almost palpable and grasp a sense of upliftment and a near ecstatic feeling of grace, quiet and purity here.

Sarnath – The Wheel of Law

Location: 12 km from Varanasi

One of the most visited places in India, Sarnath has covetable wealth in the form of religious traditions and attracts thousands of pilgrims, archaeologists, historians and students from India and overseas. Sarnath was where Lord Buddha turned the Wheel of Law in motion. In due course of time this has become a significant pilgrimage spot for Buddhists who consider it to be the birth place of Buddhism.

Having enjoyed the bliss of enlightenment for seven weeks, the Buddha got up and gazed with reverence at the sacred Bo-tree and proceeded on foot to the deer park (Mrigadava) about 250 km away at Isipatana (Rishipatana), modern Sarnath, near Varanasi.

After attaining Enlightenment at Bodh Gaya, Buddha took the decision that he should teach his Dhamma to five erstwhile companions who were then at Sarnath.

On seeing Gautama approach, the five ascetics decided to not welcome him, and said instead that 'by abandoning austerities and turning to a life of luxury Gautama has committed a sin and is not worthy of respect'. But as the Buddha neared, all the five Parivajrakas involuntarily rose from their seats and greeted him with reverence. Impressed by his dignified manners and his personality, they instinctually treated him like a distinguished guest.

An inscription from the Kushan period (AD 50) found at Sarnath gives a partial record of the Buddha's First Sermon, unfolding the new path discovered by him. The Buddha said, *"Two extremes there are, O monks, which he who strives after enlightenment must avoid."*

"Which two?"

"*A life addicted to pleasure which is vulgar and worthless, and a life given to self-mortification which is painful and equally profitless.*"

Then the Buddha enunciated the Four Noble Truths, explained the cause of suffering, its cessation, and the path leading to the cessation of suffering. And added that the way to Nibbana, emancipation, or the path that leads to cessation of suffering, higher wisdom and peace of mind is the Noble Eightfold Path, or the Middle Path. This path is:

1. Right Understanding: Free from superstition and delusion
2. Right Thought: High and worthy of the intelligent earnest man
3. Right Speech: Kind, open and truthful
4. Right Conduct: Peaceful, honest and pure
5. Right Livelihood: Not hurting or endangering any living thing
6. Right Effort: In self-training and in self-control
7. Right Mindfulness: The active watchful mind
8. Right Concentration: Earnest thought about the deep mysteries of life

The Buddha thus preached this First Sermon at Isipatana, modern Sarnath. This event is known in the Buddhist text as the Dharma Chakra-pravartana, or the 'Turning of the Wheel of the Law'. The First Sermon comprises a unique and frank intellectual statement of the basic problem of life, as well as the solution. It is universally regarded as the essence of Buddha's teachings. Sarnath naturally became the symbol and radiating center of light throughout the Buddhist world.

The five Parivajrakas, namely, Kondana, Bhaddiya, Vappa, Mahanama, and Assaji popularly known in the Buddhist texts as Panchvargiya Bhikkus, were the first members of the sangha established by the Buddha. The sixth person to join the sangha was Yasa, the son of a rich merchant from Varanasi. Following his example, 54 of his friends also became Buddha's disciples. With them and the first five monks, the Master founded the first sangha and sent 60 monks to various directions to preach his dhamma.

Lord Buddha spent here the first monsoon after his attainment of Enlightenment. Therefore, the Dharma-chakra-pravartana and founding of the sangha, as well as a number of holy temples and monasteries were constructed at this holy spot during the lifetime of the Buddha. It appears that Sarnath was not converted into a place of permanent residence by the Buddha or his disciples although Buddha visited it twice or thrice.

By about the end of the fourth century BC, Sarnath had grown in importance and when Ashoka ascended the throne, it was a flourishing Buddhist center. It is a pity we do not have any documents charting the continuous history of Sarnath after Ashoka. Fa-hian who visited it in the fifth century AD speaks of flourishing establishments here. But, the most active and prosperous period in Sarnath appears to have been between the third and seventh century as is evidenced by numerous pieces of sculptures belonging to that period. Hiuen-Tsang, the second Chinese pilgrim who visited Sarnath in AD 638, saw the Dhamek Stupa, the Dharmarajika Stupa and the Pillar of Ashoka, the main shrine and many other smaller shrines.

The fortunes here began to decline around tenth century AD and suffered a severe blow at the hands of Sultan Mahmud Ghazni in in AD 1000. The final and fatal blow came soon after in the 12th century (AD 1194). Qutub-ud-din, Viceroy of Mahamud Ghori, invaded the country and destroyed what remained of the sacred edifices, thus closing the last brilliant chapter in the history of Sarnath. From AD 1100-1600, we have no knowledge again about the events at Sarnath.

In 1794, Jagat Singh, Dewan of Benaras pulled down a tower supposed to be the Dharmarajika stupa, because he needed bricks for establishing a market at Benaras. While dismantling the stupa, two vessels of marble and sandstone were found. One of these contained some human bones, old pearls, gold leaves, etc. These bones were believed to be the earthly remains of Buddha, and were cast into the Ganga. An account of this was published by a British resident of Benaras, Mr. Jonathan Duncon, and this attracted the attention of scholars and archaeologists. A distinguished line of British excavators namely Col. Mackenzie, Sir Alexander Cunningham, and Major Killoe worked at the site and the history of Sarnath was gradually unearthed.

Places of Interest

Chaukhandi Stupa: On entering Sarnath, visitors are immediately faced with the Chaukhandi stupa in all its grandeur. It was here that Buddha met again the five ascetics who went on to become his first five disciples.

Dhamek Stupa: The Dhamek stupa earlier known as Dharmachakra stupa, is the sole surviving symbol of the ancient glory of Sarnath, and is now generally regarded to mark the original spot where Lord Buddha first encountered the five Parivajrakas and where he delivered the first sermon.

The Dharmarajika Stupa: The Dharmarajika stupa was pulled down by Jagat Singh's workmen in 1794 for transporting the building material to Varanasi for constructing a building. A reliquary within a stone box was found. The excavations revealed six stages of enlargements of the stupa, originally built by Ashoka.

▲ The Dhamek Stupa marks the place where Buddha delivered his first sermon

Two outstanding statues, viz., the colossal red sandstone Bodhisattva installed in the third year of Kanishka and the statue of Buddha seated in the attitude of preaching were found around this monument.

Mulagandhakuti (Main Shrine): Towards the north of the Dharmarajika stupa, the visitor comes to the Main Shrine, a temple surrounded by a concrete pavement. It is a replica of the famous temple at Bodh Gaya. During an excavation, an image of a standing Buddha in the Gupta style was found in the chapel, on the south side.

▲ The main shrine in Mulagandhakuti

The ruins of the Dharmarajika stupa and Mulagandhakuti mark the place where Lord Buddha lived during his stay at Sarnath. Buddha used to sit in meditation in the Mulagandhakuti, and would take a walk in the courtyard.

Ashoka Pillar: The Ashoka Pillar, stands towards the west of the main shrine. Under a flat roof and surrounded by an iron railing, this famous pillar was erected by Emperor Ashoka in 250 BC, or thereabouts. It probably stands on the very site where the Lord delivered the first sermon to his five disciples. The pillar bears three inscriptions. The earliest one is Ashoka's edict in Brahmi characters, in which the emperor warns the monks and nuns against creating a schism. In the ringing words of the Emperor, *"No one shall cause division in the order of monks."* The second inscription belongs to the Kushan period and refers to the 40th year of the Asvaghosha. He was a ruler of Kaushambi who also held sway over Banaras and Sarnath. The third record is incised in early Gupta script and mentions the teachers of the Sammitiya sect and of the Vatsiputraka school.

Mulagandhakuti Vihara: To the east of the Dhamek stupa, stands the magnificent modern Buddhist temple built by the Mahabodhi Society in 1931. The credit for making Sarnath a living shrine in modern India goes to the Anagarika Society of India. When Dharama Pala visited in 1891, he found the Holy Isipatana completely in ruins. He resolved to save the decaying Dhamek stupa and carvings from vandals. Some years thereafter, he laid the foundation stone of Mulagandhakuti Vihara in November 1922 (it opened in November 1931).

On the inside walls are magnificent paintings, depicting scenes from the life of the Master, executed by one of Japan's foremost painters, Kosety Nosu.

On the left of the Mulagandhakuti Vihara is a cluster of three Bodhi trees in the compound, planted by Anaganika Dharmapala in 1921. These saplings were nurtured from the historic Bodhi tree at Anuradhapura in Sri Lanka, which was planted there by Sanghamitra, Ashoka's daughter, in third century BC.

A small building known as the Monastery of the Bhikkus is quite close by. Here lived the late venerable Dharmapala, the founder of Mahabodhi Society. The anniversary of the Vihara takes place on a full moon day in November. The festival is celebrated every year by a spectacular assembly of monks and lay devotees representing every nationality of the world.

Kittoe's Monastery: The first place in the monastery is named after Major Kittoe who carried out excavation work here from 1834-77. Only the foundation of the monastery is intact. The building was evidently destroyed by fire.

Chinese Temple: To the east, is the Chinese temple built in the graceful Chinese style. The temple contains a beautiful image of Buddha carved from a block of pure white marble.

Maha Bodhi Vidyalaya: Opposite this temple is the Maha Bodhi Vidyalaya which is one of the several institutions of the Society where Buddhism is studied.

The **Burmese Temple** and the **Rest House** are to the west of the Main Shrine.

Kushinagar – The Mahaparinirvana

Location: 51 km from Gorakhpur

Kusinara, Kusinagari, Kusigrama or Kusavati, or present Kushinagar is identified as the place where Lord Buddha attained Mahaparinirvana and where he was cremated. In ancient times, Kushinagar was situated along an important trade route, Sravasti to Rajgir, along the west bank of the river Hiranyawati. At that time, it was a small town belonging to the Mallas who had created a park called 'Upavattana', which was the actual place chosen for the Mahaparinirvana.

The Blessed One had reached the ripe age of 80. His two disciples,

Sariputta and Maha Moggallana, had passed away three months earlier. Prajapati Gautami, the foster-mother of the Master and head of the order of the nuns, Yashodhara and the son Rahula, were no more. Finally, the Buddha moved from Vaishali.

There a severe sickness fell upon him and was the cause for much pain and agony. He was on the verge of dying, but he bore it patiently. He felt that he should not pass away without taking leave of the Sangha. When that illness had abated, the Blessed One, addressing Ananda said, "*Come Ananda, let us go on to Kushinagara.*"

The Lord, accompanied by his beloved disciple Ananda, left for Kushinagar via Pava. Rajagir, the capital of Magadha, was the starting point for the final journey of Buddha's life, which ended with the Mahaparinirvana at Kushinagar.

The Buddha ultimately decided to breathe his last, not in a renowned city like Rajagir or Saravasti, the center of his activities, but in a distant and insignificant hamlet.

"*Long ago, Ananda, there was a king, Mahasudarsana, king of kings, a righteous man who ruled in righteousness. This Kushinagar was the royal city of king Mahasudarsana, under the name of Kusavati, and on the east and the west it was twelve leagues in length and on the north and on the south it was seven leagues in breadth.*"

These were the words of Buddha to his favourite disciple Ananda, when the latter tried to dissuade him from spending his last moments in this little wattle and daub place, in the midst of the jungle, in this branch township of Kushinagara, the capital of the tribe of Mallas.

"*Go now, Ananda, and enter into Kusinagara, and inform the Mallas of Kushinagara, saying this day, O Vasisthas, in the last watch of the night, the final passing away from the Tathagata will take place. Be favourable, herein, O Vasisthas, be favourable. Give no occasion to reproach yourself thereafter, saying, in our own village did the death of our Tathagata take place and we took not the opportunity of visiting the Tathagata in his last hours.*"

These tender words bespeak the familiarity and feelings with which, he viewed the Mallas in whose territory he chose to pass the last moments of his life. The Mallas, had a very high regard for him.

Then Ananda went to inform the Mallas of Kushinagara that the Blessed One had arrived there and would pass away in the last watch of the night.

At Kushinagara, the Blessed One addressed Ananda saying, *"Spread over for me, I pray you Ananda, the conch with its head to the north between the twin Sal trees."* And the Blessed One laid himself down on his right side, with one leg resting on the other, composed, and mindful.

Speaking now to the monks, the Buddha instructed them on many important points which are recorded in the *Mahaparinibbana Sutta* or the discourse on the passing away of the Buddha, his longest discourse. All the events that occurred during the closing years of his life are recorded in this discourse.

Before the Mahaparinibbana, the Buddha gave Ananda instructions about what should be done with his remains.

The Blessed One addressing Ananda, said, *"Now it is not thus, Ananda, that the Tathagata is rightly honoured, reverenced, or venerated. But the bhikkus or Bhikkuni or the Upasaka or Upasika, who steadfastly fulfils all the lesser duties, who is correct in life, walking according to the precepts – it is they who rightly honour, revere, and venerate the Tathagata with the worthiest homage. Therefore Ananda, be ye steadfast in the fulfilment of the greater and the lesser duties, be ye correct in life, walking according to percepts. Thus, Ananda, should be right."*

To the disciples who gathered around him, the Buddha summarised his teachings. He asked if questions remained in the minds of anyone present. When all felt silent, the Buddha gave his final teaching, *"Bhikkus never forget. All compounded things are impermanent."* With these words, the breath left his body, and the Buddha entered parinirvana.

Thus preaching, passed away the greatest of the world's religious teachers at the age of 80, on the Vaisakha Purnima day in 544 BC or 488 BC lying between two large Sal trees.

Upon his passing the earth shook, stars shot from the heavens, the sky broke into flames in the ten directions, and the air resounded with celestial music.

The last rites of the Buddha were performed by the Mallas of Kushinagar in a most dignified manner. For six days, his body lay instate to enable his disciples to pay homage to the Master. On the seventh day, the Mallas carried the body of the Buddha in a procession to the Mukuta-bandhana, where they used to hold their coronation ceremonies. There the Buddha was cremated with full honours under the guidance of Ananda, and Maha Kashyapa, who had reached Kushinagar by that time.

After the bone-relics had been collected by the Mallas, they kept it in their council hall and worshipped it for seven days. The relics were ultimately divided into eight parts and shared equally by the Mallas of Kushinagar; Ajatashatru, the king of Magadha; the Licchavis of Vaishali; the Sakyas of Kapilvastu; the Bulies of Attakapa; Koliyas of Ramagrama; the Mallas of Pava; and a resident of Vethadipa. The vessel containing the remains of the Blessed One was taken by the wise Drona who was instrumental in dividing the relics to the satisfaction of all. In two centuries after the Great Decease, however, Kushinagar does not seem to have risen much in importance.

Kushinagar continued to be a living shrine till about AD 1300, as is evident from the construction of a monastery and a chapel attached to it during the reign of a local chief of Kalachuri dynasty. Thereafter, it appears to have been deserted and in due course it was completely lost to oblivion.

After a silence of more than half a millennium, we hear of the place for the first time from Buchanan, an officer of the East India Company, who visited it in the course of his survey-work early in the last century.

The site was further studied by HH Wilson, Alexander Cunningham, ACL Carlleyle, JPH Vogel, and Hirananda Shastri. Numerous brick buildings were discovered clustering round the great monuments and representing monasteries and secondary stupas and shrines. These excavations yielded indubitable proofs of the identity of Kasinara/Kushinagar and of the monuments in numerous inscriptions.

After the lapse of some seven centuries, Kushinagar thus came to life again.

Places of Interest

The Nirvana Temple: The ruins of this temple and the reclining Nirvana statue inside were discovered by Carlleyle in 1876. The present Nirvana temple was built by the Government of India in 1956, as part of the 2500th Buddha Jayanti celebrations. The 1,500-year-old Nirvana statue is 20 feet in length and is sculpted out of one block of sandstone of mixed reddish colour, probably from Chunar, in Uttar Pradesh. It represents the Dying Buddha, reclining on his right side, with his face turned towards the west. It is placed on a 24-feet-long brick throne, with posts at the corners and is faced with stone slabs on all sides. The reclining Buddha image is believed to be on the very spot where Lord Buddha breathed his last.

▲ Mahaparinirvana Temple (Top)
Reclining Buddha (Above)

The Main Stupa: The Main Stupa was excavated and completely exposed by Carlleyle in 1876. The Main Stupa, as repaired and restored in 1927, with the donations of U Po Kyo and U Po Hlaing is 75 feet high. Inside its drum, a chamber, representing a miniature replica of the original stupa, was constructed 19 feet above ground level.

The Matha-Kuar Shrine: More than a furlong south-west of the main site, by the side of the Voadi, is the Matha-Kuar Shrine, wherein is installed a colossal statue of the Buddha, measuring 19 feet in height and is carved out of one block of the blue stone in the bhumi-sparsha-mudra locally called Matha-Kuar.

Cremation Stupa (Angara Chaitya): The stupa is situated about 1.61 km to the east of the Matha-Kuar shrine and is locally known as Rambhar. The site of the Cremation stupa was a big mound when Cunningham visited Kushinagar in 1861-62. He tried to dig it out, but abandoned the attempt. The hidden stupa was discovered by Hiranand Shastri in 1910 when he exposed the eastern face of the mound and found that it represented an unusually large stupa. It is said to have been erected on the very spot where the body of the Tathagata was cremated.

Sravasti – To Heaven and Back

Location: 47 km from Baharaich railway station, 151 km from Lucknow

Sravasti has been identified with the remains of Saheth-Maheth on the borders of the Gonda and Bahraich district of Uttar Pradesh. This identification is confirmed by the discovery at Saheth of several inscriptions referring to the convent of Jetvana at Sravasti.

Saheth-Maheth consists of two distinct sites. The larger one, Maheth covering an area of about 400 acres, has been identified with the remains of the city proper and Saheth, about 32 acres in area and lying about a quarter of a mile to the south-west, is the site of the Jetvana monastery.

Sravasti, or 'Savatthi' in Pali, was the capital of Kosala, the most powerful kingdom during the sixth century BC.

Out of 45 rainy seasons, the Buddha spent as many as 25 rainy seasons there, four of them continuously at Sravasti. Since the Buddha had spent a major part of his missionary life at Sravasti, a majority of the sermons recorded in the *Tripitaka* were delivered by the Blessed One while staying at Jetvana. Here, he shaped the Sangha into a unique spiritual community based on sound moral principals and guidelines that fostered harmony while allowing unlimited scope for realisation. The locus of numerous teachings, Sravasti is sacred to the Buddhists, because it was here that the Master, in accordance with the practice of the previous Buddhas, performed the greatest of his miracles, to confound the heretic Tirthika teachers, demonstrating his mastery of the elements and the ability to reveal the true nature of his powers and abilities.

According to sacred literature, this great event consists of a series of miraculous episodes, such as *the sun and the moon shining together in the sky, fire and water emanating alternately from the upper and lower parts of the Master's body, and the Buddha creating multiple representations of Himself.* The Sravasti event has been a favourite theme in Buddhist art from very early times.

At the time of the Buddha, the King of Sravasti was Prasenjit. He erected an elegant monastery here when he became Buddha's disciple. Even in the days of the Buddha, Sravasti was an active center of Buddhism and it was here that Anathapindada built in the garden of Prince Jeta, a large monastery for the reception of the Master, which had been purchased at a fabulous price in gold. The story of the purchase of the garden and its eventual presentation to the Lord has been a favourite theme in early Buddhist art. In later times also, shrines and monasteries arose on this sacred spot and it remained a flourishing center of the faith, till a late period.

The history of Sravasti is known from the sixth century BC when it became famous owing to its association with Buddha. Sravasti continued to grow as a Buddhist shrine after the demise of the Buddha. Commemorating this holy place, Ashoka erected a tall pillar on each side of the eastern entrance to Jeta's Grove, where there once stood a seven-storied monastery. The stupas were built on the site of Ananthapidada's house, the vihara of Mahaprajapati, and the cremation place of Angulimaliya, a murderer, who became an *arhat* after his conversion to the Dhamma.

During the Kuahana rule, from the first and second century AD at Jetvana, new shrines were erected and images of Buddha installed.

Most of the stupas and temples of his period survive in ruins.
When Fa-hian visited Sravasti in the fifth century AD only 200 families were living in the city, but these stupas were still standing at Jetvana. Hiuen-Tsang, who visited Sravasti in AD 637-638 found it in wild ruins. Among the deserted buildings he saw the stupas of Sudatta and Angulimala, and the vihara of Prajapati, all seen earlier by Fa-hian. In addition to these, Hiuen-Tsang noticed the ruins of the 'Hall of Law' built by King Prasenjit. By the time of Hiuen-Tsang, Jetvana had decayed much and there was no one living in the monasteries.

After Hiuen-Tsang's visit, there appears to have been a revival at Jetvana. A number of inscribed sealings and Buddhist sculptures such as the images of Loknatha, Trailokya-vijaya, Avalokitesvara, Simhananda Lokeshvara, and Jambhale have been discovered, which belongs to the eighth and ninth centuries.

The last patrons of the Jetvana shrines, were the Gahadavala Kings of Kanauj, Madanapala and his son Govindachandra. Inscriptions referring to their reign were found in Jetvana in a monastery which, to this day, are quite well preserved.

After AD 1300 Jetvana shrines were lost into oblivion and completely forgotten.

The twin ruins of Saheth-Maheth were first identified with the ancient Sravasti by Sir A Cunningham. Some improvements were made at Sravasti by the government in 1956 during the celebration of 2500 years of Buddhism.

Places of Interest

Jetvana (Saheth): Within a furlong to the north of the Balrampur-Baharich road lie the ruins of the Buddhist establishment of Jetvana. The most important shrines at Jetvana as we see today are Temples 11 and 12.

Temple and Monastery 19: It is one of the largest buildings in Jetvana and contains a shrine, a well within the courtyard, 21 cells for the use of monks, and a portico. In some of the cells of the monastery were discovered a clay tablet representing Buddha seated in dharma-chakra-mudra and the Buddhist creed in three lines, in Gupta script; a number of Buddha images, of which one is in bhumi-sparsha-mudra with Avalokitesvara; and Maitreya carved in miniature and another sculpture showing Buddha receiving a bowl from a monkey.

The Eight Stupas: The space adjacent to the east and north-east of Monastery 19 seems to have been specially utilised for the erection of stupas, of which eight are visible. One of them yielded an inscribed seal with the name of Buddhadeva in the characters of the fifth century AD. To the north-west of these stupas is an octagonal well.

Temple 6 and 7: To the north of the octagonal well are the remains of two temples of which Temple 7 is bigger and better preserved, and contains a shrine room.

Stupa 17 and 18: On the east of the aforesaid shrines lies Stupa 17. A relic-pot containing a gold wire and bead and other crystal objects were discovered which are linked to the Kushana period i.e. first century AD. An inscribed relic bowl containing fragments of bone, stone beads and pearls also belonging to Kushana period have been discovered from the adjacent Stupa 18.

Bodhi Tree: This Bodhi tree stands immediately in front of the ruins of the Jetvana monastery. The story of the tree is written in the *Pujavaliya*. Lord Buddha spent only three months in the year there, during the monsoon, and the rest of the year, he was on tour carrying the message of hope he had discovered, to each and every hamlet of the vast country. His followers in Sravasti desired his permanent residence in the city and they begged him for some token so that they may at least venerate it during his absence.

To satisfy the craving of the people, Ananda obtained the Lord's permission to plant a sapling of the Bodh Gaya Bodhi tree. Mahomoggallana, who was famous for his supernatural powers volunteered to bring the sapling, and did so by flying to the Bodhi tree. After the sapling was brought, Anathapindika was selected for the honour and, with great ceremony, he planted it in front of the monastery he himself had built. Lord Buddha blessed and sanctified it by passing one whole night under it in meditation. From that time, it took the place of the teacher during his absence for the devotees to make their offerings.

Temple 2: Temple 2 marks the site of the original temple called Gandhakuti, built by Anathapindika, as part of the Jetvana monastery. Gandhakuti is one of the most sacred temples in Jetvana, having been hallowed by the Buddha's presence.

Temple 3: Temple 3 lies to north of Bodhi tree and faces east. In front of the temple, are two brick terraces erected on the original promenade used by Buddha for his walks. A large Boddhisattva image discovered near the building bears an inscription from the first century AD. It says that the image was set up at the *chankama* of Buddha at Kosambakuti by Bala in the reign of a Kushana king.

Stupa 11: This stupa seems to have been vested with particular sanctity, as it marks the place where Lord Buddha would sit during discourses for the Buddhist monks and laity. Portions of the stupa may go back to the Gupta period, and its lowest foundries are likely to have been made at a still earlier date.

Stupa 8: This structure consists of two stupas erected one over the other in different periods. An inscribed Bodhisattva image is found here and dates back to the Kushana period.

Adjacent to Stupa 8, to its west, are remains of a similar medieval stupa, Stupa 9.

Another interesting relic of the past Jetvana is the well from where the Buddha would have water drawn for his personal use. This well has once again been put to use, and pleasantly enough, has very sweet water which the visitors drink and believe it to be Buddha's blessing.

Sravasti city – Maheth

City Wall and Gates: To the north of Jetvana, outside the city, visitors can go to the site of the ancient city by taking the road which enters it by the Sobhanath Gate, one of the openings made in the recent past in the high rampart that encompasses the city. The huge mud fortifications run along a circuit of 5.20 km, in the shape of a crescent. The inward curve of the crescent faces northeast along the old bank of the Rapti (Achiravati) river. The rampart varies considerably in height, the top is everywhere strewn with large bricks. In the rampart, there are many openings giving access to the interior, the four important ones being Imli Darwaza (south-west), Rajgarh Darwaza (north-west), Nausahra Darwaza (north-east) and Kand Bhari Darwaza (south-east).

The Temple of Sobhnath: As one enters the precincts of the western part of the city from Jetvana, the building that first comes to view is the temple of Sobhnath, set on a high mound. The spot is hallowed as the birth place of Sambhavanatha, the Jaina Tirthankara.

Pakki Kuti: From the Sobhnath temple, the road leads to Pakki Kuti, which is one of the two largest mounds inside the city area, the other being Kachchi Kuti. Pakki Kuti has been identified by Cunningham as the remains of the Angulimala Stupa, as seen by the Chinese pilgrims in the fifth century AD.

Kachchi Kuti: Kachchi Kuti is the most imposing monument in this area. It owes its modern name to a renovation during which kachcha bricks were used to make the topmost shrine, by a sadhu who lived there.

Sankisa

Location: 45 km from Farukhabad, 200 km from Agra

Sankisa, a holy spot that has links to the life of the Master, was earlier known as Sankasya, where the Buddha is said to have descended to earth from the Tryastrimsa Heaven or Tushita heaven (Heaven of the Thirty-Three Gods) where he preached the Abhidhama to his mother and other gods. This event is said to have occurred after the Great Miracle performed at Sravasti, as it was a fixed law that all Buddhas would resort to the Heaven of the Thirty-Three Gods after performing their greatest miracles. According to Buddhist legends, the Lord came down by a triple ladder, accompanied by god Brahma and Sakra, and the incident forms a favourite motif in Buddhist art. The story of the Buddha's descent from heaven at Sankisa has been a popular theme in early Buddhist art.

On account of these sacred associations, Sankisa become an

important Buddhist shrine and a number of stupas and monasteries were erected there in ancient times. 'Sankasya' has been identified with 'Sankisa', also known as 'Sanisa Basantpur', in the Farukhabad district of Uttar Pradesh.

Both Fa-hian and Hiuen-Tsang visited Sankisa and have written interesting accounts of the important monuments. Due to long periods of neglect, now all the monuments are in ruins. After centuries of oblivion, the ancient Sankaysa was identified by Sir A. Cunnigham in 1842 with the modern village of Sankisa.

Places of Interest

The present village is perched on a mound, locally known as the fort, 41 feet high and extending within an area of 1,500 feet by 1,000 feet. An important relic at Sankisa is the stump of the broken Ashoka pillar surrounded by the elephant capital. It has beautiful carvings of lotus flowers and leaves of the Bodhi tree. About 20 yards to the south of the Ashoka pillar is another mound, composed of solid brick work and surmounted by a temple dedicated to Bisari Devi. It is believed that the Buddha had descended from heaven right here.

Nearby, is a small modern Buddhist temple under the Bodhi tree. It was constructed in 1957 by Ven. Vijaya Soma, a Buddhist monk from Sri Lanka. The modern shrine has a standing image of Lord Buddha flanked by Brahman and Sakra, who are believed to have accompanied the Buddha as he descended from heaven.

The Buddhists visit Sankisa in large numbers every year on the Asvina (Sharad) Purnima in October, when a religious congregation takes place.

Rajgir

Location: 11 km from Nalanda, 100 km from Patna

Modern Rajgir was known in ancient times as 'Rajagriha' meaning the home of royalty.

Today, Rajgir is a hill-girt town in the midst of lush green forests. The city was situated in an area enclosed by hills and was known with different names as is noted in early literature, but is now known as Vaibhara, Vipula, Ratna, Chatha, Udayagiri, and Sonagiri. Rajgir was the capital of the powerful kingdom of Magadha, constituted as the first recorded capital in Indian history and is sacred to Buddhists for reasons more than one. Not only did the Master visit the city several times, but this was where Devadatta, his wicked cousin, made many attempts to kill him. Moreover, in this city, in the Satapani (Saptaparni) cave of the Vaibhara hill the First Buddhist Council (Sangiti) was held, just after Buddha's Parinirvana. The Vinaya and Dharma/Dhamma were discussed in the Council and were fixed with the assistance of Upali and Ananda. The principal points of the Creed and Discipline were thus agreed upon and the stability of the new religion assured. It was at Rajgir, that Sariputta and Moggallana met the Blessed One. They were delighted by the doctrine preached by the Venerable Assaji. After meeting the Buddha, they became the chief disciples of the Buddha.

From Gaya, Buddha in accordance with the promise made to the King Bimbisara before his Enlightenment, went along with his large retinue of arhant disciples to Rajgir. Here he stayed at the Suppatittha Shrine in a palm grove at Yesthivana, now identified with modern Jethian, about 15 km south of Rajgir.

Places of Interest

Ashokan Stupa: To the west of new Rajgir on the other side of the Saraswati stream, is a large mound which marks the site of an Ashokan stupa, according to Hiuen–Tsang.

Bimbisara's Prison: About a kilometre south of the Maniyar Math, is a place about 60 m square, enclosed by a stone wall about 6 feet thick. This place has been identified with the prison in which King Bimbisara was imprisoned by his son Ajatashatru.

Cyclopean wall, or outer fortifications: Built by King Bimbisara with a different elevation and extending over a length of about 40-48 km along the crest of the hill.

According to Pali texts, Rajgir is said to have 32 main gates and 64 minor ones. Once the gates were closed, no one could enter the city. Parts of these walls can still be seen at the point of entry towards Gaya and the main gate in the north.

Gridharakuta Hill: One of the highest hills surrounding the city, the Gridharakuta hill was the Buddha's favourite resort and was witness to many of his important sermons.

King Bimbisara made a flight of steps to reach the monastery situated on top of this hill. Also, there are two natural caves atop the hill. Inside one of these caves was found a number of terracotta plaques of seven past Buddhas and Maitreya, the Future Buddha, seated in two rows and the Buddhist creed inscribed below each figure.

It was from the summit of this hill that Devadatta hurled a stone at Lord Buddha who narrowly escaped death here. The Sukhara Khanna cave where Pariggaha Sutta was delivered to Dighanaka, the former teacher of Sariputta and Moggalana, is also situated on this hill.

Maniyar Math, or Ancient Chaitya: A stupa in the center of the valley is called Maniyar Math, so named after a small shrine that existed on the mound before the place was excavated. The worship of the nagas was the primitive religion of the people of Rajgir. This Maniyar Math is probably the Temple of the Maninaga (probably the guardian deity of the city). During the excavation in 1861-62 by Sir A Cunningham, several pieces of Buddhist sculptures, the figure of a five-hooded nagi, and jars with spouts all around them were found.

Sonabhandar Cave/Saptaparni Cave: This famous cave, now known as Sonabhandar, is situated on the inner slopes of the Vaibhara hill. This cave is where some authorities say that the First Buddhist Council was held shortly after Gautam

▲ The Sonabhandar Caves were believed to be King Bimbisara's treasury

Buddha's death. According to legend, this was King Bimbisara's treasury.

Jarasandh ki Baithak, or Pippala Stone House: On the eastern slope of the Vaibhara hill is Pippala cave, described in Pali texts as the residence of Maha Kashyapa, the president of the First Buddhist Council. It is said that on one occasion Buddha visited Maha Kashyapa when the latter was lying sick in the Pippala cave. It is also associated with the primeval king of Rajgir, Jarasandha, who, it is said, had his *baithak*, or open sit-out here.

Jivaka's Mango Garden: Jivaka was the most famous physician of his day and was attached to the royal court of Bimbisara and Ajatashatru. Bimbisara presented his extensive mango garden to Buddha and built a monastery there. It is said to have been his favourite retreat. It was here that Jivaka helped heal Buddha when he was injured by Devadatta.

Ranbhumi Area: About a mile south-west of the Sonabhandar caves is an open area called Akhara, or a battlefield, where, the people believe, the famous duel between Jarasandha and Bhima was fought during the Mahabharata.

Tapoda Nadi Hot Water Springs: 'Tapoda' in the *Mahabharata* refers to the hot water springs in Rajgir. The Tapoda springs are situated on the slopes of the hills to the right, as one enters the basin of Vipula hill from the direction of Gaya. These have been in existence from the time of Buddha, who has mentioned them in his sermons.

About 150 metres to the north of the hot springs, is a large tank now identified with Karnada tank where the Buddha used to take his bath. Today, these springs attract not only the pilgrims and tourists, but the sick and infirm as well.

Venuvana: Venuvana, the Buddha's favourite resort was a royal park gifted by King Bimbisara.

Vishwa Shanti Stupa: The Venerable Nichidassau Fuji, the founder of the Japan Buddha Sangh, has built a stupa on the Ratnagiri hill, adjacent to the Gridharkuta, which is known as the Vishwa Shanti Stupa, or the World Peace Pagoda. It was built during the Second World War, when atom bombs completely

▲ The Vishwa Shanti Stupa

destroyed the prosperous cities of Hiroshima and Nagasaki in Japan. To prevent a recurrence of such a disaster, the Guruji decided to propagate the philosophy of world peace and started the construction of Vishwa Shanti Stupas in several countries.

Prof. Minoru Ohoka from Japan and the noted Indian artist, Upendra Maharati, have designed the 160 feet high, gold-topped pagoda, with great care and attention to aesthetics. The stupa is almost double the dimensions of the Sanchi stupa.

To get to the top of the 11,000 feet high hill, the Japanese have installed an aerial ropeway chairlift with 114 chairs. The lift takes about seven minutes to carry a passenger from the bottom to the top, near the stupa. There is a big park and a monastery for Japanese monks, and a helipad.

Rajgir is also very sacred to the followers of the Jain religion. Vardhman Mahavira, the 24th Tirthankara, spent 14 monsoons here and resided here for many years. Many hilltops here are crowned with Jain temples. The Swarnabhandar caves, a short distance from Maniyar Math were built by the Jain saint Vairadeva. Practically on every hilltop in Rajgir there are small temples that hold great importance to the Jain community.

There is evidence that Rajgir remained a popular Buddhist shrine till about the 12th century. Thereafter, it fell to ruins and was largely forgotten. The present Rajgir comprises a part of the new Rajagriha built by Ajatashatru. Rajgir is a popular tourist destination, and the archaeological authorities undertake excavations to unearth the ancient monuments in the area. The monuments that have been discovered are being preserved by the government.

Buddha spent many years at Rajagriha, which was the chief center of propagation in the early years of his spiritual administration.

Buddha's administration of the city and its environs is summed up in the *Digha-Nikaya*, where he says,

"*Delightful is Rajagriha;*
delightful is the Gridhrakuta hills;
delightful is Gautama – Nyagrodha;
delightful is Chaura – Prapata;
delightful is the Saptaparni Cave on the side of the Vaibhara;
delightful is Kalasila on the Rishigiri side;
delightful is Tapodarama;
delightful is the Kalandaka in Venuvana;
delightful is the mango-grove of Jivaka;
delightful is the deer park in Mardakukshi."

Vaishali

Location: 56 km from Patna

Vaishali ranks among the few rare places in history that reflect the pride of ancient India.

As the scriptures record, the city of Vaishali itself was a place of great beauty, inhabited by people respected throughout northern India for their love of freedom, their harmonious interactions and their prosperity.

Before the time of the Buddha, the Licchavis, the Mallas, the Videha, and the other tribes had formed this confederacy for mutual protection against their powerful neighbours in Kosala on their western border and in Magadha to the south. Vaishali is supposed to be the first republic state in the world, having a collected body representative and an efficient administration as early as the sixth century BC and was the largest city of the Vaijjian confederacy.

Lord Buddha is said to have visited Vaishali thrice during his lifetime. He had also spent two retreats (Vassa) – fifth and 45th at Vaishali. Many distinguished Licchavis had become Buddha's disciples. It is said that during one of his visits, a monkey offered the Buddha a pot of honey, which is one of the four miracles in the life of Buddha. It was in Vaishali that the Buddha decided to admit his foster mother Gautami and Yashodhara into the order of the Bhikkunis.

On the Buddha's first visit to Vaishali after his Enlightenment, he ended a great plague that was devastating the city, and won the respect and love of the people.

Amrapali, the chief courtesan donated her mango grove for the residence of the monks. A number of his teachings had been delivered in this mango grove (Amravana).

It was in this mango grove that before leaving Vaishali, the Buddha announced on Maghi Purnima that after three months he would attain Nirvana. Thereafter, he set out on his last journey to Kushinagar. Buddha spent his last, the 45th, rainy season at Vaishali.

Vaishali is also known for the Second Buddhist Council held 100 years after the Mahaparinirvana. It is said that the monks in Vaijji had started practising the Ten Points (dassa vathani), which was regarded as an unorthodox indulgence by some monks led by Yasa. To settle this dispute, the Second Council (sangiti) was convened at Vaishali. Seven hundred monks met under the Presidentship of Venerable Sabhakami. In a unanimous verdict, the council declared the conduct of Vaijjian monks as unlawful. The Vaijji monks, however, refused to accept the verdict. This resulted in a schism in the Sangha and the secession of the Mahasanghikas (Vaijji monks). The Second Council, therefore, led to a new development in Buddhism.

The Licchavi nobles erected a grand stupa over their share of the holy relics of the Buddha, which they later brought from Kushinagar.

Both Fa-hian and Hiuen-Tsang visited the city. They saw a large number of Buddhist monuments including the stupa which had been erected by the Licchavis and which had been opened up by Ashoka for its relics, and also the stupa built by Ashoka himself.

In present times, Vaishali is represented by the ruins of Raja Bisal ka Garh at Basrah and the adjoining region in the Muzzafarpur district of Bihar.

The site of the Raja Bisal ka Garh is believed to represent the citadel of the ancient city of Vaishali. It consists of a large brick-covered mound, about 8 feet from the ground level, and slightly less than a mile in circumference. The most interesting finds are a large number of clay seals, official and private, the latter bearing the names of individuals or guilds of merchants, bankers and traders. The official seals indicate that in the Gupta period, Vaishali was an important administrative headquarter; and an interesting seal, engraved in characters from the Mauryan period, refers to the patrol outpost at Vaishali.

At Kolhuna, two miles to the northwest of Raja Bisal Ka Garh, there stands a monolithic pillar (locally known as Bhimsen ki Lath) of highly polished sandstone topped by a bell-shaped capital that supports the standing figure of a lion on a square abacus. It is about 22 feet above the present ground level, a considerable portion having sunk underground through the ages.

▲ Several remarkable ruins dot the landscape in Vaishali, such as this Ashokan Pillar

The line of pillars in the Champaran and Muzzafarpur districts – Rampurwa, Lauriya, Araraj, Lauriya Nandgarh, and Kolhua – is believed to mark the stages of the royal journey form Patliputra to Lumbini, which Ashoka undertook in the 20th year of his consecration. Nearby, to the south, is a small tank, called Rama Kund, identified by Cunningham with the ancient monkey's tank or markata-hraka.

Other Important Buddhist Sites in Uttar Pradesh
Kapilvastu
Location: 32 km from Varanasi

Today's Piparahwa, 20 km from Siddharthnagar, is identified with ancient Kapilvastu where Lord Buddha spent 29 years of his early life. Kapilvastu was the capital of the Sakya clan whose ruler was the father of Lord Buddha, and therefore Lord Buddha is also called Sakyamuni. The Sakya domain was one of the 16 Janapadas of that time.

THE JANAPADAS

Magadha	Modern district of Patna, Gaya and some parts of East Bengal
Kosala	In north-west of Magadha with its capital at present Sravasti
Kasi	Region around Varanasi on the banks of river Varuna and Asi
Vajji/Vriji	Licchhavis was one of the important clans, of eight allied races with its capital at Vaishali
Chedi or Cheti	Mountains of Nepal and Kushambi in Bundelkhand
Vatsa or Vamsa	Modern Allahabad in Uttar Pradesh
Kuru	Thanesar, state of Delhi and Meerut district of Uttar Pradesh
Panchala	Located between Himalayan ranges and river Ganga
Matsya/Macheha	Jaipur in Rajasthan, including Alwar with some portions of Bharatpur
Sura Sena	Around Mathura and west side of river Yamuna
Assaka/Ashmaka	Located on the banks of river Godavari, roughly present Maharashtra
Avanti	Western India, roughly where the present state Madhya Pradesh is located
Gandhara	On the banks of river Kunha till the river Indus
Kamboja	Was said to have been located on either side of Hindukush mountain ranges
Anga Videha	Bihar and some parts of West Bengal

Today, two sites claim to be ancient Kapilvastu, Tilaurakot in Nepal, and Piparahwa in India. Important finds have been made at both sites that link them with the Sakyas, the Buddha's family, precise identification is elusive. Since monasteries were built at each site, both may have been traditionally venerated as holy places.

The capital city of the Sakya clan, and one of the earliest republics, it was in Kapilvastu's opulent environs that the holy soul of Prince Siddhartha spent his childhood. Here he saw sorrow and pain, and death. Then, finally when he saw a radiant sadhu who had conquered all these, he decided to renounce all worldly riches and pleasures to seek truth and embark on the path of salvation.

Today, Kapilvastu in India comprises several villages, mainly Piparahwa and Ganvaria. Meandering their way through Kapilvastu, the devotees feel as though they have travelled back in time, to an era thousands of years ago, when young Prince Siddhartha set off to find salvation.

▲ Early India 600 BCE

Places of Interest

Stupa: This is the main archaeological site which was discovered during an excavation in 1971-73. Some seals and other artefacts of historical importance were unearthed from the site. An inscription on the lid of a pot discovered on the site reads, *'Om Deoputra Vihare Kapilvastu Bhikshu Sanghasa'*. The title 'Deoputra' refers to Kushana ruler Kanishka, a great patron of Buddhism who built the biggest Vihara at Piparahwa and renovated the main stupa.

Ganwariya Archaeological Palace Site: Excavations carried out by archaeologist Dr. KM Srivastava have indicated the ruins here to be that of the palace of King Shuddhodhan, the father of Prince Gautam. It is said to be the place where Lord Buddha spent the first 29 years of his life.

Salargarh Archaeological Site: Near Piparahwa, excavations have revealed a monastery dating to the Kushana period. A small stupa was also attached to the monastery.

There is a small monastery run by Sri Lankans and a temple of Mahendra, in the vicinity of the ruins.

Kaushambi

Location: 60 km from Allahabad

Lord Buddha visited Kaushambi in the sixth and ninth year after attaining Enlightenment. It has therefore been an important place for Buddhists. When Lord Buddha travelled widely to convey the message of universal brotherhood and humanity, his sojourn here also glorified Kaushambi.

During the time of Lord Buddha, Kaushambi was the capital of the famous Vasta kingdom, ruled by King Udayan. It was also known as Kosam, Vasta Desha, etc.

A large number of architectural relics, ruins, sculptures, figurines, coins, and other finds highlight the importance of the city during ancient times. The site has also yielded a large number of punch-marked and cast coins and unique terracotta articles that have been preserved in the museum of the Ancient History Department of Allahabad University and in Allahabad Museum.

A large part of the site is contained within an irregular area, no less than 1.5 km on the north, south and east. The entire periphery is demarcated by ramparts with regularly spaced bastions; there was also a deep moat, and the walls around it were originally of earth, but were later surfaced with brick-work. Gates with guardrooms were set up on all four sides. There are remains of a stone altar, possibly used for fire sacrifices, which have been found outside the gateway on the east; the altar was laid out in the form of a large eagle.

Places of Interest

Old Fort: Believed to be built during the sixth century BC by King Udayan on the banks of the river Yamuna.

Ghoshitaram Monastery: The ruins of Ghoshitaram monastery prove that once this place was a renowned religious and commercial center. It was one of the most famous monasteries in Kaushambi.

Ashokan Pillar: This Ashokan pillar has many rare edicts. Though its upper part is missing, it is of great historical value.

Within the walled area, excavations have revealed of continuous occupation from about the sixth century BC until AD 700. Among the identified remains are a paved road, brick habitations, mud walls and wells, brick-lined tanks, and pottery drains. At the south-west corner, the remains of a large structure has been identified tentatively as a palace complex. There was also a large brick monastery with a stupa in the middle and chambers all around it.

Kaushambi is also an important place for Jain devotees. As per the Jain scriptures, the sixth Tirthankar, Lord Padma Prabhu, was born here. Also, Lord Mahavir Swami sojourned and meditated here for a considerable period.

Prabhosa

Location: 1 km from Kaushambi

Prabhosa is about a kilometre from Kaushambi. Buddha spent his sixth rain retreat here. The Chinese pilgrim Hiuen-Tsang visited Prabhosa and mentioned a stupa constructed by Emperor Ashoka. There are caves and rock shelters here, the largest cave called Sita's Window, was probably where the Buddha stayed during his visit.

Mathura

Location: 62 km from Agra

Mathura, traditionally recognised as the capital of the Braj Bhoomi, is the land where Lord Krishna was born and spent his youth. The region is richly interwoven with the legend of Lord

Krishna, kept alive today by millions of devotes who believe him to be the most endearing incarnation of Lord Vishnu.

Situated on the banks of the river Yamuna, Mathura had assumed great significance during the Mauryan era. It also received great stimulus under the rule of Emperor Ashoka. Later, under the Kushans, it became a center of trade and learning and was practically their southern capital for two centuries. The city's strategic location at the crossroads of various trade routes made it the meeting point of many cultures. It was here that the Buddhist sculptural art took birth and reached its zenith.

Braj and Mathura also find mention in Buddhist literature, including the Pali *Tripitaka and Atthakathas*, the Sanskrit *Avadana*, the Vinaya text of the Mula – *Sarvastivadins*, the travel accounts of Chinese pilgrim Fa-hian and Hiuen-Tsang.

Buddhist sculptures, railings, and potshards belonging to the Kushan period have been found in the Chaubara mound, Jamalpur mounds, Govindnagar mounds, Chaurasi mounds, Girdharpur mound, Chamunda mounds, and the Jaisinghpura mounds.

Excavations in areas and villages around Mathura including Isapur, Ganesra, Maholi, Salempur, Pali Khera, Mansa Tila, Nauganwa, Hakimpur, Sonsa-Shahpur, Govindpur-Sarai Azamabad, Kota, Kota Chharera, and Bajna have also brought to light Buddhist relics.

Other Important Buddhist Sites in Bihar
Nalanda

Location: 11 km from Rajgir, 90 km from Patna

Nalanda is India's contribution to world culture and heritage as the first residential university in the world.

Strolling down the steps of Nalanda is like stepping back into a delightful and near forgotten era. Here lie the ruins of the world-renowned Nalanda university. It offered accommodation to about 10,000 students and 2,000 teachers, and attracted students from all over the world. The courses of study included scriptures of

Buddhism (both Mahayana and Hinayana Buddhism), Vedas, Hetu Vidya (logic), Shabda Vidya (Grammar), Chikatsa Vidya (medicine), etc. The university received patronage from the great Emperor Harshavardhana of Kannauj AD 606, and also the Pala kings. From eighth to tenth centuries, Nalanda's wonderful reputation spread all over the east, especially as a center of Buddhist theology and other educational activities. All necessary arrangements for the student's boarding, lodging, and education were made by the university, free of charge. This was made possible by the munificence of the ruling princes who made liberal endowments to this university.

The name 'Nalanda' was current during the 24th Jaina Tirthankara Mahavira and the Gautama Buddha (circa sixth century BC). The meaning of the word Nalanda has been traced to three sources. First two Sinhalese words, 'na' meaning an iron (wood or trees); 'landa' signifying high ground with a low jungle/scattered jungle. This locality might also have been so named on account of the lotus stalks (nala) which grew there in plenty. Hiuen–Tsang, says that according to tradition, the place owed its name to a Naga of the same name, who resided in a local tank. But he also conjectured that it was more probable that Buddha, in one of his previous births as Bodhisattva, became a king and this was his capital, and that his liberality won for him and his capital the name 'Nalanda' or 'charity without intermission'.

In pre-Buddhist India, education had two basic features. Firstly, it was restricted to the upper strata of society and secondly, it was essentially based on an individual teacher with his small group of pupils, i.e. the 'gurugriha' (teacher's house) system. The Buddhists revolutionised both these concepts.

Since the time of Buddha, the bhikkus were always encouraged to study the various arts and sciences.

▲ Strolling down the steps of Nalanda

Learning was greatly encouraged as it served dual purposes – knowledge and practice. The monks, therefore took to learning so that they might practise it and teach Dhamma perfectly and thereby enrich the masses. Buddhists made this learning open to all and also introduced the system of organised schools in the monasteries. These monastic institutions later gave birth to well-known Buddhist universities.

Of all the Buddhist universities, Nalanda was the first and grandest university in India. Its importance as a monastic university continued until the end of 12th century. The glory faded, but the legacy lives.

▲ Nalanda was originally a monastery built by Ashoka, it became a university much later

Nalanda was in Buddha's time, a lovely resort of saints and ascetics, students and teachers Lord Buddha visited Nalanda several times and delivered some important sermons. Moreover, Sariputta as well as Moggallana, the two chief disciples of the Buddha, were born close to Nalanda. Sariputta also attained Parinibbana/ Parinirvana in his parents' home in Nalanda.

Though Ashoka the Great had built a monastery in Nalanda in the third century BC, yet it emerged as a university much later. While Nagarjuna's name is associated with the Nalanda University since its start in AD 100, Arya Deva, it seems, gave it a definite shape in AD 300.

Under the Guptas and the later monarchs of Magadha, Nalanda, as an educational center, attained a magnificent status. The Nalanda University became famous on account of its galaxy of well-versed professors and the high standard of teaching. Nalanda produced a large number of eminent philosophers, grammarians, logicians, and leaders of religion whose writings are extant to this day. Some famous scholars who studied in Nalanda were Nagarjuna, Aryadeva, Asanga, Vasubandhau, Dinnaga, Dharmapala, Shilabhadra, and Dharmakirti.

From AD 750 in the Pala period there was much emphasis on Tantric teachings. Nalanda was visited by a number of visitors in the next important political epoch in eastern India. Under the Palas (AD 700), Nalanda rose to even greater prosperity and fame.

The Pala and Sena emperors held East India from AD 700-1100, and were noted for their patronage of Buddhism. At the same time, they established other monasteries at Vikramshila, Sompura, Odantapura, and Jagaddala.

Nalanda was visited by a large number of foreigners. Hiuen–Tsang was very warmly received at Nalanda and resided there for a long time. He took the master of law degree there.

Nalanda university consisted of three grand buildings called Ratna Sagara, Ratna Dadhi, and Ratna Ranjaka, respectively. The Ratna Dadhi, a nine-storey building, contained sacred scripts. The libraries were vast and widely renowned, although it is said that there was a huge fire in which many texts were destroyed and some irrevocably lost.

The university of Nalanda continued to grow and remained the greatest seat of learning for 700 years. To study, or to have studied in Nalanda was a matter of great prestige. Even in the 12th century, it had several thousand students from India and abroad.

Whatever fame a place may win for itself, it cannot escape from the working of the law of Anicca, which is a cardinal doctrine of Buddhism. Nalanda too was not exempt from this inexorable law. The end of Nalanda came owing to the disappearance of Buddhism from India. The great blow was delivered by Mughal invaders in the 12th century, when they drove away the monks and destroyed their main religious residences.

Places of interest

The following are the main sites of interest:

— The row of stupas in front of the monasteries

70 BUDDHIST INDIA *Rediscovered*

— The monasteries and the university building
— The archaeological museum

There are about 10 monasteries and five temples including the main temple here. The monasteries are all almost similar in layout and general appearance.

Row of Stupas: The stupas were built with a planned layout of nine Buddhist monasteries facing four temples.

Main Temple Site 3: This temple is a huge solid structure standing in the middle of a court surrounded by a number of small votive stupas, many of which were built twice or thrice, one over the other, on the same spot.

Monastery Sites 1A and 1B: To the east of the main temple are the remains of two monasteries. The buildings are on all four sides with small cells, the shrine chamber is in the middle.

Monastery Site 1: There are nine levels here, each is indicated by concrete pavements and superimposed walls and drains. The lower monastery, consisting of a number of monk's cells with wide verandas in the front, is believed to have been constructed in the reign of Devapala, the third king of the Pala dynasty. The main shrine of the lower monastery originally contained a colossal figure of the seated Buddha, indications of the crossed legs and drapery still exist.

Monastery Site 4: This monastery is worth mentioning on account of two interesting features. The first is the opening in the wall adjoining the staircase. The second is the discovery of a coin belonging to the reign of King Kumargupta (AD 413-415). This is one of the earliest coins discovered at Nalanda.

Monastery Site 5: There are two rows of cells here, one behind the other, the cells in the front two communicating with each other through corbelled doorways.

Monastery Site 6: This too was a double-storied building. A peculiar feature of this monastery is the double-set of ovens in the middle of the courtyard. There are two shrines in the lower courtyard and one in the upper.

Monastery Site 7: There are several monasteries built on the same site, each one upon the ruins of a previous one, following a similar plan.

Monastery Site 8: This is a very spacious and imposing monastery.

Monastery Site 9: There are six ovens in the courtyard. In the south-west corner is a staircase with a skylight, charred layers of wood were found on the steps of the staircase showing that they had originally been built of wooden sleepers which were subsequently destroyed by fire.

Monastery Site 10: This monastery is interesting due to the use of arches for doors. Mud mortar is used here in a clever manner.

Monastery Site 11: This monastery is in a very bad condition. The architectural features are more or less like other monasteries.

Temple 12: This monastery shows features belonging to two different periods of construction, a later building having been erected directly upon the ruins of an earlier one. In the front are votive stupas of different sizes.

Temple 13: This temple now lies nearly in ruins. The site is important on account of the discovery of a furnace used to manufacture metal figurines.

Temple Site 14: The outer walls of this temple show two periods of construction, plain walls have been erected at many places upon earlier ones with beautiful mouldings. An interesting feature about this temple is the existence of paintings in the niches of the pedestal, the only extant specimen of mural painting in Nalanda. The specimens are, however, much too fragmentary and what now remains shows the figures of a deer and a lion.

Temple Site 2: This stone temple site is interesting on account of the 211 sculptured panels over the moulded plinth. These panels depict people in various postures, including Kinnaras playing musical instruments, Makaras, Agni, Kuvera, Gajalakshmi, Kartikeya on his peacock, etc. Among the Jatakas represented here is the *Kacchapa Jataka*. These sculptures belong to AD 500-600.

For centuries, Nalanda lay in ruins, unknown and unidentified. The first European account of the village Baragaon containing the ruins of Nalanda was given by Buchanan Hamilton, who visited the place in the first quarter of the 18th century and found Brahmanical and Buddhist images. But it was only in the 1860s that Alexander Cunningham identified the place with ancient Nalanda based on the distance and directions given by Chinese pilgrims and some images and inscriptions that he found here. Cunningham published his findings in the *Ancient Geography of India,* in 1871, and thus put Nalanda once again on the world map. The remains of this great university bear witness to the spacious grandeur of a bygone age.

Barabar Hill Caves
Location: 25 km from Gaya

▲ The inscriptions in the Barabar Hill Caves claim that Ashoka donated the caves to the monks

The great series of Indian cave temples begins with the group of Mauryan caves situated in the Nagarjuni and Barabar Hills, about 25 km north of Gaya. These two caves consist of two narrow parallel ridges, about a kilometer from each other, the rock being a loose-grained granite. They are locally known as Sat Ghara (seven houses), and these caves are divided into two groups, the southernmost in the Barabar group, being the older.

Karna Kauper Cave: It is situated in the north face of the ridge. This cave, carved out of granite was excavated by Emperor Ashoka in the nineteenth year of his reign and bears an inscription which says that it was donated by Ashoka for the use of the monks.

The Sudama (Nyagrodha) Cave: This cave is hewn in the same granite ridge, but directly opposite the Karma Kauper Cave. This cave is different from others on account of its circular hall and hemispherical dome.

Lomas Rishi Cave: Of the four caves here, the most significant one is the Lomas Rishi cave. The façade of the cave has been based on the architecture of the thatched huts, which used to house ascetics in the ancient period. This cave was handed over to the Ajivikas by Dasarath, a grandson of Ashoka, as mentioned in the inscription. The fourth cave in the Barabar group is the Visava Jhopri.

Gopika is the most important cave in the Nagarjuni hill group. This was given over to the Ajivikas by Dasaratha, Ashoka's grandson, and this is mentioned in the inscription. These caves are worthy of notice not only on account of their probably being the first caves to be made in India, but because they bear witness to the kindness of Buddhist kings who generously donated some of them to non-Buddhist sects also.

The remaining caves, known as the Vahiyaka and the Vadthika, are small and of no special interest. They both bear inscriptions about Dasaratha.

Aurangabad/Aungyari/Kurkihar/Baragaon

Location: 60 km from Bodh Gaya

Aurangabad, Aungyari, Kurkihar, and Baragaon are easily accessible from Gaya. The first mention of this site was by the archaeologist Buchanan Hamilton. Innumerable shrines are found in this area. During my visit in September 2011, I was informed that Kurkihar is protected by the Department of Archaeology and digging more than five feet into the ground is not allowed here, since these places contain a veritable wealth of shrines, statues, and cultural wealth. There are temples and ponds behind the temples. Many statues of Hindu deities as well as statues of Buddha have been found in these ponds and installed in temples in the respective areas.

In a group of hills near Madanpur between Aurangabad and Sherghati, on the Grand Trunk Road, traces of Buddhist shrines were found among the rocks. Burhi, nearly 3 km to the east, has yielded several sites with the chaitya and large viharas. Viharas contains five statues of Buddha and some smaller Buddhist figures.

▲ Aungyari Buddha Statue

Aungyari

Location: 35-40 km from Bodh Gaya

There is a Buddha statue in the Surya temple, alongside other statues of the Sun God.

Baragaon

Location: Adjoining Nalanda

Baragaon has a small hamlet containing a nine-foot tall statue of Buddha in the bhumi-sparsha-mudra. The same statue is worshipped as Teliya Baba by Hindus as well as Buddhists. Worshippers offer oil to the statue and believe that skin diseases can be cured if one makes offerings with true devotion. Very recently people from Thailand have begun visiting Baragaon to worship the statue with the same devotion as Hindus.

▲ Kurkihar Buddha Statue

Kurkihar

Location: 22 km from Gaya

The large mound over which this village lies, consists of the remains of a very old Buddhist monastery. The village also has two Hindu temples and is quite famous for a rich collection of Buddha statues and Bodhisattvas. Approximately 148 bronze artefacts were excavated from this area in the 1930s.

The excavated items consisted of statues of Buddha and Bodhisattvas in all shape and sizes, bells, stupas, and a number of ritual objects. All the items that were unearthed exhibit the highest degree of workmanship.

A sizeable number of items, excavated over the years, have been kept in a Hindu temple in Kurkihar village. Amongst all the relics, the most splendid one is the statue of Akshobhya-buddha, placed just outside the entrance of the temple. Some of the antiquities excavated here, have been put up on display in the Patna Museum and some others are in the Indian Museum, Kolkata.

Champanagar

Location: 220 km from Patna

Lord Buddha visited Champanagar a number of times. It also served as the venue for a number of sermons that he delivered. He conveyed the Kandaraka Sutta (from the middle length discourses), the Sanadanda Sutta (from the long discourse) and numerous other significant discourses at Champanagar.

The place derives its name from the numerous Champaka trees here. One of the attractions of Champanagar is a lake known as Gaggara's Lotus Tank, popular for the splendid lotuses that grow there. On the banks of the lake is a huge plantation of Champaka trees, which used to be most favoured by Lord Buddha. To the left of the lake is a large water body, known as Saravana Talab. A number of Buddha statues were found here in the 1990s, when the lake was cleaned.

Don

Location: 140 km from Patna

There is a legend associated with Don. It is believed that after Buddha's death a number of kings demanded a portion of his relics for their state. The argument that ensued was resolved by a Brahmin called Dona. Dona distributed the ashes in a very equitable manner.

Dona built a stupa to enshrine the holy vessel in which the ashes had been stored. Known as Dona's stupa, it is now reduced to a grassy mound. Over this mound, a Hindu temple which houses the statue of Tara, carved in AD 800, is worshipped as a Hindu goddess.

The entire episode relating to the distribution of the ashes as well as the presentation of the vessel is mentioned at the end of the *Mahaparinibbana Sutta*.

Gurpa

Location: 33 km from Gaya

Gurpa is associated with Maha Kashyapa, the successor of Lord Buddha. It is believed that Maha Kashyapa was on his way to Kukkutapadagiri, his favourite hill resort, when he realised that his life was drawing to an end. Throughout the way, rocks kept hampering his procession. With his staff, he made the rocks give him way. The moment he reached the top of the mountain, the rocks drew apart. He went inside the opening and fell into a deep meditative trance and the rocks closed around him. The legend goes that when Maitreya (the future Buddha) comes into the world, he will go to Kukkutapadagiri. There, he will wake up Maha Kashyapa and receive Buddha's robe. Only after this, he will start announcing new dispensation. This sacred mountain of Kukkatapadagiri is now called Gurpa.

A few Hindu and Buddhist shrines and antiquities are located at the top, near the cave.

Ghosrawan

Location: Near Rajgir

Ghosrawan is the site of a large Buddhist monastery, probably the Kapotaka vihara visited and mentioned by Hiuen–Tsang. In the outskirts of the village, beside the lake is a Buddha statue nearly 10 feet high, carved out of a shiny black stone. The village Tetrawan has a marvellous and valuable collection of carved Buddhas and Bodhisattvas. Nawada, also close by, is home to a worn out museum with a small display of Buddha statues that were found in the surrounding areas.

Hajipur

Location: 10 km from Patna

In ancient times, Hajipur was known as Ukkacala and was the first village one came to after crossing the river Ganga from Patna.

The village Hajipur gained significance since it was the venue of one of the discourses given by Lord Buddha. Buddha preached the *Cula Goplalaka Sutta*, a middle length discourse here.

It also houses some of the ashes of Ananda, the closest disciple and personal attendant of Buddha.

There is a legend associated with the Hajipur village. It is believed that when Ananda realised that his end was drawing near, he decided to move towards the north Rajgir town. As soon as Ajatashatru heard about this, he went after Ananda, and escorted him with his entire staff. Soon the news of Ananda's arrival reached the people of Vaishali and they gathered along the banks of Ganga to welcome him. By the time King Ajatashatru caught up with Ananda, he was already in the middle of the river.

From one bank, the people of Vaishali, and from the other King Ajatashatru requested Ananda to come over to their side. In order to avoid disappointment and any possible conflict, Ananda rose into the air and disappeared into a ball of flames. His ashes fell on both banks of the river. On either bank, a stupa was built where the ashes fell. With the river changing its course over time, the stupa on the southern bank got washed away. Even the one on the northern bank is now a grassy mound. Over this mound, a Hindu temple has been built, known as Ramchura Mandir.

Indasala

Location: Near Rajgir

The Indasala cave near Rajgir lies at the base of a sharp cliff, halfway up the side of Giritek Mountain. On the top of the mountain stands the Hansa stupa. The Hansa stupa holds the distinction of being the most complete stupa in India, till date. The stupa as well as the story behind it finds mention in Hieun Tsang's travelogue.

The Indasala cave is an important Buddhist pilgrim destination in India, as it was the venue for one of the most thoughtful discourses given by Buddha, known as the *Sakkapanha sutra*.

Also, a number of verses of the *Dhammapada,* namely 206, 207, and 208 were given here by Buddha. The Indasala caves also served as the residence of Buddhasrijnana, the famous commentator on the *Guhyasamaja Tantra,* for some time.

Jethian

Location: Near Rajgir

Jethian, a small village near Rajgir, in ancient times used to be known as Lativana, or the Palm Grove. In the seventh century AD, Jethian also served as the seat of influence of Jayasena, the famous saint. Even Hiuen-Tsang spent two years of his stay at Jethian, as the disciple of Jayasena.

King Bimbisara met Lord Buddha for the first time in this village. It is said that after coming from Sarnath and Bodh Gaya, Buddha left for Rajgir, to meet King Bimbisara. As soon as the King heard that the Buddha was on his way, he went to the outskirts of the city, along with his staff, to welcome Lord Buddha.

There are numerous Buddhist structures as well as Buddha statues in and around Jethian. As one moves towards the village, one comes across a large mound and a tank. The mound is believed to be the remains of the stupa built over Supatittha Chaitya, the place where Lord Buddha stayed, during his stay at Jethian. There is also a huge and impressive statue of Lord Buddha and Padmapani here.

Do not miss the Chandu Hill, located 3 km from Jethian. This hill is quite popular as it houses the large cave of Rajpind – which has been mentioned in the *Tripitaka*.

Kesaria Stupa

Location: 140 km from Patna

Kesaria is marked by the tallest Buddhist stupa in the world, which dates back to the sixth century AD.

Legend says that when Lord Buddha was on his last journey from Vaishali towards Kushinagar, he spent a memorable night at Kesaria, where he made great revelations, which were later recorded in a Buddhist *Jataka* story. The story says that in his previous births, Buddha ruled as a Chakravartin (i.e. a powerful emperor). According to the legend at Kesaria, Lord Buddha asked the Licchavis, who were accompanying him through his last journey, to return to Vaishali, after he gave them his begging bowl. From Kesaria, Lord Buddha proceeded to Kushinagar in Uttar Pradesh where he is believed to have died. It is also believed that the stupa in Kesaria known to the locals as 'Raja Ben ka Deora' was built by the Licchavis of Vaishali to remember the important event when Lord Buddha gave them his begging bowl.

This stupa is the largest in the world, as high as 105 feet, and attracts lots of Buddhist pilgrims from all over the world. Excavated in 1998, the stupa is a rare example of Buddhist architecture and archaeological preservation. The stupa is slightly taller than the stupa of Borobodur (103 ft.) in Java, Indonesia, a world heritage site.

It is believed that the stupa of Kesaria was originally 123 feet high, but collapsed during the famous earthquake in Bihar in 1934. The Chinese pilgrim Hiuen–Tsang has mentioned this giant stupa in his travelogue.

The striking similarity between Kesaria and Borobodur is that both stupas have six floors or terraces, and the diameter of the Kesaria stupa is equal to that of the stupa in Borobodur.

The place is reminiscent of Lord Buddha's last few days and his humanitarian approach towards all, independent of caste and creed. His simple and ethical principles also come to mind when one looks at this huge brick monument, which is nearly twice as large as that of the Sanchi stupa in Madhya Pradesh.

Lauriya Nandangarh

Location: 22 km from Bettiah district

Lauriya Nandangarh houses the Ashokan pillar, comprising six Ashokan edicts. As per the version of the historians and archaeologists, as many as forty pillars were built there by Emperor Ashoka. However, today only one pillar exists in complete form, at its original location. The height of the pillar is 12 metres.

Even after so many years, the Mauryan polish used on the pillar still retains its radiance and shine. The pillar is carved with six Ashokan edicts, issued by the Emperor in 244 BC. The top of the pillar is adorned with a squatting lion. The face of the lion is partly destroyed since it was hit by a canon in AD 1660. One of the major attractions here is a large stupa, considered to be one of the biggest in India. The massive stupa is 24 metres high, and has a circumference of almost 457 meters.

Patna

Turning over the pages of early Indian history, one comes across the name of the pre-eminent city of Patliputra located at the site where Patna is today. This city saw the rise and fall of India's first major kingdoms. Its period of glory spanned a thousand years from from 500 BC to AD 400.

Ajatashatru, second in the line of Magadh Kings, built a small fort at Pataligram close to the Ganga. This later became the famous metropolis of Patliputra and was ruled by Chandragupta Maurya (a contemporary of Alexander) and his son Ashok.

Buddha came here while on his last journey to Kushinagar. The Third Buddhist Council was held in Patna under the patronage of Emperor Ashoka.

Kumhrar, or Kumrahar, is the remains of the ancient city of Patliputra, located 5 km from Patna Railway station, on Kankarbagh Road. Archaeological remains of the Mauryan period (322-185 BC), have been discovered here. The findings date back to 600 BC, and mark the ancient capital of Ajatashatru, Chandragupta, and Ashoka, and collectively the relics range from four continuous periods from 500 BC to AD 400.

Pragbodhi Caves – Dhungeswara Hills

The hill is situated about three miles to the north-east of Bodh

Gaya on the eastern banks of the river Falgu. The name 'Pragbodhi' literally means 'Prior to Enlightenment'. The hills were identified by Cunningham with the Pragbodhi mountain known in Buddhist literature, where the Buddha is said to have lived for six years before he proceeded to Uruvela, i.e. modern Bodh Gaya. The cave is shaped like a crescent, 37' x 5' with a small entrance 3'2" wide and 4'10" high, where Buddha is said to have meditated.

Today, the mountain has been renamed Dhungeswara. As per the legend, Prince Siddharth spent the time of his asceticism in a small cave half-way up this mountain. The same spot now houses a small temple looked after by Tibetan monks. A number of ancient stupas adorn the top of Pragbodhi mountains.

Somapuri

Location: Near Bodh Gaya

Somapuri, built in a remote region east of Vikramshila and distant from trade routes, was intended to be a place of retreat. Its history is the most fragmentary of the four monastic centers that were the jewels of the Pala dynasty. Here Kanhapa, a Mantrayana scholar, was initiated into the practice of Hevajra, and the great siddha Virupa was ordained and attained siddhi.

Somapuri's fortunes were closely linked to those of the Pala kings, all of whom strongly supported Buddhism. During the reign of Mahipala (AD 900), Somapuri's temple was completely renovated and votive stupas built with a shrine for Tara.

In the 11th century, local disruptions and external invasions weakened the Pala rulers and possibly damaged Somapuri as well.

Vikramshila

Location: 40 km from Bhagalpur, 291 km from Patna

Vikramshila houses the famous Vikramshila University, the main intellectual as well as learning centers for Tantric Buddhism.

Tarantha, a Buddhist text, records that Vikramshila was located in Magadha, at the top of a hill overlooking the Ganges. Its central monument is said to have been encircled by 53 smaller temples dedicated to Guhya Tantra and 54 ordinary temples, forming a complex of 108 temples surrounded by a boundary wall, King Dharampala provided for a staff of 108 pandits and six administrators. Out of these, almost 53 temples were dedicated to the study of the Guhyasamaja tantra. Each pandit was responsible for teaching a special aspect of the doctrine, and the head of the monastery was charged with watching Nalanda as well.

The university was built under the patronage of King Dharampala, a Pala king. Also known as Paramasaugata (meaning the chief worshipper of the Buddha), he was a great follower of the Mahayana sect of Buddhism. The center of the university once had a huge temple, adorned with a life-sized copy of the sacred Mahabodhi tree.

The entrance to the main temple stands between two brilliant statues of Nagarjuna and Atisa Dipankar.

Uttar Pradesh and Bihar have remained central to the major activities of Buddhism since the time of Buddha himself.

The main airports to start your journey from are Delhi, Patna, and Varanasi. The main railway stations to start your journey from are Patna or Varanasi. Both the states have a network of trains like the Rajdhani Express, Shatabdi Express, and other mail trains that link most places, or places close to them, on this pilgrimage.

All major sites are connected with good motorable roads, hotels, private and public transport facilities and many tour operators and travel agents operate here. Travelling through Buddhist pilgrimages around this area is an experience one must have at least once in a lifetime.

Air Taxi – An air taxi service connecting Buddhist sites in Bihar will be launched soon. The State Tourism Department is likely to sign a Memorandum of Understanding (MoU) with Pawan Hans to start helicopter services.

All major cities, sites, airports and a few railway stations have tourist offices, they can also make arrangements for guides. Local English and foreign language speaking guides are also available.

General Information

Bihar

Area: 94,163 sq. km

Capital: Patna

Boundaries: Jharkhand, Uttar Pradesh, West Bengal

Country – Nepal

Chief Languages: Hindi, Urdu, Bhojpuri, Magadhi, Maithili, Angika

Major Towns: Patna, Gaya, Bihar Sharif, Bhagalpur, Muzzafarpur, Motihari, Siwan, Mumger, Bhagalpur, Ara, Chhapra, Sasaram, Buxar

Air: *Airports* – Patna

Rail: Main Railway Stations – Patna, Muzzafarpur, Gaya, Katihar, Samastipur

Road: Road length – 13,412.80 km (in 2001); NH – 2461.74 km; SH – 10,951.07 km

84 BUDDHIST INDIA Rediscovered

General Information
Uttar Pradesh
Area: 2,40, 928 sq. km
Capital: Lucknow
Chief languages: Hindi and Urdu
Boundaries: Uttarakhand, Himachal Pradesh, Haryana, Delhi, Rajasthan, Madhya Pradesh, Chhattisgarh, Jharkhand, Bihar
Country – Nepal
Major Towns: Lucknow, Allahabad, Kanpur, Varanasi, Gorakhpur, Agra, Jhansi, Meerut, Ghaziabad, Aligarh, Faizabad
Air: *Airports* – Lucknow, Kanpur, Varanasi, Allahabad, Agra, Jhansi, Bareilly, Ghaziabad, Gorakhpur
Rail: Main Railway stations – Lucknow, Agra, Kanpur, Allahabad, Mugalsarai, Jhansi, Varanasi, Tundla, Faizabad
Road: Road length – 1,18,946 km; NH – 3,869 km; SH – 9,097 km; District roads – 9,911km

4

ANDHRA PRADESH

Buddhism had been a strong force in the social and cultural history of Andhradesa for about 1000 years, this new gospel was responsible for uniting the Andhras into a single race, and in return the Andhras played a remarkable role not only in its geographical extension, but also in developing and enriching the Buddhist philosophy, religion and art.

The Andhras appear to have been in the forefront of all movements that took place in the development of Buddhist doctrine. It is doubtless that Buddhism entered Andhra during the lifetime of Lord Buddha. Buddhism had a glorious history till AD 500, and till the close of AD 1100, Buddhism continued to have worshippers in Andhra.

Buddhism was patronised initially by the commercial and well-to-do classes who built a series of structures that included monasteries, stupas and refectories, by following a standardised plan probably contrived during the life time of Buddha.

Though the image of the human form of Buddha became popular only after the first or second century AD, his symbolic representations, important episodes in his life and Jataka tales pertaining to his previous births were profusely painted on the walls and the surface of the stupas and monasteries even during pre-Christian times. Till the introduction of the image of Buddha around AD 150, in the Krishna valley, symbols like that of his pada (feet of Buddha) and the chaitya or stupa were worshipped.

The Andhras started worshipping the relics of the Buddha. The major stupas of Andhradesa such as those at Dhanyakataka, Amaravati, Bhattiprolu, and Sriparvata Nagarjunakonda were built on the genuine corporeal relics of the Buddha. At Bhattiprolu, Dhanyakataka and Salihundam the Dhatus are

◀ Buddha idol made of sandstone — Sankaram

preserved in crystal caskets.

The Andhra Buddhists not only enshrined the relics of Buddha in their stupas, but certain religious concepts were harmonised with the architectural requirements of the stupa. Since the spread of Buddhism started with King Ashoka, the wheel became a main feature in Buddhist art. Most of the chaityas are wheel-based and might be inspired by the idea of the dharma chakra in some of the chaityas, the swastika-inset is found in the center. All over the country, the belief in the erection, decoration, and adoration of the stupas led to the practice of donating votive stupas both by monks and by devotees. Donating votive stupas means a small-sized stupa offered to pay reverence to Buddha.

Andhra Pradesh, untrodden by Buddha, received the faith most probably only during the reign of Ashoka. Ashoka was instrumental in propagating the religion on a large scale, as a part of his religious expedition (Dhammavijaya), after the conquest of Kalinga, which subsequently became a mass religion in the sub-continent. Mauryan Emperor Ashoka, ushered a revolution during the third century BC for the first time in India. He standardised the Brahmi-script and popularised the same in Prakrit or Pali language throughout the length and breadth of India. The entire literary output of Buddhism was originally compiled in Prakrit, a language of the people, which was easy for communication.

Andhra Pradesh witnessed a phenomenal growth in Buddhist religion, art and architecture in the centuries immediately preceding and following the Christian era.

In Andhradesa, the period of Satavahana rule (200 BC to AD 200) witnessed the growth and development of Buddhism and Buddhist art, besides maritime trade. The Satavahana kings made valuable gifts to the Buddhist monks and monasteries, and several caves and religious structures were built during this period.

The art of Amaravati and its influence was keenly felt in the sculptures of the contemporary south-eastern India. The zone of its influence extended along the coast further south and south-east till it reached Sri Lanka (Ceylon) and limits of south-east Asia.

After the Satavahanas, Buddhism continued to receive patronage by their successors, viz., Ikshvaku, Salankayana, Vishnukundin and other minor dynasties, who, however, were staunch adherents of Brahmanical religion.

After the Vishnukundis, Buddhism lost its ground, mainly due to the lack of royal support and hence many settlements were deserted. This fact is also confirmed by the account of the Chinese pilgrim Hiuen–Tsang who visited Andhradesa during AD 600.

One after another, the Buddhist centers of Andhradesa started closing down. During the post-Ikshvaku era, and the revival of Brahmanical faith, the patronage for Buddhism declined. While royal support which was its mainstay, witnessed a downward trend, its survival as a religion, in some parts of Andhradesa, continued even up to late medieval times.

The subsequent rulers who ruled Andhradesa were strong supporters of Brahmanical religion. Furthermore, the infiltration of Vajrayana, with great emphasis on the female element and large scale practice of tantric Buddhism, led to laxity in discipline and moral fervour. There was a pronounced tendency towards the creation of saktis or consorts. As such, most of the institutions have lost their importance.

Andhradesa, however, maintained its sanctity till the fag-end of Buddhism in India. Up to AD 1300, it attracted pilgrims from Sri Lanka. Several Buddhist sculptures in the characteristic style of the early and later schools of Amaravati were found in Sri Lanka. The Buddhist architecture of Andhradesa had a lasting effect on this island.

Thus, Buddhism in Andhradesa flourished for over 1000 years as one of the important religions, right from 500-400 BC to AD 1400-1500, as is attested by literary, epigraphical, and archaeological accounts.

Buddhist Sites

Andhra Pradesh has a rich Buddhist tradition. There are about 144 sites spread all over the state which have withstood the ravages of time. It is from here that Buddhism spread to the Far East including China, Japan, and Sri Lanka.

Hyderabad

Hyderabad, the capital of Andhra Pradesh has developed as an important Buddhist pilgrimage site, after the installation of the world's largest monolithic statue of Buddha (26ft tall and weighing 320 tonnes) on a rock in the Hussainsagar Lake. This gigantic sculpture of the Enlightened One, presiding in supreme bliss on Hyderabad's Rock of Gibraltar, flags you off in the right spirit to explore the destinations in the Buddhist circuit. The Andhra Pradesh Tourism Development Corporation's boating unit takes tourists to the statue.

The State Archaeological Museum at Hyderabad has enshrined a Buddha relic. The Ananda Buddha Vihara at Mahendra hills, Secundarabad, is the religious and cultural center of Buddhism in Hyderabad. This temple, built along the lines of a Buddhist Vihara, has a temple, museum, and library.

Cuddapah District
Nandalur

About 10 km from Rajampet town is Nandalur. Excavations on a hilltop, locally called Lanja-Kanuma (the mound of prostitutes) brought out an inscribed Satavahana shard in Brahmi script, a Buddhapada slab depicting asthamangala symbols, with naga carvings, a hoard of Satavahana lead coins, mahachaitya, a chaityagriha and 15 smaller stupas, besides early historic pottery. In 1978, the Department of Archaeology and Museums, Govt. of Andhra Pradesh, conducted excavations at the site.

East Godavari District
Adurru

Near Nagaram in Razole taluka, is Adurru, where remains of a mahastupa 17 feet in diameter with a raised platform running all round the drum and ayaka platforms on cardinal sides was discovered by the Department of Archaeology in 1925, on a mound locally known as Dubaraju Gudi. From the brick debris it is evident that the monastic establishments connected with the stupa must have covered a large area.

Erravaram

While on the way to Visakhapatnam, 45 km from Rajamundry is Erravaram.

On the eastern side of the village is a hillock locally known as *Dhanla-dibba*, littered with early historic cultural materials. A survey on the hilltop resulted in the discovery of caves, rock-cut cisterns, remains of viharas, stupas, pillared congregation hall, and a mahastupa, besides early historic pottery datable to AD 100. The famous pilgrimage center of Annavaram lies at a distance of 33 km from Erravaram.

Rampa Errampalem

The Rampa Errampalem Buddhist monastery is situated on a steep hill in the Gokavaram mandal of the east Godavari district. The historian BV Krishna Rao first discovered the site in 1934. It is popularly called *Pandavulakonda* or the abode of the Pandavas. Locals offer obeisance to the Pandavas who they think constructed the rock-cut caves. On the summit of the hill are two lofty stupas entirely cut from rock along with remnants perhaps of a brick structure of which there is no other trace. A less steep western slope used to carve three huge cells each has a votive stupa at the entrance.

▲ Lofty stupas in Rampa Errampalem

Korukonda

Korukonda along with Rampa Errampalem is second in the series of three sites on the northern banks of Godavari. The site at Korukonda is actually situated on a hill in a hamlet called Kapavaram in the outskirts of the small town. On the broad summit of the hill are remnants of a huge brick structure with a mahastupa, apsidal chaityagrihas, circumambulatory paths, and a refractory. These seem to be the earliest structures that date back to the pre-Christian era. The construction plan is very similar to the site in Pevurallakonda series. The monastic order, probably of Theravada affiliation seems to have thrived right into the Christian era when the establishment witnessed a Mahamaya phase.

The rock-cut vihara complex could be dated to around AD 200. By far, these are newest additions to the other rock-cut cave complexes, very rare in costal Andhra. In all, there are seven huge cells with a common corridor that is connected to the summit of the hill through stairs chiselled from rock. The name Korukonda or Carved Hill may have been derived from these rock-cut caves. One important find at Korukonda is a fine carved image of Hariti belonging to AD 300.

Guntur District

Amaravati

Amaravati is about 35 km from Guntur town. In ancient times, it was known as Deepaladinne (mound of lamps). The well fortified town Dharanikota which flourished as the capital city of the Satavahanas, lies 1 km away from the present Amaresware temple complex. The Prakrit, Sanskrit, and Telugu inscriptions refer to the site as Dhamnakada, Dhanyakataka, Dhanya Vatika, Dhanyankapuram, Dharanikota, Dhamakadaka, Dhannada, etc.

▲ Remains of a stupa in Amaravati

It was an important inland port town during the pre-Christian era, through which, high-quality glass ornaments were imported from the Mediterranean region. The maritime trade activity at this site, during the early centuries of the Christian era is also well attested by the occurrence of rouletted and arretine wares, Roman amphorae, and a good number of Roman coins. Amravati also known as Dhanyakataka ('Dhanya' means grain, and 'Kataka' means place) was a famous grain-producing center. It remained a flourishing Buddhist center from 300 BC to AD 1300 as is attested by a large number of inscriptions found at the site. The nucleus of the main stupa, called Mahachaitya, which formed the principal focus of Buddhist establishment, dates back most probably to the third century BC, from AD 300-200 ascribed by the earliest donative's records, some of them incised on granite uprights and plain limestone copings and cross-bars of the early railing around the stupa.

The discovery of a good number of stone and bronze images of Buddha and also of the stone figures of Buddhist deities like Maitreya, Manjusri, Lokesvara, Vajrapani, Heruka and others, belonging to the sixth to the 11th century AD, testify not only to the prosperity of the Buddhist art and religion during the period, but also to the gradual transformation of Buddhism in its final Tantric Vajrayana form.

Even as late as the 14th century, Amaravati retained its international position in the Buddhist world, as is evident from the Gadaladeniya (District Kandy, Sri Lanka) rock inscription, dated 1344, in which Dharmmakirti, a sthavira, is credited with the restoration of a two-storeyed image house of Dhanyakataka.

The Mahachaitya is one of the largest and magnificent Buddhist edifices (158 feet in diameter) in Andhra Pradesh, comprising a brick built circular vedika or drum with rectangular ayaka platforms (23x8 feet). It seems that five octagonal pillars were planted on each platform, to signify the principal events from the Master's life. The drum and dome were veneered on the exterior with sculptured slabs. The original Mahachaitya was perhaps a modest earthen mound, enlarged afterwards, during different periods, and decorated by limestone slabs and provided with a railing and gateways. The renovation of the rail pattern at Amaravati, according to an inscription, was attended by Ven. Buddharakshita.

Some of the sculptured slabs comprising panels of stupa and railings which found their way to London are displayed along the walls of the grand staircase of the British Museum.

Bhattiprolu

▲ Brahmi inscription found in the remains of the stupa in Bhattiprolu

Bhattiprolu known as *Prathilapura* in ancient times is perhaps the site with the oldest stupa.

The stupa is now an irregular mass of brick-work with concentric courses of bricks visible at places. Both in respect of sanctity and dimensions it was at one time next only to the Mahachaitya of Amravati, as it contained the corporeal relics of Buddha.

There are also other mounds here, locally known as *Pedda lanjja-dibba, Chinna lanjja-dibba,* and *Vikramarka Kota-dibba.*

Goli

The sculptures from the excavated stupa were acquired for the Chennai Museum, where they are now displayed. The sculptures have a close relationship to those of the Nagarjunakonda which is commonly assigned to AD 200.

Kesanapalli

About 12 km from Dachepalli (Nadikude) is Kesanapalli. The mound outside the village yielded remains of a stupa and vihara. The finds include a broken octagonal shaft containing an inscription in four lines and a few limestone slabs bearing lotuses.

Nagarjunakonda

Nagarjunakonda or Nagarjuna's Hill, now transformed into an island, is situated on the bank of the river Krishna. The Valley, now completely submerged under water, also came to be known by the same name. The name Nagarjunakonda is of medieval origin and is often conterminous with the hill fort perched on the hill. In ancient times as the inscription (dating from the third-fourth century) shows, the valley was known by the name Vijayapuri.

Nagarjunakonda means the hill (konda) of Nagarjurna who is usually identified, on the basis of a Tibetan tradition, with the famous Buddhist teacher of that name, contemporary of a Satavahana king of AD 100. The teacher is said to have spent his last days in a monastery on the Sariparvata, the latter identified with the chains of the hills (offshoots of the Nallamalai range) around Nagarjunkonda on the evidence of the inscription of Buddhisiri. The association of this particular teacher with this site, however, still remains uncorroborated by archaeological finds.

▲ Remains of a stupa, Nagarjunkonda

The Buddhist establishment at Nagarjunkonda/Vijayapuri was a prominent center for Buddhist monks from AD 100-500.

Excavations conducted at different places in the valley, brought to light a number of structures belonging to both Brahmanical and Buddhist faith, dated to AD 200-300. Excavated remains have been well preserved and displayed in the museum atop the hill.

In order to salvage the remains from submergence, due to the construction of the Nagarjunasagar dam across the Krishna, an excavation on an unprecedented scale was undertaken in 1954 and went on for seven years.

Before the valley was converted into a reservoir, a few important monuments had been reconstructed with ancient material on the Nagarjunkonda hill and on the eastern bank of the reservoir. Small-scale replicas of several monuments have also been erected on the hill. The antiquities found in the excavations are in the Archaeological Museum constructed on the hill.

Anupu

Located a stone's throw from the mammoth Nagarjuna Sagar Dam, Anupu enshrines a true testimony of faith, with its perfect reconstruction of Buddhist monuments, brick by brick, with diligent devotion. With a view to utilise the supposed wastage of Krishna water flowing into sea and to develop the dry areas of the lower Krishna valley, a huge dam was built at Nagarjunakonda in the Palanadu area of Guntur district some 29 km away from the ancient capital of the Ikshvakus.

After long years of exploration and excavations, the Buddhist antiquities found at Nagarjunakonda were curated at a museum after the valley was submerged. The best part of the conservation work was the recreation of an ancient university complex at Anupu. Among the most interesting aspects of the site presently is a Roman style amphitheatre with a seating capacity of at least a thousand people. The amphitheatre was probably used for staging performances of the *Jataka* tales, or for ceremonial readings of Buddhist texts. The amphitheatre was possibly part of a large institution meant for novice monks called the Nissayas, along with senior monks who probably studied Buddhism.

Nandayapalem

It is an extensive early historic site, 4 km from Chandavolu. The habitation area covers the present villages, namely Karlapalem, Buddham, Etravaripalem, and Pata Nandayapalem. A good number of sculptural and architectural pieces were recovered at the site and it was found that some of the sculptured panels contain Brahmi label inscriptions assignable to the first century AD.

Penumaka

Penumaka is 10 km from Vijaywada on the Vijaywada-Amravati road, and it is an ancient Buddhist site belonging to the first century AD, the present habitation site is encompassed by a rubble fortification wall. Outside the fortification on the slopes of the hillock are 20 rock-cut cisterns in various shapes and sizes. On the northern side of the habitation is a high mound, probably a

Mahastupa. The discovery of brick-bats, dressed stones, and early historic pottery suggests the existence of a Hinayana Buddhist site on the hill-top.

Vaddamanu

Location: About 34 km north-east of Guntur and 10 km south-east of Amravati is Vaddamanu.

The western and north-western parts of Chinnakonda and Peddakonda near the village, are perched on ancient remains. Excavations resulted in unearthing a mahastupa, several votive stupas, viharas, pillared halls, elliptical structures, a fragment of a crystal lid, Brahmi label inscriptions, coins, art motifs and a good number of inscribed pot shards etc., ranging in date from post-Mauryan to Vishnukundin times (300 BC to AD 600). During the excavations, a fragment of the upper lid of a crystal casket, along with other early historic materials, were found in the slope of the hillock.

From 1981-85, the Birla Archaeological & Cultural Research Institute, Hyderabad conducted excavations here and brought to light a well-established monastic complex, coupled with early historic cultural materials. On the hill-top of Peddakonda, near one of the cisterns, came to light a Brahmi label inscription engraved in typical Ashokan characters, i.e. third century BC.

Vaikunthapuram

Location: Vaikunthapuram is 20 km away from Vijaywada on the Vijaywada-Amaravati road.

Fragments of a harmika and chhatra carved in lime stone, rouletted ware, inscribed pot shards, celadon ware, terracotta moulds for making punch marked coins, etc., datable to first and second centuries AD have been unearthed here. Recently, a sculpture of Buddha carved on black basalt stone in bhumi-sparsha-mudra was recovered from the eroded bank of the river. On stylistic grounds, it is dated to AD 900. The above evidences suggest that the site might have existed as a Buddhist center from first to 10th centuries AD.

Karimnagar District

Kotalingala

A small village in Laksettipet taluk is well-fortified with brick bastions on four corners. Inside the fort area, excavations yielded brick built walls, drains, granaries, apsidal houses with rubble foundations, early historic pottery, and Brahmi label inscriptions, besides a good number of punch-marked, pre-Satavahana, and Satavahana coins.

Khammam District

Nelakondapalli

This place is popularly known as the birth place of the celebrated devotee Ramadas (Kancherla Gopanna) and is about 20 km from Khammam. Here lies an extensive, early historic site encompassed by a mud fortification wall covering nearly 100 acres of land. The habitation site is locally known as Bairagulagutta and the stupa area as Virataraja-dibba.

Excavations unearthed foundations of brick viharas, wells, cisterns, a mahastupa, terracotta figurines, a bronze image of Buddha and nine stone idols of Buddha, a miniature stupa carved in limestone and other early historic materials belonging to AD 200-300.

Besides these, the other remains are votive stupas in limestone and a pedestal in black basalt, decorated with triratna symbols and lotus motifs. A Brahmi label inscription is incised on the miniature votive stone stupa.

Krishna District

Allure

Allure is 5 km from Yerrupalem railway station on the Vijaywada-Hyderabad line. The excavations undertaken at this site, exposed a stupa with a drum measuring 76' 8" diameter. Two inscriptions in Brahmi characters, datable to AD 200 have been found here. According to these inscriptions, Allure might have flourished as a trade route connecting the Maisolia region with the west coast via Paithan.

Ghantasala

Ghantasala was once a renowned Buddhist center, teeming with monuments of great beauty. It is 21 km west of Machilipatnam and 75 km from Vijayawada. The prosperity of Ghantasala was mostly due to the sea trade. Ptolemy (in the middle of the second century AD) made a specific mention of the 'Emporium of Kontakossyla' in the region of Maisolia (Machilipatnam). The site is in close proximity to the sea on the east coast of Andhradesa towards south. It has attracted many people from far away lands. It enjoyed close cultural contacts with many neighbouring Buddhist centers.

Here, the remains of an important Buddhist stupa and sculptural slabs were brought to light in 1919-20. The main scene is portrayed in a circular medallion in the style of Amaravati sculptures and shows the return of Kapilavastu, of the horse and groom of the Bodhisattva Siddhartha after the latter's renunciation. The slab must have originally formed part of a casting slab of a Buddhist stupa.

▲ Dharmachakra and Buddha

The Buddhist mound at that place had, however, been reported as early as 1871 by an archaeologist known as Boswell. The stupa had a cube of solid brickwork in the center with cross walls meeting the outer circular wall. It also had a procession path along with a projection on cardinal directions. The unique cubic centerpiece of solid bricks, which adorns the stupa excavated here, is a rare discovery. Interesting inscriptions of the 12 zodiac signs are another rare attraction here.

A number of gold coins and hundreds of copper and lead coins of the Satavahana, with the ship motif found here are now the only remnants left by the flood of Indo-Roman trade. Indeed, one of the inscriptions, in characters from AD 100, found here, records the gift of an ayaka-pillar by the wife of a mahanavika (master mariner).

In and around the village, lie several mounds locally known as Yennammapadu, Ghantakamalapalli, Kota-dibba, and Lanja-dibba. Recently, a hoard of Kshetrapa coins were also reported from this place, and is now in the State Museum, Hyderabad.

Gummandidrru

Location: About 10 km from Madhira Railway Station on Vijayawada-Hyderabad is Gummandidrru.

Excavations in 1926, brought to light an extensive Buddhist settlement, comprising a mahastupa, votive stupas, apsidal chaityagrihas, and other secular and religious structures. The cultural milieu includes sculptured panels, beads, two lead coins from the Andhra period, a casket and early historic pottery. The discovery of an inscription datable to AD 100, engraved on a votive stupa and 127 inscribed clay tablets, belonging to the Buddhist creed in Nagari characters of late medieval period, clearly suggest a prolonged life for the site.

Inside the main stupa, was found a damaged metal casket containing relics, 15 pieces of a necklace in gold, kept in an earthen pot. It also contained a fragment of a bone.

Peddaganjam

Close to Chinna Ganjam in Krishna district is Peddaganjam. The three mounds located a mile to the north of village, familiarly known as Frangula-dinne (the mound of the Franks). Bhogamdani-dibba and Sakaladani-dibba (the mounds of the prostitute and the washer-woman) yielded broken statues of the Buddha, limestone slabs carved with recurrent Buddhist themes and motifs with label inscriptions datable to the third century AD. A seated Buddha, with dwarfs beneath and some sculptured lions belonged to a stupa, were exposed at Frangula-dinne.

Kurnool District
Erragudi

Location: Erraguddi is a village 8 km from the nearest town of Gutty on the Anthapur and Kurnool district borders in Rayalaseema.

On a mound locally called Erugulakonda are engraved eight major and five minor edicts of the Mauryan Emperor Ashoka. The edicts were probably engraved here sometime between 256 and 253 BC. To the west of Erragudi there were gold and diamond mines that came under the Mauryan reign soon after the conquest of Kalinga.

Medak District
Kondapur

Kondapur village is situated in the Kalabgur taluk of the Medak district. The ancient site is to the south of the village in a circular mound spanning 84 acres. Several antiquities and structural remains have been brought to light during the course of the excavations conducted at this site. The important finds include 1,800 Andhra coins, terracotta figures, seals, inscribed pot shards, carved lime pieces, punch-marked coins, and pottery of various designs and shapes datable to first century AD. The structures exposed are stupas, chaitya halls, monasteries alongwith a blacksmith area where two furnaces and moulds of coins were recorded.

Nalgonda District
Phanigiri

About 50 km from Jangaon Railway Station is Phanigiri where there is a Buddhist monastic settlement on a flat hill in the north-east of the village. It has more than 30 stupas. Most of these brick structures, were raised on squarish rubble basements and found on the

▲ These intricate carvings depict events about the Boddhisattva

western slope of the main vihara. The excavation at Phanigiri revealed many fragmentary carvings on limestone including a broken figure of a male with bulbous eyes wearing a turban. The elongated ear lobes carrying heavy metallic ornaments are resting on the shoulders. On a pilaster is a figure of a dwarf with a protruding belly, holding a thick staff in the left hand.

In another pilaster, a human figure was depicted in between a racing humped bull and chasing elephant, beneath an intricately carved lotus medallion. More than 60 Satavahana coins, dating to the first and second centuries AD, were found here during the excavation.

Nellore District
Island of Pulicat

Recent archaeological investigations in the Island of Pulicat Lake in Nellore district, resulted in the discovery of two sculptures of Buddha – one carved in black basalt at Kollapattu village (hamlet of Damarai) and the other carved in granite at Kunthuru village in Sullurupet mandal. A survey in and around the island, resulted in the discovery of brickbats and medieval pot shards. Both the images represent the Buddha as Amitabha (dhyanamudra) with a prominent flaming usnisha on the head. They are rare sculptures so far not reported in Andhradesa. Similar examples are reported from Tamil Nadu and south east Asian countries. Based on their style, they are dated to the late Chola period AD 1100-1200.

Prakasam District
Chandavaram

At Chandavaram in the Prakasam district, is a very interesting stupa constructed on elevated terraces, which is the first of its kind in the whole of Deccan and the second of its kind in the whole of India, the other being at Sanchi. It is probably the biggest in the whole of south India in elevation, and can be compared with the Dharmarajaka stupa at Taxila. The excavations here revealed 24 beautifully decorated slabs with Buddhist designs, some of which were also inscribed. Excavations also unearthed viharas, votive stupas, Satavahana coins, Brahmi label inscriptions and other early historic cultural materials datable from second century BC to second century AD.

Srikakulam District

Dantapuram

Dantapuram is an early historic fortified site, 8 km from Srikakulam railway station, on the right bank of the river Vamsadhara. It lies in between the villages Rottavalasa and Ravivalasa in Sarbujjili mandal of Srikakulam district.

The site is encompassed by a mud rampart rising about 35 feet high, which is about 60 feet thick. Inside the fort-like area, are several high mounds.

▲ These shards of pots are believed to go back as far as the third century BC

Based on the references in Jaina, Brahmanical, and Buddhist literature, the Department of Archaeology and Museums, Government of Andhra Pradesh, conducted excavations inside the fort area, in 1994 and 1999, which resulted in the discovery of traces of stupas built from bricks.

Associated with the structures, a good number of pot shards of polished black ware, knobbed ware, red ware, red polished ware, black and red ware, ivory comb, iron objects, lamp stands, etc. datable from third century BC to second century AD were collected. The city might have survived as a Janapada during the lifetime of Buddha.

From Dantapuram, the left canine tooth relic of Lord Buddha was carried to Sri Lanka, which was mentioned in the Pali text *Daladavamsa* (third century AD).

Kalingapattnam

South of the village Salihundam, lies another Buddhist site at

Kalingapattanam. Excavations brought to light a large stupa about 85.5 ft in diameter, along with its structural components. The stupa is built on a wheel-shaped pattern with ayaka platforms. To the west of this mound, a smaller stupa, devoid of the hub and wheel design was excavated. Associated with the structure a good number of early historic cultural materials datable to the first century AD were collected.

Mukhalingam

The famous pilgrimage center Mukhalingam, is located on the left bank of the river Vamsadhara. According to literature, it was the principal city in the region of ancient Kalinga familiarly known as Trikalinga. About 2 km away from this place is an ancient port-town called Nagarikatakam, which might have served as an urban center like Dhanyakataka and Salipitaka, in the early centuries of Christian era. Earlier explorations on the bank of the river, i.e. behind the Lord Madhukesava temple, resulted in the exposure of several brick structures and early historic pottery, besides Satavahana coins. Recent renovation works near the temple complex also brought to light early historic vestiges datable to first and second centuries AD. Here, in the precincts of the temple complexes were found three sculptures of important figures in the Buddhist pantheon (datable to ninth century AD) viz. Buddha as Aksobhya, Buddha as Amitabha, and a figure of Usnishavijaya belonging to the Vajrayana pantheon of Buddhism. Based on the available cultural materials, it is quite reasonable to conclude that the Buddhist settlement might have survived right from the early centuries of Christian era to the medieval times.

Salihundam

Salihundam is 5 km west of the old sea port town of Kalingapattanam, and is a Buddhist settlement perched on a hill top. It looks very imposing, and oversees the river Vamsadhara. Salihundam is an Oriya word meaning *the hill of rice*. It was originally called *Salipataka*, which probably meant, rice market. It might have been linked to the nearest port town of Kalinga-pattanam, which was in ancient times the capital of Kalinga.

Salihundam was probably established immediately after the Kalinga war and could have been directly patronised by the Mauryan reign. A label inscription was found during the 1954 excavation with a legend *Dahramarano Asokasirino,* which could be translated to mean 'belonging to the great king of Dharma Asokasiri'.

The script of the label however belongs to the second century of the Christian era and there was no other king with such a name ruling the area during that time. Probably it was to mark the memory of Ashoka, who established and patronised the site when the monastery was upgraded in the second century. The river Vamasadhara provided for all the needs of the monks on the hill. It was also the time when the monastery came under the influence of Mahayana.

Periodical scientific digs yielded not just inscribed stones, but also inscribed rouletted ware, a terracotta relic casket with gold flowers with a piece of bone in it, inscribed conches, stone and crystal relic caskets, coins and seals. These excavations brought to light apsidal and circular chaityagrihas, pillared mandapas, viharas, images of Buddha, votive stone stupas and platforms, spoked stupa, terracotta receptacles, and a good number of inscribed Brahmi pot shards and sculptures of Tara, Manjushri, Marichi, etc. belonging to the Vajrayana phase.

From the inscriptions, it is believed that the original name of the village Salihundam was *Salipetak* (emporium of rice) and the hill on which Mahavihara was situated was known as Maha Uga Parvate or 'the hill near the great sea'. The inscriptions range in date from second to about sixth century AD. The Kormi plates of Anantavarma Chodaganga (AD 1100) mentioned this was a holy place known as Mundu Marri. It means the place is famous for 'mundiya monks' (monks with clean shaven heads).

Visakhapatnam District
Bavikonda

About 16 km away from Visakhapatnam town is a site that has a large mahastupa and a number of monastic cells dating to the start

106 BUDDHIST INDIA Rediscovered

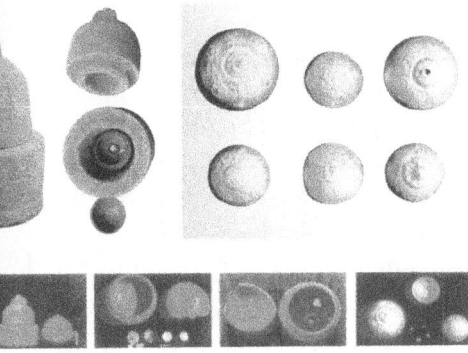

▲ This casket containing Buddhist relics has been recently unearthed

of the Christian era. It was discovered when a naval reconnaissance helicopter was scouting for a place to build an airbase in 1983.

Bavikonda was probably called *Senagiri* going by inscriptional evidence from the neighbouring Thotlakonda where a couple belonging to the area near Bavikonada donated a water trough. 'Syenaka' in Sanskrit denotes a mythical eagle that is of great significance in the *Jataka* tales.

Excavations (1982-87) on the hill top brought to light an extensive Buddhist establishment consisting of a mahachaitya, embedded with relics caskets, large vihara complex, a number of votive stupas, a stone congregation hall, rectangular halls, a refectory etc. The vihara consists of three arms in the layout of a Trisala, a big congregation hall, where lectures and debates must have been held. In association with these structures were recovered a Satavahana lead coin, three Roman silver coins, fragments of Brahmi label inscriptions, Buddhapada slabs decorated with the asthamangala symbol and other early historic cultural milieu, datable from third century BC to third century AD.

While attending to the conservation work of the Mahachaitya, five receptacles containing silver and gold caskets were recovered.

Gopalapatnam

On the left bank of the river Tandava, about 12 km from Tuni, is Gopalapatnam. Recent excavations revealed a Chhatussala type of vihara complex, a mahastupa on a terraced platform, votive stupas and other early historic materials such as polished black knobbed ware, black and red ware, decorated pot shards, stone sculptures, and inscribed Brahmi labels, which range in date from second century BC to fourth century AD.

Kottur

The earliest reference to the village called Kottur, which is 52 km from Visakhapatnam town on the left bank of the river Sarada near Elamanchili, is found in the Allahabad pillar inscription of Samudragupta (fourth century AD) wherein it was mentioned as *Kotura* (Girikottura). During this period, the region was under the political control of the local King Svamidatta.

On the slopes of the Panchardhara hills, there is an early historic mound littered with brick bats and pot shards. Excavations have brought to light a stupa and a vihara complex. The stone receptacle found here is made out of khondalite. In the outer container of the receptacle, was embedded a green-coloured soapstone reliquary, a small crystal phial, gold foils, silver flowers, and beads. A red coloured bead incised with a rampart lion is an important find in the casket. A Brahmi label inscription is engraved on the soap reliquary datable to the second century BC.

Pavurallakonda

Pavurallakonda or Pavurallabodu is about 30 km from Visakhapatnam near Bhimili, it is the local name of a hill, popularly known as Narasimhaswamykonda. During the course of explorations here, nearly 14 to 16 rock-cut troughs or cisterns were found hewn into the bedrock. Near the entrance of the tank were found Brahmi label inscriptions. Trial excavations in the habitation here, revealed foundations of viharas with cells and a common veranda, circular chaityagrihas, votive stupas, halls etc.

Associated with the structures were two Satavahana coins, a Roman coin, inscribed pot shards, besides black and red ware, black polished ware, beads etc. A casket in two parts, i.e. the upper lid and the lower container, was recovered while exposing the votive Stupa 1 situated near the tank. The rivulet locally known as Gosthani flows near the northern periphery of the hill and joins the sea, thus forming a vast confluence at the foot of the hillock, which served not only as water resources for the inhabitants of Pavurallakonda, but also as a navigational point for inland trade during early centuries of Christian era.

Sankaram

About 3 km north of Anakapalle railway station are the twin hillocks locally known as Bojjanajakonda and Lingalametta, Sankaram, is a corrupt form of Sangharamam. The rivulet Sarada flows by the side of the village, which is the principal water source for both trade and drinking.

The twin hillocks locally known as Bojjanajakonda and Lingalametta were for the first time noticed by Alexander Rea (1970-78). The hillocks were elegantly dotted with a row of rock cut votive stupas, resembling Shivalingas and hence were familiarly known as Lingalametta.

On the top of the hillock Bojjanajakonda, lies the main stupa, and a host of votive stupas made of bricks, viharas, rock cut cells, apsidal rock cut shrines etc. The main stupa consists of a square platform approached by a flight of steps, a drum and dome commanding a panoramic view of the fertile countryside.

On the eastern side of the hillock is perched a brick structure, whereas the western and northern sides of the summit are peppered with scooped out caves. The caves on the western side, which are wider and larger in dimension, contain exquisitely carved Buddhist sculptures.

The other antiquities recovered from the site include 70 copper coins of the Eastern Chalukyan dynasty, seals and sealings, inscribed clay tablets with Dharanis, one local Satavahana coin, one gold coin of Samudragupta, images of Buddha, Vajrayana images etc.

Based on the architectural features of the monastic complex and other early historic cultural material, the foundation of the site may be assigned to second-third centuries AD and it seems to have flourished up to the ninth-tenth centuries AD.

Thotlakonda

About 16 km away from Visakhapatnam along Vizag-Bheemili beach road is the Buddhist settlement on the hill top of Mangamaripeta, locally known as Thotlakonda. The excavations unearthed an extensive monastic complex, comprising a mahastupa, apsidal and circular chaityagrihas, votive stupas, rock cut cisterns, a congregation hall, pathways, Roman and Satavahana coins and stucco pieces datable from third century BC to fourth century AD. Altogether, 12 Brahmi label inscriptions engraved on chattra pieces, stone troughs, stone steps etc. have been reported, ranging from second-third century BC to second-third century AD.

Vijayanagaram District
Ramatirtham

Ramathirtham is a huge monastic complex situated on a granitoid hill very close to the Nellimarla town in Vijayanagaram district. Here, on one of the hills known as Gurubhaktakonda, the extensive ruins of a Buddhist monastery were laid bare. Besides, a number of chaityas and stupas were also found. Some of the brick chaitya halls may be quite ancient. A large number of early historic pottery was also recovered, from the excavations.

Situated in the west and connected with Gurubhatakonda is the hill known as Durgakonda, which also originally contained Buddhist monuments, but was subsequently occupied by the Jainas and thereafter by the Hindus. Excavations conducted by Rea brought to light images of Buddha, a Satavahana lead coin, clay seals, votive stupas etc. One of the clay seals contained the name of the local King Sri Siva (maka) Vijaya Rajia Selasaghasa who ruled the area in the first-second century AD. A similar name also occurs in one of the label inscriptions at Amaravati. From this, it appears that the King Siva (maka) Vijaya was a local chieftain, who most probably ruled over this area for some time, after the eclipse of the Satavahana kingdom.

Warangal District
Dhulikatta

The Adilabad-Karimnagar-Warangal region was peppered with a large number of early historical settlements, some of them fortified with mud ramparts.

Here, the Buddhist stupa and the vihara was constructed over a prominent mound at the confluence of two perennial rivulets one coming from the west, one from the north merging together to flow towards the east. The stupa constructed during the last quarter of the third century BC was sufficiently enlarged during the first quarter of second century BC. During the first phase, the stupa was enclosed by a square platform to buttress the stupa as well as serve as a circumambulatory path.

The enlarged garbha of the stupa was bedecked with more than 50 carved slabs, most of them found intact. One of the slabs the Muchilinda Naga – a five-headed cobra protecting the Lord Buddha, symbolically represented by his feet, was exquisitely delineated. At the top of the Naga, over the embossed frame, is an inscribed label in early Brahmi script datable to circa 175 BC. Punch marked Satavahana and Roman coins, ivory combs, seals, a silver portrait coin of Pulumar, beads and bangles, terracotta figurines etc, were also recovered.

Dhulikatta may be one of the 30 walled towns in the Andhras mentioned by Magasthanese, a famous ancient Greek traveller. The settlement is located on an ancient trade route leading from Vidarbha, south Kosala and Andhra to Dhanyakataka.

West Godavari District

Arugolanu

Arugolanu is in the Tadepalligudem sub-division of west Godavari district. Excavations here revealed the extensive remains of a large vihara, with two small stupas, votive stupas, and Mahachaitya. At Pedda Lanja-dibba, the ruins of rectangular buildings, and two relic caskets were discovered.

Guntupalle

About 120 km away from Vijaywada is Guntupalle. Situated on a hillock, surrounded by serene natural beauty, the site holds some of the most unique rock-cut Buddhist shrines, chaityas, stupas, and viharas.

Dignaga, the great Buddhist logician, is believed to have lived here in his arama (place of rest).

The picturesque horseshoe-shaped hill range which is an offshoot of eastern ghats overlooking the village, contains rare early rock-cut caves which can be compared with the earliest known Mauryan examples of Sudama and Lomas rishi caves (third century BC) at Barabar hills in Bihar. Excavated in a row, all along the slope, the caves are simple and facing east and north. About 2 km north-east of caves are located another group of caves which formed naturally due to erosion and disintegration of the rock. The remains are spread over three huge hills and the foothills towards the present habitation space.

▲ A ruined chaitya on the top of Guntupalle

At the entrance to the hill on the right is a huge natural cavern running into the core of the hill. It appears that the cavern was enlarged in the front to provide space along with a portico and stairs leading down. This natural cavern was probably the first layer of occupation much before the first brick structures came up on the hill. The first rock cut caves could have also belonged to a much later period, between first and second century AD.

Prominent among the caves is the vritta (circular) chaitya situated at the southern end of the ravine. The chaitya contains a rock-cut circular stupa at the center leaving space for a pradakshinapatha around the holy place. The chamber measures 17 feet in diameter and the domical ceiling with its circular ribbed framework is 14 feet in height.

The remarkable feature of this shrine is its vaulted ceiling with ribs, converging at the apex, resembling a wood hut (kuta) with carved rafters.

Another noteworthy feature of the cave is the horseshoe-shaped arched façade of the cave entrance with projecting rafters all cut into the living rock, an imitation of the contemporary original wooden prototypes. The chaitya is known as Dharmalingeswara as the local people believe it to be a huge Shivalinga.

The rock-cut viharas at Guntapalle are invariably rectangular with an arched façade. The façade of the vihara cell has usually one main entrance in the center, flanked by two small windows. The cells have a rock-cut seat along the rear wall with a backrest. These cells served as living rooms for the monks.

Besides the above mentioned rock-cut caves perched on the hill, are structural stupas and mandapas in stone and brick. More or less of the same period as the rock-hewn chaitya is a brick-built circular chaitya. The other small stone stupas here are mostly votive in character. Three standing images of Buddha are found here carved on limestone, these sculptures are depicted wearing heavy lower garments, which typify the Amaravati school of art.

A complex of more than 40 votive stupas strewn on a semi-flattish terrace made of either brick or khondalite stone blocks is testimony to the popularity of the site. For structural stupas, the dome part was encased with curvilinear slabs with no ornamentation, rock-hewn cisterns served as storage tanks for rainwater.

The excavated finds from this site, such as a free-standing statue of Buddha, stone relics casket, golden beads, terracotta finials and iron objects are kept in the Government Museum, Chennai.

There can be no doubt that Guntapalle is the biggest Buddhist site in Andhra Pradesh. Since it is shaped like a horseshoe, like the Ajanta caves, Guntapalle is called the 'Ajanta of Andhra Pradesh'.

Pedavegi

About 12 km north of Eluru town is Pedavegi. In ancient times it was known as 'Vengipura' the capital city of the Salanukayanas. A few Brahmi label inscriptions were reported from the excavated mound, locally known as Dhanam-dibba. All the labels are datable to pre-Salankayana times.

Jaggayyapeta

The venue of the Buddhist establishment here is a low hillock (locally called Dhanabodu or 'hill of wealth'), the Velagiri of yore. In ancient times, its original name was Velagiri, which afterwards became Vedagiri and Elagiri, as can be seen from inscriptions found at the site. Later on, over this mound was raised a village known as Betavolu. Subsequently, Raja Venkatadri Naidu of Chintapalli, developed it into a town and named it Jaggayyapta, after his father. Excavations here brought to light a Mahastupa embellished with architectural and sculptural slabs, as at Amaravati, and a processional path.

The fallen fragment of the outer railings, near the pathway, suggests that it possessed a decorated stone railing. The occurrence of epigraphs, besides sculptural carvings depicting such beauty as winged animals, capitals, pilasters and other early historic antiquities, can be dated from second century BC to sixth century AD.

The discovery of a few carved slabs from one of the brick mounds here in 1818 revealed the existence of a group of ancient stupas. The fragments of the images of Buddha and also the carved base of a votive stupa of the type usually found in the apsidal chaityagrihas leave no room for doubt about the existence of the shrines in the immediate vicinity of the mahachaitya.

One of the relics of the Buddha bears, below the feet, the record of Chandraprabha the disciple's disciple of Nagarjunacharya, in characters of the sixth or seventh century AD, proving thereby the continued existence of Velagiri as a Buddhist center at least up to that period.

The following year, the place had been so long dug for bricks and slabs that traces of only one stupa were left. The stupa after excavation was found to be 30 ft in diameter and had slabs of the same materials as those at Amaravati. The rail around the stupa had entirely disappeared. Inside the casing, the stupa was made of earth and bricks.

The slabs surrounding the base of the stupa were mostly plain, very few of them having any carving except a small pilaster up the edge. Some of the sculptures on the pilasters closely resemble in style the Bharhut sculptures, and also the earliest ones at Amaravati. The capitals are heavy and roughly bell-shaped and show double-winged animals like that at Pitalkhora. Some of the slabs were inscribed in characters of Mauryan type ascribable to the beginning of the second century BC.

Gudivada

Gudivada is 32 km northwest of Machilipatnam. The existence of a stupa here was brought to notice by Boswell in 1870. Alexander Rea undertook some excavations here in 1894 and found traces of circular courses of brick work. Remains of an ancient township are also reported on the outskirts of the village wherefrom bricks, pottery, coins and beads were collected along with some coins belonging to the Satavahana dynasty.

General Information

Area: 2,75,069 sq.km.

Capital: Hyderabad

Boundaries: Maharashtra, Chhattisgarh, Karnataka, Orissa, Tamil Nadu, Bay of Bengal

Chief Languages: Telugu, Urdu

Main Towns: Hyderabad, Secundarabad, Karimnagar, Sirpur, Visakhapatnam, Vijayawada, Cuddapah, Kakinada, Anantpur, Adilabad, Warangal, Nellore, and Rajahmundry.

Air: Hyderabad, Tirupati, and Visakhapatnam.

Rail: Rail route length – 5107 km. Main Railway Stations – Hyderabad, Secunderabad, Guntakal, Warangal, Renigunta, Vijayawada, Visakhapatnam.

Road: National highways in A.P. are 4,647 kms., and State highways cover 61,488 km. There are 1,18,235 km of Panchayati roads.

APTDC operates buses to certain Buddhist sites. Other means of transport include private taxis. For further information, contact the tourist office, or travel agents. Major cities have very good hotels that suit every budget.

Andhra Pradesh has a rich Buddhist tradition with over 140 Buddhist sites and nearly 96 sites under development. APTDC has created beautiful resorts and public amenities at the Buddhist sites to make the visitors comfortable. APTDC is in the process of developing the Buddhavaram Theme Park covering 279 acres near Nagarjuna Sagar.

Hyderabad, Vijayawada, and Visakhapatnam are the focal points from where the Buddhist sites of the state can be visited.

Hyderabad Buddhist Circuit: Nagarjunkonda, Phanigiri, Gajulabanda, Kondapur, Dhulikatta.

Vijayawada Buddhist Circuit: Amaravati, Vaddamanu, Battiprolu, Ghantasala, Chandavaram, Guntapalli, Adurru, Jaggayyapeta, Gummmadidurru, Nelakondapalli, Dhanyakatakam.

Visakhapatnam Buddhist Circuit: Salihundam, Dantapuram, Ramatirtham, Kothur, Thotlakonda, Bavikonda, Pavuralakonda, Magamaripeta, Sankaram.

I am grateful to Prof. P Chenna Reddy, Director of Department of Archaeology and Museums, Government of Andhra Pradesh. During my visit to his office at Hyderabad, he readily made available information about Buddhist sites, which enabled me to write captioned information. For further details contact: chennareddyp@gmail.com

I am also grateful to Sashi Sekhar, for allowing me to use pictures from his book *Wheels and Its Tracks*.

5

GUJARAT

Gujarat, a state on the west coast of India, has its own interesting character and a glorious history. The history of Buddhism in Gujarat is spread over nearly 1,800 years. All the phases of Buddhism were experienced in Gujarat, as they were elsewhere in India.

The real history of Buddhism in Gujarat begins with the establishment of the Mauryan dynasty's rule here. Long before Ashoka proclaimed Buddhism to be the state religion, the first Mauryan dynasty, had spread its power over the north-west frontiers of India, northern India, and the greater part of the Kathiawar peninsula. The continuity of the Mauryan rule and the advent of Buddhism in Gujarat are proved by 14 edicts installed by Ashoka, the grandson of Chandragupta, on a rock in Junagadh. It is probable that from the earliest times, Mount Girnar, near Junagadh, was considered a sacred place and it is probable that for this reason Ashoka used a large stone near the foot of it for carving one of his most complete set of edicts.

The coastal region of Gujarat stretching from Kachchh to Saurashtra and up to Bharuch is dotted with several caves. These caves were excavated between second century BC and sixth century AD. It is believed that most of them were excavated during the Kshatrapa rule, especially the first century BC.

There are indications in old Pali scriptures that a few people in Gujarat had become Buddhists even during the lifetime of Gautam Buddha. In the *Theragatha* we find the names Vaddha Thera, Malitavamba, and Vaddhamata Theri of Bharuch. There are several references to Bharuch in Vinayapitaka. Several places in Gujarat are frequently mentioned in the oldest Buddhist literature.

◀ The subterranean caves in Uperkot are decorated in Indian and Greek style

Early Beginnings

It is well known that Purna of Sopara had brought Buddhism to Maharashtra during Buddha's lifetime. Purna's conversation with the Buddha regarding his intention to preach the Dhamma in Sunaparanta (Sopara) is well-known. Sopara and Bharuch were very closely connected by sea. As revealed by the *Jataka* stories and by other sources, there used to be heavy traffic between Sopara and Bharuch. Since Buddhism had reached Sopara during the lifetime of the Buddha, it is possible that Buddhism must have entered Bharuch during Buddha's lifetime too, because of the influence of Purna in the country of Aparanta.

The famous city Avanti was not far away from the border of Gujarat. It was on an important trade route joining northern cities like Rajagriha (Rajgir), Vaishali, and Sravasti with Bharuch and Saurashtra. Therefore, the influence of Mahakaccana's presence in Avanti must have been felt in Gujarat also. Mahakaccana was one of the most eminent disciples of Buddha. He was considered the chief among the expounders of the complete sayings or teachings of the Buddha. It is possible that Buddhism might have trickled into Gujarat during Mahakaccana's time there from Avanti.

Influence Wielded by Rulers

The Mauryan empire ruled Gujarat from Patliputra for nearly 130 years, up to 184 BC. Even during the Sunga period, the descendents of Ashoka ruled Gujarat for a long time as independent rulers. After the end of the Mauryan rule, the Greeks ruled over Gujarat for some time during the third century BC.

As is well known, the prominent Greek ruler Minander had accepted Buddhism as his religion. Minander's rule extended from Sialkot to south Gujarat. Minander's coins were discovered in Saurashtra near Junagadh and in south Gujarat near Bharuch. His coins were current in Bharuch even up to the third century AD. A large number of Greek Buddhist names appear as donors in the caves of Maharashtra. A Roman author, Strabo, in his *Geography of India* has written about a Bhikku from Briach (Bharuch) who died in Athens at the time of Augustus Caesar, in the beginning of the first century AD. The Greek's hold over Gujarat began to decrease by the end of the first century AD and they were replaced by Partho-Scythians, or the Kshatrapa family. Buddhism became popular in Gujarat during the Kshatrapa rule, from first-sixth century AD and it continued to flourish during the Maitraka rule.

The Buddhists lost their great patrons with the downfall of the Maitraka rulers and thus they suffered a severe setback in Gujarat. Still, there is sufficient archeological, epigraphic, and literary evidence to show that Buddhism flourished after the end of the Maitraka dynasty and in the post-Maitraka period and existed even up to the 13th century AD. Saindhava rulers, who ruled from Bhutambilika, or Ghumali, in western Saurashtra between AD 735-920, had given liberal grants to Buddhist viharas.

In the 13th century, a minister, Asraja of the Solanki king Viradhavala, is described as a Buddhist monk. This perhaps is the last reference about the existence of Buddhism in Gujarat.

Buddhist Sites in Gujarat

Most Buddhist monuments in Gujarat are situated along the Saurashtra coast and around Junagadh. Junagadh seems to be a prominent center for Buddhism in this state since Ashoka's reign.

Saurashtra Region
Junagadh

'Junagadh' literally means old fort. It was the capital of an erstwhile Muslim princely state Saurashtra, of the same name, and was an ancient city in the pre-Christian as well as early historic Saurashtra era, and enjoyed considerable importance. The city and its surrounding hills have Buddhist caves.

In the vicinity of Girnar Hills, at the entrance of the valley, near the edge of what was once the Sadarsana Lake is a huge rock (third century BC) now known as the '14 Rock Edicts of Ashoka'. This rock edict is a huge boulder and the inscriptions in the Brahmi script in Pali language oppose greed and animal sacrifice and preach principles of purity of thought, devotion, secular thinking, kindness, and gratitude. The rock edict found near

▲ This huge rock has inscriptions in Brahmi script urging people to value purity of thought

Junagadh is conical in shape, about 12 feet high, and the perimeter is 75 feet. At the end of the fourteenth edict, the words *'Sarvalokasubahar – sveta – hasti'* are written, which refer to Lord Buddha.

There are groups of rock excavations, which were excavated by Buddhists for their congregations and monastic residences. There were numerous Buddhist cave monasteries and even as late as the seventh century AD. Hiuen–Tsang mentions the presence of as many as 50 Buddhist convents where nearly 3,000 monks of the 'Sthavira' sect of the Mahayana order lived, in the capital of Saurashtra, near which is the mountain he called Yen-Shen-Ta (known as Urjayanta or Girnar).

Junagadh Caves

The caves in Junagadh fall into three groups:

- The Khapra Kodia Caves
- The Baba Pyara Caves
- The Buddhist Caves at Uperkot

The Khapra Kodia Caves

To the north of the city is a series of large excavations known as Khengar's or Khapra Kodia's palace. On the basis of scribbles and short cursive letters on the wall, Khapra Kodia caves are datable to third-fourth century AD. The Khapra Kodia Caves are the plainest of all cave groups. When Hiuen–Tsang visited Junagadh, he found many Buddhist monasteries and convents around this area.

The Baba Pyara Caves

This group of caves lies to the eastern side of Junagadh, close to Modhi-math, and is also known as Baba Pyara's caves. The caves are arranged in three groups, with the first group in the north facing southwards, featuring the largest cave on its west. The second group of caves is chaityagriha, facing an open courtyard. The verandah in front of the chaityagriha has a winged lion at each end and six pillars with lion capitals. The southern cave in the group has a sunken courtyard, a verandah and two cells. It is marked with Buddhist symbols and figures. The third group has five caves, each of which has a hall with a central pillar supporting its roof.

▲ The Baba Pyara caves are marked with Buddhist symbols and figures

The Buddhist Caves at Uperkot

The most important excavations at Junagadh are the subterranean caves within the fortified area of Uperkot simply known as the 'Buddhist Caves'. The cave group is a three-storeyed complex with the main hall at the bottom. The hall, partially open to the sky, is the most decorated in the entire complex. The decoration style shows the influence of both contemporary Indian art and Scythian and Greek art, and is datable to the second century AD.

There are three important structures belonging to the medieval period in Uperkot, namely the Adi-chandi vav, Navghan vav, and the Jami Masjid. Of these, the first two have been cut deep into the soft rock. Jami Masjid was originally the center of activities for Chudasama rulers and is indeed known as Ranak Devi Mahal after the Queen of Ra Khengar, and had been converted into an extensive Jami Masjid by Mahumud Beghara in the first flush of his final victory over the princely vestiges in Saurashtra in 1470 AD.

Boriya Stupa

According to a report by the Royal Society of Bengal, a stupa was recovered which was a lofty burnt brick structure that rose up to 80 feet in height, it is now preserved in the museum in Junagadh. The Boriya stupa was excavated by archaeologists Camphel and Cousens at Junagadh in AD 1885. The aim of this excavation was to retrieve a casket from the stupa.

A shaft dug in the center of the stupa revealed a stone casket. Within it there was another smaller stone casket which in turn contained a copper box. Within the copper box, they found a silver casket that contained a gold box which contained a small piece of bone (about the size of a finger nail), a small piece of wood, and five semi-precious stones. All these are now kept in the museum at Junagadh.

Archaeologists also discovered the remains of a marble vedica (railing). The remains are very similar to that of the Sanchi vedica, which is characterised by the horizontal cross-bars, lenticular in section, fitted in vertical pillars and topped by rounded canopying. This is the earliest known stupa found in Gujarat which belongs to the second century AD.

Intava Vihara

The Intava vihara at Junagadh was excavated by archaeologist GV Acharya and the report was published in a Gujarat daily. The six rooms of the vihara that were excavated looked over a verandah. These might be a portion of a square vihara like those at Devni Mori. The most important find here was a small clay seal embossed with the words, *'Mahraja Rudrasena vihare Bhikshu Sanghasya'*. *'Rudrasena'* refers to Rudrasena I (AD 200-222). The vihara dates back to the second or third century AD.

Sana Rock-cut Caves

Location: 24 km north of Una railway station

The caves are situated in a wild and desolate part of the country close to a perennial stream. A little to the east of these caves in the Lor hill are some natural caverns which certainly show signs of having been occupied and close to them is a perfectly plain excavation, probably a Buddhist ascetic's cell.

In these hills, more than 60 caves have been found, believed to date from the first century BC to the second century AD. The most impressive is Ebhal Mandap, which is about 22 meter (70 feet) wide, 5 meter (16 feet) high and 20 meter (64 feet) deep. The Bhimachory cave, sometimes written as Bhima-Churi, facing the north-east has octagonal pillars and a stone bench. It is believed to have been a vihara. Near the cave is the chaityagriha which has a plain stupa, about 2.3 meters in diameter, and has an apsidal rear.

A Sitaram Bapu temple has been built on a hill which has many caves connected to one another by rough hewn rock steps. A kund or water tank found near the Sana hill may have been the source of water for the cave's residents.

Bhavnagar District
Talaja Rock-cut Caves

To the south-east of the Saurashtra peninsula, on the north-west face of the Talaja hill, near the mouth of the Shatrunji river, is a series of about 28 rock-cut Buddhist caves and 20 *pondis* or cisterns.

The frontage of most of the excavations has crumbled away and the cutting of a passage to the extensive Jain establishment on the top of the hill has destroyed several caves.

One of the largest of these caves and the only one that now presents any remains of ornamentation is at a height of a hundred feet.

The large hall, without any cells in its sidewalls, has four octagonal pillars in the front, but none inside to support the roof; nor has it a wall. It seems to have been constructed as a place of assembly for religious instructions, a dharmashala in fact, where the early Buddhist missionaries preached new doctrines to the people. Outside the entrance are wells or tanks on both sides, and several cells. On its façade are fragments of modified, perhaps a very primitive form of a horse-shoe or chaitya-window ornament, and of the Buddhist rail pattern, but this is the only sculpture traceable in these caves.

The ruined Chaitya No. 3 consists of an open verandah and a long hall with a plinth on either side. A single chamber in the rear contains the remains of a dagoba.

The courtyard has benches on all sides, beneath which have been excavated large cisterns for water, whose openings are flanged for fitting wooden, or stone covers.

Valabhi

Maitraka kings were originally Buddhist and Buddhism reached the peak of its glory while they held sway over the state. The Maitraka period was one of the most glorious periods of Buddhism in Gujarat.

Bhattaraka is considered to be the founder of the Maitraka dynasty that ruled Gujarat for more than 300 years from AD 470-789. There were separate monasteries for Bhikshus (monks) and Bhikunis (nuns). Under the fostering care of this dynasty, the Buddhist educational center of Valabhi grew to be as reputed as Nalanda. Valabhi is now a pretty township, and local tradition has it that many centuries ago it spread right down to the coast through the river Ghala and the main artery of outward bound merchant traffic. Valabhi was in commercial intercourse with Persia and Rome. Broken pieces of red polished ware of non-Indian make and a number of scattered Buddhist antiques were found, small images of Buddha's head, and tiny terracotta tablets called 'Dharnagutikas' with the formula of the Buddhist creed – *'Ye dharma hetu prabhava'*, etc. inscribed on them.

Jamnagar District
Dhank Caves

Location: 55 km north-west of Junagadh

A few caves are still preserved here, which are likely to be Buddhist caves, but are claimed to be Jain caves. According to local tradition, a temple of Mancesvaridevi was here, later it was converted into a Shiva temple. Mancesvaridevi is the corrupt form of the name of the Buddhist god of wisdom, Manjusri.

Near Dhank, at Siddhasar, is a ravine called Jhinjhuri-Jhar in Saurashtra. A few Buddhist caves here are still in good condition. Inscriptions on some stones helps date them to the second century AD.

▲ The author at the Dhank caves

Rajkot District
Khambalida Rock-cut Caves

Location: About 21 km south of Gondal, off the National Highway leading to Porbandar, is a road to Badar Dam that continues to Khambalida.

▲ The most popular cave – Khambalida with breathtaking statue of Avalokiteswara at the entrance

Khambalida has one of Gujarat's most impressive Buddhist caves. Steps lead down to a cluster of 15 caves in the center of which is a chaityagriha. The entrance to this cave is flanked by sculptures of Bodhisattvas identified as Avalokiteswara (Padmapani) who is much revered by Buddhists as an embodiment of compassion, and Vajrapani, one of the earliest bodhisattvas of Mahayana Buddhism. Vajrapani is integral to Buddhist iconography as one of the three protective deities surrounding the Buddha. This cave is of considerable interest as it is the only one in Gujarat with perfectly identifiable carvings of Bodhisattva, beings who assist people in achieving complete enlightenment or Buddhahood. This cave is believed to date to the fourth century AD, and also has remains of a stupa.

There is a group of small caves here, the only one in Kathiawar which contains many mythological sculptures, but they are of a very crude description and very weathered, some are probably of a later date.

North Gujarat Region
Mehsana District
Taranga Hill

Location: 20 km from Vadanagar

On the Aravali range, Taranga hill seems to be an important center for tantric Buddhism. The main idols enshrined in the Taranmata and Dharanmata temples are of Buddhist Goddess Tara. Broken terracotta images of Buddha, four carved images of Dhyani-buddha on a stone plate, stone and brick walls inside rock shelters, etc. have been discovered here. Recently, the Gujarat State Archaeology Department located a Buddhist sanctuary at the site.

▲ The view from Taranga Hill where there are several Buddhist artefacts, and (inset) a statue of Buddha

Vadanagar

Location: 30 km from Mehsana and 104 km from Ahmedabad

Vadanagar is probably the Anandpur described by Hiuen-Tsang which was said to be an important Buddhist site. This site is geographically important as it falls between the important Buddhist sites in Malawa and south-east Rajasthan and those in western Gujarat.

Excavations have yielded a Buddha statue in the Mathura style, coins, toys, and brick structures. Excavations are in progress at Vadanagar. Vadanagar holds an important place in the history of Gujarat, the Solanki Rajput rulers built temples here which are known for their profusely carved *toranas* – tall towering structures with supporting arches.

Eastern Region
Sabarkantha District
Devni Mori
Location: 2 km from Shamlaji

▲ A relic casket found in Devni Mori, contained some items belonging to Gautama Buddha

The remains of Devni Mori are situated in a picturesque vale on the bank of the Meshvo near well-known Shamalaji, where the river enters the plain after cutting through the outliers of the Aravalis. Just south of Shamlaji on NH8, a bridge leads off to the Ahmedabad–Udaipur highway across the Meshvo river. The path from here leads to the village Devni Mori. This village came into the limelight in the early sixties because of the excavations here that revealed the presence of a substantial Buddhist site with stupas and viharas.

The stupa of Devni Mori could have been of special significance, as an inscription on a relic casket found at the site states that it contains the relics of Gautama Buddha.

The copper box inside the casket contained a gold bottle, burnt sandalwood, beads, gold and silver foil, and silk. The ashes found in the gold bottle of Devni Mori may not weigh more than four or five grams.

While the original casket and most of the other finds at Devni Mori have been moved to MS University in Vadodara, a replica of the casket and a model of the stupa with its elongated dome as depicted in the plaque have been exhibited at the nearby Shamlaji Museum, which also displays some of the Buddhist sculptures found in Sabarkantha district.

South Gujarat Region
Bharuch District
Jhagadia

Location: 20 km from Ankleshwar, 105 km from Vadodara

En route from Ankleshwar to Jhagadia, a trail leads off from Jhajpor to Kadia hill, the site for seven Buddhist caves and a monolithic lion pillar. The presence of a veranda in front of each of the caves and the benches hewn into rocks at the rear of the caves suggest that these caves were viharas. The highest located caves on the hill have figures of elephants and monkeys as well as inscriptions written in Brahmi characters.

The first cave is more than 8 feet high and seven feet wide and has a depth of about 24 feet. The relics of a vedica or railing can be seen leading from the veranda at the entrance. The second cave has steps leading to the veranda. Its veranda is noteworthy. The seven caves seem to belong to the first and second century AD. A number of ruined brick structures and utensils dating to the fourth century BC to the first century AD have been found in the vicinity of the hill.

Eight brick structures found in the forest surroundings and a lion pillar appear to be remains of viharas and stupas. Based on its ground plan, one of them seems to be a hemispherical brick stupa.

Kadia Dungar Caves

Location: Near Bharuch

There are seven caves here – four facing the east, two facing the west, while the last one is facing the south-east direction. Caves 1 and 2 bear some inscriptions in Brahmi, which have not yet been deciphered. There's another inscription in a cave nearby, which is almost obliterated, but the name of Kshetrapa king Virasena can be read, which indicates that the inscription was carved around 288 AD. A brick stupa was also found in the foothills.

These caves were in use during the first and second century AD. There is also a monolithic lion pillar near the caves. These caves can be reached from Zaspor railway station.

Kachchh District

Siyot Rock-cut Caves

Location: 125 km from Bhuj

On the highway from Bhuj to Lakhpat is the village of Ghaduliya from where a road leads past the village Siyot to a cave with an east-facing sanctum and an ambulatory which is said to date to the first century AD. It is believed that this may have been a Shiva temple before the Buddhist monks occupied the cave. Siyot must have been one of the 80 monastic sites that the seventh century Chinese traveller reported seeing at the mouth of the Indus river, at walking distance from the cave.

Ranapur

Location: 30 km north-east of Porbandar near Ranapur village.

Most of the caves here are very simple and without ornamentation. One group of caves has been exploited by contractors as a stone quarry. A few caves have been converted into temples of Hindu gods and goddesses.

Buddhist Circuits in Gujarat

- Ahmebabad, Vadanagar, Taranga, Devni Mori
- Rajkot, Dhank, Junagadh, and places around Junagadh, Sana, Talaja, Khambalida

Gujarat has 25 districts, and the Gujarat state transport bus system connects all these districts. Private buses ply between major cities of Gujarat and cities of connecting states like Maharashtra, Rajasthan, and Madhya Pradesh. Tourist taxis, and local transport is available.

An International Seminar on Buddhist heritage was held at the Maharaja Sayajirao University of Baroda from January 14-16, 2010, to highlight the Buddhist tradition in India in general, and in Gujarat in western India, in particular.

The Chief Minister of Gujarat Mr. Narendra Modi was the chairperson of the seminar and was blessed by His Holiness the Dalai Lama who also attended the seminar. The Government of

Gujarat and Gujarat Tourism Development Corporation are now actively involved in promoting Buddhist sites in Gujarat. For current developments, contact Gujarat Tourism Development Corporation at Ahmedabad, or Maharaja Sayajirao University at Baroda.

I feel proud to mention here that I was the only person to read the paper on the subject 'Developing Buddhist Tourism in Gujarat' during the seminar.

I must thank Mr. YS Rawat, Director of Archaeology, Government of Gujarat, for his help in providing information and making corrections where required.

General Information

Area: 1,96,024 sq. km

Capital: Gandhinagar

Boundaries: Rajasthan, Maharashtra, Madhya Pradesh, Daman-Diu, Dadra Nagar Haveli

Country – Pakistan. Sea – Arabian sea

Chief Language: Gujarati

Main Towns: Ahmedabad, Vadodara, Bhavnagar, Bhuj, Surat, Jamnagar, Kandla, Mehsana, Porbandar, Rajkot

Air: *Airports* – Ahmedabad, Vadodara, Bhavnagar, Bhuj, Surat, Jamnagar, Kandla, Keshod, Porbandar, Rajkot

Rail: Main railway stations – Ahmedabad, Vadodara, Bharuch, Valsad, Navsari, Surat, Dahod, Nadiad, Anand, Rajkot, Himatnagar, Palanput

6

HARYANA

During the long span of a little less than half a century after His Enlightenment, it may be said that Buddhism reached Haryana with the Buddha himself.

The Buddhist text *Vinaya of the Mulasarvastivadins* refers to Buddha's long journey with Ananda from Hastinapura to Rohitaka via Mahanagara, Srughna, Brahmanagrama and Kalanagara and from there to Gandhara and Uddiyana and back with Yasaka Vajrapani. Rohitaka is undoubtedly modern Rohtak and Srughna was rightly identified by Alexander Cunnigham as Sugh village near Jagadhri.

The *Mahavastu* attributes 60,000 cities to the Kuru kingdom, but the specific names of places mentioned in the Buddhist literature, besides Indapatta and Hatthinipura are only a few – Thullakotthita, Kammasadamma, Kundi, and Varanavata. During the time of Buddha though the Kuru kingdom may not have been very important politically, yet culturally it seems to have been a prominent state. The *Jatakas* mentions the Kuru kings and princes (Dhanajaya Koravya, Koravya, and Sutasoma) whose historicity remains to be confirmed by further evidence. The reigning dynasty belonged to Yudhitthila gotta, i.e. the family of Yudhisthira, Kuru chief Koravya (son of Kuru magnate) is said to have paid a visit to Rattapala, who had become a disciple of the Sakhya Sage. *Dipavamsa* refers to Buddha's visit to a city in the Kuru country where he received alms on the banks of the Anotatta Lake, which he crossed. The city may have been Kurukshetra, if the Anotatta Lake is Anyatahplaksa of the *Satapatha Brahmana*.

Thulliakotthita and Kammasadamma find repeated references in Buddhist literature as the place where Buddha stayed during his sojourns to the Kuru country. Buddha delivered numerous discourses here. During His visit to the Kuru country, Buddha usually stayed at Kammasadamma, which was a celebrated trade center.

It is generally believed, perhaps erroneously, that Buddhism disappeared from the land of its birth because of the hostility of the Hindus. Post-Harsha Buddhist relics are rather rare. The discovery of an eighth century bronze image of Buddha in bhumi-sparsha-mudra amongst a large hoard of Jain images found from Hansi some years back; a sandstone head of Buddha from Sanghi in district Rohtak ascribed to the same period; a broken Buddha head from Rohtak and another from Adi Badri datable to ninth-tenth centuries; indicate that Buddhism did not disappear altogether from this part of the country.

That it continued to exist in Haryana as late as about the 14th century is proved by an image recovered from a temple at Taraori in district Karnal showing Buddha seated on a lotus pedestal in bhumi-sparsha-mudra.

Buddhism flourished in Haryana only during the reign of Ashoka.

▲ The remains of stupas in places like Agroha need the attention of historians

It continued to be an important religion during the Sunga, Indo-Greek, and Sakhya rule and touched its all time high in Haryana during the Kushana period.

Buddhist sites at Adi Badri, Agroha, Asandh, Chaneti, Kurukshetra are known locally, but still they need the attention of historians and archaeologists from all over the world.

The best way to visit the Buddhist sites in Haryana, is from New Delhi.

Haryana Transport Organisation operates regular buses to all major towns of Haryana.

General Information

Area: 44,212 sq. km

Capital: Chandigarh

Boundaries: Punjab, Chandigarh, Himachal Pradesh, Uttaranchal, Uttar Pradesh, Delhi, Rajasthan

Chief Languages: Hindi, Punjabi

Main Towns: Karnal, Rahtak, Panipat, Hisar, Yamunanagar, Gurgaon, Faridabad, Rewar, Bhiwani

Air: *Airports* – Pinjore, Karnal, Hissar, Bhiwani, Namaul

Rail: Main railway stations – Ambala, Panipat, Kurukshetra, Jakhal

Road: Road length – 31,901 km; NH1 – Murthal to Delhi border to Karnal; NH2 – Balabgarh to U.P. borders

Private taxis are available from New Delhi and also from major towns in the state. Major towns offer accommodation to suit every budget.

For further information, contact the tourist office, or travel agents.

I must thank and introduce my colleague Mr. Sidharth Gauri, who is an activist and has dedicated his life to the mission – 'Save Buddha, Save Stupa'. I request readers to refer to the website www. thebuddhistforum.com and join the venture. You could also email him at sidharthgauri@gmail.com

7

HIMACHAL PRADESH

Himachal Pradesh has nurtured Buddhism through the ages. A necklace of Buddhist monasteries and gonpas are etched across its landscape.

Buddhism is said to have entered Lahaul and Spiti in the early centuries of the Christian Era even though it was introduced in the Himalayan region in the third century BC by the missionaries led by Ven. Majjhima who were deputed by Ashoka to preach the Dhamma. Ashoka had issued a number of pillars and rock edicts throughout India. One such rock edict has been found near the confluence of the Yamuna and Tons river.

Buddhism in Himachal Pradesh, as everywhere else in north India, received further impetus during the reign of the Kushana King Kanishka (AD 78-101), a great patron of Buddhism after Emperor Ashoka. The Kushana dynasty continued to rule till about AD 225. Significantly enough, a number of archaeological remains from the second century AD have been discovered in Himachal Pradesh.

Buddhism continued to flourish in Himachal Pradesh in the subsequent centuries as is confirmed by the monastic sites and the images of the Buddha that date to the fifth and sixth centuries AD. We can gauge the state of Buddhism in Himachal Pradesh from what Hiuen-Tsang saw in AD 653 at Tamsavana (modern Raghunathpur or Sultanpur) and Kuluta (modern Kulu). Tamsavana or 'Darkness wood' has been identified with Sultanpur in the Kulu valley, situated at the confluence of Beas and Serhari. Kuluta is the modern city of Kulu and the areas around the upper valley of the Beas river. In this valley is a celebrated place of pilgrimages, Trilokanath, situated on a hill in the village Tunda on the left bank of the Chandrabhaga (Chenab) river. It contains an

◀ The Key monastery where Lamas receive their training

image of Avalokitesvara Bodhisattva with six hands, now worshipped as an image of Mahadeva. Lord Buddha is said to have come here and converted a Yaksha who later built a monastery. In earlier times a stupa called *chi-chi-tope* stood here, which contained a relic of the Buddha. Ashoka had also erected here a stupa, which was still intact when Hiuen–Tsang visited Kulu in August AD 635.

The presence of Buddhism in Himachal Pradesh became stronger when the famous Padmasambhava sojourned in these valleys on his way to Tibet in AD 747-748. One of the greatest preachers of Buddhism in this area was Rin-Chen-Bzang-Po (AD 958-1055) who is said to have been born at Sumra in Kinnaur. Rin-Chen-Bzang-Po was the greatest scholar and translator produced by Kinnaur who not only preached and propagated the Dhamma in the Guge kingdoms, but also in Tibet. The ancient monasteries in this region go back to the 11th century and are believed to have been founded by him. The two most important monasteries among them are the Alchi Monastery in Ladakh and the Tabo Monastery in Spiti.

Some gonpas go back to the time when Buddhism was a shadowless sapling in the region. The seed for its rise in the area had been sown in the seventh century AD when the Tibetan king Sondtsen Gompo (Sron-b-Tsan Sgam-po) was influenced by two of his wives, Cheng from China and Bkrikuti Devi from Nepal. A century later King Trison (Khri-Sron-Ide-btsan AD 755-797) embraced the way of the Buddha and from India came masters like Santarakshita and the famous teacher and tantric Padmasambhava. The ninth century witnessed a break in the spread of Buddhism, but the tenth and eleventh centuries witnessed a grand revival and it was the age of great teachers – Atisha, Marpa, Milarepa, and Rin-Chen-Bzang-Po. With the passage of time, Buddhism became the major religion of Tibet, Ladakh, Lahaul, and Spiti. It also extended its influence in neighbouring areas like Kinnaur. Apart from their religious influence, the gonpas also became the fount of power and the repositories of the region's art and manuscripts. A millennium old, Tabo in Spiti, is one of the area's most venerated monasteries.

The travel accounts of Tibetan pilgrims throw light on the condition of Buddhism in Himachal Pradesh in the 13th century. These pilgrims came to Punjab to pay their homage to the second Nagarjuna (AD 600-650) the founder of Vajrayana.

There are monasteries barely a few decades old that came into being after 1959, when His Holiness the Dalai Lama left Tibet along with several followers and came to reside in India.

The Buddhists of Lahaul, Spiti, and Kinnaur follow the Tibetan form of Buddhism. Owing to its proximity to Tibet, the impact of the Tibetan culture on the people of this region is quite significant and is visible in many ways. Their temples, gonpas, monasteries have Tibetan names.

And as surely as the chant of prayers accompanied with rhythmic drum beats, and interspersed with the roll of cymbals ring out of their hallowed halls, they bless the land and welcome every pilgrim and traveller.

The remote valleys of Lahaul, Spiti, and Kinnaur have strong Buddhist traditions. Splendid gonpas, Buddhist monasteries, built along the bare mountainside seem a part of the rugged terrain. These are the repositories of the wealth of Buddhist art and culture and the dim cool interiors of ancient monasteries glow with the brilliance of painted murals, stuccos, and elaborate thangkas framed with rich borders of silk.

Monasteries in Lahaul Valley

Kardang Monastery

The 900-year-old Kardang Monastery is located at an altitude of around 15,000 feet in the Kardang village. The location of the monastery with the stunning backdrop of the bare mountains of the Rangcha massif ensures maximum sunlight during the winter. Kardang is the erstwhile capital of Lahaul and the monastery here is one of the biggest and oldest. It was renovated by Lama Norbu in 1912.

The architecture of the monastery reflects the style, which typically belongs to Lahaul and Spiti. The multi-storeyed structure has four temples, including one that contains a silver coated

▲ Kardang Monastery

chorten with the ashes of Lama Norbu.

Kardang's library is well stocked with volumes of the *Kangyur* and *Tangyur* texts in Bhoti language; its walls are decorated with tantric paintings. There are excellent colourful frescoes and murals. Additionally, the monastery also houses a huge repository of some exquisite thangka paintings, old weapons, and a collection of musical instruments like lutes, drums, horns etc.

The monastery is associated with the Red Hat sect and has a Naroba as its head Lama. Equal rights are granted to both nuns and monks. The lamas of this monastery are allowed to marry. During summer they live with their families and work in the fields while in the winters they return to the monastery.

Guru Ghantal Monastery

Location: 8 km from Keylong

Lahaul's pre-eminent Gompa Guru Ghantal was established by Guru Padmasambhava around 800 years ago. It is said to be located at the site where Guru Padmasambhava meditated before going to Tibet in AD 747. The word 'Gandhola' in Tibetan means the 'Pure House' and refers to the holy site of Buddha's enlightenment at Bodh Gaya. This monastery was believed to be the site of Padmasambhava's enlightenment and therefore came to be known as Guru Gandhola. In the course of time, this name was distorted by the foreigners and the monastery came to be known as Guru Ghantal. The monastery is also known as the Triloknath. The monastery is located on a precipice above the village Tandi, where the Chandra and Bhaga river join to form the Chandrabhaga.

Guru Ghantal is a double-storeyed structure made of wood with pyramidal roofs and a big dukhang. The monastery is particularly interesting for its black stone image of the Hindu goddess Kali, locally known as Vajreshwari Devi, assimilated into the Buddhist pantheon under Padmasambhava's tutelage.

The highlight of this monastery is that unlike the other monasteries of the state, the idols here are made from wood and not clay. The monastery has a wooden image of the Buddha which is said to have been installed in 11th century AD by Lama Rin-Chen-Bzang-Po. Within the monastery there are images of Padmasambhava and Vajreshwari Devi (Do-je- Lha-mo) along with numerous images of other lamas.

The gonpa is surrounded by a large number of rock caves and locals claim that Guru Padmasambhava had meditated in one of these before leaving for Tibet. The monastery was extensively renovated in 1959.

In the earlier days, a festival called Ghantal was celebrated in this monastery wherein the visiting lamas and thakur feasted for a day. This festival is not celebrated today. The monastery's annual festival, held on a full moon day in June, sees pilgrims perform the 29 km parikrama around Drilburi, a sacred peak.

Shashur Monastery

Location: 3 km from Keylong

Shashur Monastery, located on the Macchu slope was founded by Lama Deva Gyatsho of Zanskar in the 17th century. 'Shashur' in the local parlance means 'in the blue pines'. This is a very apt name as good patches of blue pines can still be seen around the monastery. Lama Deva Gyatsho was a missionary of the King of Bhutan. The monastery belongs to the Red Hat sect of Tibetan Buddhism. The gigantic thangkas, some over 15 feet tall, and numerous wall paintings, including that of the 84 siddhas of Buddhism indicate the influence of the Red Hat sect. The stucco images of deities in the dukhang have been kept in a glass enclosure in order to prevent thefts. On the first floor, Shashur's walls are covered with very well-preserved murals, while even the columns and beams are decorated with floral and other motifs.

Shashur's Tseshe festival, held between June and July, is most popular in Lahaul and consists of Chham dancing and ritual plays by lamas dressed in traditional costumes and elaborate masks.

Tayul Monastery

Location: 6 km from Keylong

'Tayul Gonpa' in Satingiri village derives its name from the Tibetan for 'Chosen Place'. Tayul Monastery was established by Dongpa Lama, Serzang Rinchen of the Kham reign of Tibet in the 17th century.

It is famous for its 15 feet tall statue of Padmasambhava. The local legend maintains that the main prayer wheel rotates on its own accord on sacred events. According to resident lamas, this last happened in 1986. There is also a library in the monastery which houses 108 volumes of the sacred *Kangyur* text and thangkas reflecting the life of Lord Buddha.

Monasteries in Spiti Valley

Dhankar Monastery

Location: 29 km from Kaza

On the left bank of the Spiti river, at a distance of 32 km downstream from Kaza, near Shich (a peak about 12,400 feet high) nestles the citadel of Dhankar, the official capital of Spiti. Even from a considerable distance, Dhankar, situated 29 km from Kaza, stands out because of the solidity of its construction.

Dhankar, originally called Dhankar ('Dhak', cliff and 'khar', palace), literally means 'Palace on a Cliff'. It is believed that Dhankar was once the capital of Spiti, which perhaps accounts for the fortified nature of its monastery. Dhankar is also of historical importance for art lovers.

Founded between the seventh and ninth centuries AD, Dhankar complex occupies the southern part of the steep mountain slope of the village. It is known as O-pa Gonpa (Monastery of the followers of the Lha-O).

The monastery consists of a number of multi-storeyed buildings that stand together, giving it a fortress like impression. An image of Vairocana or dhyana-buddha, consisting of four complete figures seated back to back is the highlight in this monastery. There are Buddhist scriptures in Bhoti language and relics such as paintings and sculptures. Two gonpas are housed in this monastery – Lha Opa Gonpa and Lkhang Gonpa. The former is supposed to date back to the 12th century. The second gonpa is more prominent with its splendid mural that represents the life of Buddha.

Lhakhang is decorated with depictions of Sankyamuni, Tsongkhapa, and Lama Chodrang on the central wall, making it Dhankar's main attraction.

There is also a freshwater lake about 2.5 km from the village, at a height of 13,500 feet. Set amidst lush green pastures, the lake offers a prefect idyllic camping site.

Dhankar is approachable by a motorable road, good for small vehicles only, that branches off for Dhankar from the main Kaza-Samdu road at a point around 24 km from Kaza. The branch road to Dhankar is 8 km long.

Lha-Lun

Location: Lha-Lun is a two-hour drive from Dhankar

Lha-Lun is believed to have been constructed overnight by the gods after Lotsava Rin-Chen-Bzang-Po planted a willow tree here, and said that if it lived through the year, a temple should be built next to it. The tree stands outside the gonpa to this day. The name Lha-Lun literally means the 'Land of Gods', from 'lha', 'god' and 'lun', 'area'. According to belief, the Lha-Lun god is head of all deities in the Lingti valley and emerges from the

▲ The Lha Lun monastery

Tangmar mountain located beyond the village in the valley. This mountain changes colour from time to time, in conformity with the god's moods.

There is a dark passage around the temple meant for circumambulation of the inner sanctum.

Key Monastery

Location: 7 km from Kaza town

Situated at an altitude of 13,500 feet and in a place that is known as Little Tibet is Key Monastery. The entire monastery complex is located on the slope of a hill in tiers. The gonpa is approached by road from Kaza (12 km). However, it is only a 8.5 km trek.

Key monastery dates back to AD 1000, There have been several attacks on it. In the 17th century, the Mongols were the first ones to attack. The 19th century saw three more efforts to ruin the monastery. Perhaps its location, on the main commercial roads, made it susceptible to conquest. This continuous onslaught on the monastery resulted in frequent renovations and reconstruction work, which in turn has given rise to an irregular box-like structure, and now looks like a fort rather than a monastery.

The monastery is a wonderful example of monastic architecture and came into prominence during the 14th century, because of the Chinese influence. Regular invasions have led to temples built one over another. There are low rooms and narrow corridors. The passages are not very well lit, the staircases are difficult and small doors lead to prayer rooms which themselves do not conform to a single design.

The walls of the monastery are decorated with beautiful paintings and murals, which instantly attract the attention of visitors. A beautiful image of Buddha in the dhyana-mudra can be seen in the monastery.

Hundreds of lamas receive their religious training in the monastery. Key is also a vibrant center of Buddhist cultural tradition and houses many musical instruments, along with a collection of fabulous thangkas and a set of murals based on the *Jatakas*. Its elaborate dukhang was rebuilt after the original was destroyed in the earthquake in 1975. Its library contains a collection of *Tangyur* and *Kangyur* texts.

Kalachakra or the 'Wheel of Time', for Buddhists, is 1000 years. The Key monastery was established in AD 1000 and in 2000, it became exactly thousand years old. His Holiness the Dalai Lama was part of the millennium celebration. The ceremony was hugely sacred for the Buddhists and pujas and religious congregations were organised.

The ceremony focuses on the main subjects – cosmology, psychophysiology, initiation, and Buddhahood. A Kalachakra Mandala with Vishwatma deity in union with his consort guide the disciple through the tedious process of initiation. Gustor the annual Chham festival in Key is held in the first half of July.

Kibber Monastery

Kibber is located at a height of 14,200 feet in a narrow valley on the summit of a limestone rock.

Kibber Monastery is named after Serkang Rimpochhe of Tabo. The Lama breathed his last in Kibber in 1983 and when he was being cremated a source of water erupted from the spot. Even today the water is used by the villagers. There is a traditional trade route from Kibber to Ladakh over Parang La. The Spitians go to Ladakh to barter their horses for yaks, or sell them for cash.

Kungri Gonpa

Spiti's second oldest monastery Kungri is located in the Pin valley. One of the results of sectarian strife in Spiti was that most monasteries here are of the Gelukpa order. Only in Spiti's Pin valley does one find monasteries of the Nyingmapa tradition, at Kungri and Mud – perhaps because this region was relatively isolated, the only entrance to it being through the Pin river. The Kungri gonpa has a large retinue of monks in residence.

The Kungri gonpa was erected in the first half of the 14th century. The dilapidated, mud-walled old building is flanked by a recently built hall decorated with paintings and woodwork. Within the gonpa, attractions include silk paintings of various Buddhist deities on the inner wall, huge statues, and over 300 volumes of the sacred Tibetan texts preserved carefully in white muslin.

Further along the pine riverbed are Mud structures, with two Nyingmapa nunneries, meditation caves and shelters. Phukchung, on the shores of Parahio river, also has a nunnery.

The Kungri gonpa acquired attention after it received large foreign donations for its renovation. Kungri represents unmistakable evidence of the tantric cult of Buddhism. Kungri gonpa is the main center of Nyingmapa sect in Spiti. The gonpa consists of three detached rectangular blocks facing east. The curious looking buzhens perform a sword dance and are perhaps the only branch in Buddhism in which use of weapons is practised.

Tangyud Gonpa

Location: 26 km from Kaza

The 500-year-old Tangyud monastery at Komic, at an elevation on 14,700 feet, is one of the highest in the world. Built around the early decades of the century it belongs to the Sakyapa sect and is of historical importance.

According to legend, its construction was foretold in Tibet as a monastery built between two mountains, one shaped like a snow lion and the other like a decapitated eagle. The space between the mountains would resemble the eye of a snow cock, and, the name Komic in fact derives from this – 'ko' means snow cock and 'mic', eye. About a three-hour walk from Komic, down the mountain, are the ruins of a Sakyapa monastery at Hikkim village built near the confluence of three streams and yet, ironically, abandoned because of severe water shortage.

Kaza Monastery

Kaza, the headquarters of the Spiti subdivision, has a newly built Sakyapa Monastery with fine contemporary woodwork and wall paintings. The monastery was renovated and enlarged for the Kalachakra festival held there in 2008.

Kaza serves as the starting point for trips to the gonpas of Key and Komic. Foreign tourists can collect inner-line permits here.

Tabo Monastery

Location: 47 km from Kaza

The Tabo Monastery known as Chos-khor is the largest monastery in Spiti. It has as many as nine temples. Of these, at least five temples are traced back to the 11th century AD. The three most important temples are – the Golden temple, the large temple of Drompton, and the temple of Enlightened Gods. The Golden temple has beautiful murals of the divinities and the protective deities on the walls. The ceiling of the temple is painted with gandharvas, birds, and floral motifs.

The large temple of Drompton has a large painted figure of the Buddha flanked by Sariputta on the right and Maha Moggallana on the left. The sidewalls have figures of the eight Medicine Buddhas. Medicine Buddha is one of many Buddhas who, through eliminating all negativity and perfecting all positive qualities, has attained the state of perfect enlightenment for the benefit of all sentient beings. The sky blue body signifies omniscient wisdom and compassion as vast as limitless space and is particularly associated with healing both mental and physical sufferings. The temple of Enlightened Gods has the largest number of images.

Tabo is the best illustration of a mandala, in the center of the assembly hall of the temple of the Enlightened Gods. The assembly hall itself is a vivid representation of the *Vajradhatu Mandala*, with the four-fold Vairacana in dharmachakra pravartana pose sitting at the far end and flanked by 33 vajrayana deities.

The sanctum sanctorum houses Amitaprabha on a lion, with Ramapani on the right and Mahasthanaprata on the left. The change of mount from peacock to lion is significant and deliberate as it signifies the elevation of Pratyeka Buddha to Bodhisattva who meditated on the Vajradhatu mandala.

Known locally as Tabo Chos Khor, its name means 'sacred doctrinal enclave of Tabo'. Located in the valley of Spiti at an altitude of 9,760 feet, it spreads over an area of 6,300 sq. m and is surrounded by high boundary walls.

Tabo was a royal monastery, founded and renovated by two of the most famous royal lamas of the distinguished line of kings of

Purang-Gunge in Tibet. The renovation inscription of the monastery tells us that the temple was founded by the Bodhisattva (the royal Ye-she-O) and renovated 46 years later by his grandnephew. But the tradition attributes Tabo's founding to the Great Translator Rin-Chen-Bzang-Po. According to an inscription on one of the walls, the monastery was founded in AD 996.

The monastery has a distinct boundary – a wall made out of mud brick, called 'cags-ri' in Tibetan. Tabo's central temple is surrounded by smaller structures at the four cardinal points. Inside, there are nine temples, four decorated stupas, and the cave shrine contains 23 chortens, a monk's chamber and an extension that houses the nuns' chambers.

On the sheer cliff-face above the enclave are a series of caves, which were used as dwellings by the monks and also as an assembly hall. Faint traces of the paintings that once embellished the rock face can be discerned. Even today, Tabo holds the distinction of being the largest monastic complex in Spiti, constructed in AD 996.

Tabo has treasures in its dimly-lit interiors. Tabo is famous for its exquisite murals and stucco sculptures which bear a striking resemblance to the paintings and sculpture in the Ajanta Caves, which is why it is known as the 'Ajanta of the Himalayas'. Sharp lines, earthy colours, and distinctly Indian features are characteristics of the paintings from this early period. The dukhang is the most elaborately decorated, with its walls divided into three tiers. The life of the Buddha is depicted on the lowermost tier, followed by 32 stucco images on a pedestal in the middle tier, and three rows of Bodhisattvas on the uppermost tier.

A thousand years ago, Tabo served as a meeting place between two cultures, which is graphically represented in art. Indian pandits and Tibetan scholars came to Tabo to learn Tibetan and Indian Buddhist works respectively. This interaction germinated in the seeds of a new art statement best defined as Indo-Tibetan.

Tabo Monastery is one of the most famous Buddhist monasteries regarded by a large number of followers as second only to Tholing Gonpa of Tibet. Tabo is the oldest continuously functioning

Buddhist monastery in India and the Himalayas with its original decorations and iconographic programme intact. Tabo monastery contains the largest number and the best preserved group of Buddhist monuments in Himachal Pradesh.

Even today, the monastery is keeping up its image of an efficient and effective learning center by opening up schools to impart modern education to the new generation.

Inside the Monastery Complex

The monastery complex houses nine chapels, four decorated stupas, and the cave shrine contains paintings that date to the 10th-11th century (main temple), 13th-14th century (stupas) and 15th-20th century (all other chapels). Except for the main temple and the painted interior of the stupas, all other extants are attributed to periods following the Gelupa/Gelukpa ascendancy.

The Temple of the Enlightened Gods: (g Tsung Lha-Khang) This is the most important temple in the complex and occupies the central position. It is also called the assembly hall or dukhang, within it, there is an assembly hall, a vestibule, and a sanctum. Right in the center of the temple is the four-faced figure of Vairocana. He is regarded as one of the five spiritual sons of Adibuddha, a self-created primordial Buddha. The imposing figure is placed around 2 meters above the floor and is seen turning the wheel of law. A figure, popularly known as the Vajradhatu Mandala, surrounds the central image. The walls of the temple are full of paintings that depict the life of the Buddha in various stages. The paintings, it is believed, were done by the artists specially invited from Kashmir. The sanctum of the temple houses five Bodhisattvas of the Good Age.

The Golden Temple: (gSwr-Khang) The temple was initially believed to be layered with gold. However, the 16th century saw extensive renovations undertaken in this temple at the orders of the Ladakh rulers, Senge Namgyal. The walls and the ceilings of the temple are adorned with excellent mural works.

The Mystic Mandala Temple or Initiation Temple: (dKyil-hKhor-khang) This is where devotees are initiated into monkhood. The temple houses an impressive painting of Vairocana surrounded by eight Bodhisattvas. It adorns the wall that faces the door. Mystic mandala occupies the rest of the portion.

The Bodhisattva Maitreya Temple: (Byams-Pa Chen-Po Lha-Khang) An imposing six meter high image of the Bodhisatta Maitreya dominates this temple. It is divided into a hall, vestibule, and sanctum. Murals adorn the walls depicting the monastery of Tashi-Chunpo and Lhasa's Potala Palace.

The Temple of Dromton (Brom-ston Lhakhang): The temple lies on the northern edge of the complex and is said to have been founded by Dromton (AD 1008-1064), an important disciple of Atisha. The doorway is intricately carved and the inner walls are covered by murals. These shrines are said to be the oldest in the Tabo complex and the following are later additions.

The Chamber of Picture Treasures (Z'aloma): This is an anteroom of sorts attached to the Temple of Enlightened Gods. It is covered with Tibetan style paintings.

The Large Temple of Dromton (Brom-Ston Lha-khang): It is the second largest temple in the complex with a floor area of 220 sq. ft, while the portico and niche add another 42 m. The front wall has the figure of the Sakyamuni, flanked by Sariputta and Maha Mongollana. The other walls depict the eight medicine Buddhas and Guardian Kings. The wooden planks in the ceiling are also painted.

The Mahakala Vajra Bhairava Temple (Gon-Khang): The temple is sometimes referred to as the temple of horror. This temple enshrines the protective deity of the Geluk-pa sect. Fierce deities people the room and it is only entered after protective meditation.

The White Temple (dKar-abyum Lha-khang): Noteworthy in the temple are the walls that adorn and have a dado for the monks or nuns to lean against.

The importance of this monastery can be judged from the fact that its significance is second only to the Tholing Gonpa in Tibet in the entire Himalayan region. Even today, the monastery is keeping up its image of an efficient and effective learning center by opening up schools to impart modern education to the newer generation.

Monasteries in Kinnaur Valley

Kanum Village

Location: 30 km from Pooh

Of all the Buddhist temples in Himachal Pradesh, those at Kanum, a tiny village in Kinnaur, are most important on account of their architecture, wall paintings, and literary treasures. Situated in the lap of the hills at an elevation of 9,600 ft, Kanum is about 225 km from Shimla. Kanum is a wholly Buddhist village. It has as many as seven monasteries and the Kanum monastery extends across the entire village, divided into three buildings. One of these is attributed to Rin-Chen-Bzang-Po. The main hall has an image of Buddha, and his meditation is illustrated in tablets along its walls. The third hall is the library, with an extensive collection of *Kangyur* and *Tangyur* texts. The renowned Hungarian Tibetologist Alexander Csoma de Koros studied these texts from 1826-31, and his pioneering work on Tibetan texts is well-known.

In Rarang, near Kanum, is the Tashi Choeling monastery, which has a functional nunnery. Within is an ancient stucco image of Manjushri Manjughosha.

Kangyur Monastery

The Kangyur Monastery, the most ancient in Kanum, is situated in the heart of the village. Its two-storey building houses a very fine library which contains 108 volumes of *Kangyur* and 225 volumes of *Tangyur* books written in Tibetan script.

Lundup Ganfel Gonpa

This is the biggest monastery in Kanum and is situated on the top of the village. This monastery is also called Kache-lha-khanq, i.e. the Kashmiri temple, by the local people. According to Rahul Sankrityayan, it was built by Maha Pandit Shakya Virbhadra of Kashmir, the last Sangharaja of India, who fled from India in about AD 1213 and lived for 10 years in Tibet. On his way back to his birthplace in Kashmir, he stayed at Kanum and constructed a vihara. The present monastery was built on the site of the old temple by Lama Tomo Geshe who lived in Kinnaur for about 100 years.

This gonpa has on its walls the nicest and most beautiful mural paintings depicting various phases of the life of Buddha. The monastery has also a good collection of religious books and Buddha statues made of clay and sandalwood.

Lachao Labrang or Lha-Khang Locahlama

This monastery commemorates the visit of Rimpoche Locha Lama of Tashilhunpo, Tibet, who visited Kanum in AD 1897 when he came to consecrate the Buddhist temple built at Rampur by Tikka Raghunath Singh of Bushahr.

Kano Village

This monastic complex of four large temples is called the Lotsaba Lha-Khang after its founder, Rin-Chen-Bzang-Po who was a great Buddhist revivalist in this region in the 11th century AD.

Kulu-Kangra valley
Nako

Nako is known for its ancient murals and beautiful Buddhist paintings, dated from the 11th century, and for a rock said to have the footprints of Guru Padmasambhava.

Nako monastery is also known as 'Lotsava Lhakhang', meaning 'Complex of the Translator'. Of Nako's four halls, the oldest and the largest is the dukhang. Walls are adorned with fully developed mandala with gates, fire-circles, and non-Buddhist deities in attendance.

East of the dukhang is a smaller hall, with an unusual stucco image of Yellow Tara. Its walls and ceilings are also decorated with mandalas. The third hall has a four-faced figure of the Vairichana.

Of Nako's remaining temples, one is dedicated to a local divinity, Purgyal, who is said to be the spirit of the mountains. Its Lhakhang has images of the five Dhyani Buddha carved from clay, along with a collection of other idols arranged along the walls.

A few kilometres before Nako, on the road from Spiti, is a gonpa in Chango. Its main attraction is a giant prayer wheel measuring over 11 feet in diameter, made of yak skin.

Pooh

Location: 40 km from Nako

Pooh has a temple dedicated to Rin-Chen-Bzang-Po. This gonpa has preserved an extremely valuable illustrated volume of the *Prajnaparamita* (Book of Wisdom), dated 11th-12th AD. According to local belief, this gonpa was built on the spot where an inscribed stone slab mentioning Rin-Chen-Bzang-Po and Atisha, and the lower half of a human figure, was found.

Dharamshala

The higher snow-clad Dhauladhar ranges of the Himalayas are a magnificent backdrop for Dharamshala, a beautiful and peaceful town, spread over different levels. Dharamshala is variously known as India's Scotland, the Queen of Hills and Little Lhasa – Sanctuary of Righteousness.

Macleod Ganj: Originally home of the semi-nomadic Gaddi tribe, Macleod Ganj, is today the residence of His Holiness the Dalai Lama. This mid-century place was developed as a British Garrison. The Dalai Lama resides in Macleod Ganj and this has turned Dharamshala into the Buddhist capital of the world. It has a school of Tibetan studies, with rare manuscripts and ancient texts, and the Tibetan Institute for the performing arts and handicrafts center.

The large population of the region and the presence of traditional architecture design has enhanced the beauty of the area.

Places of Interest

The Presidence of Dalai Lama: The Dalai Lama settled in Macleod Ganj in 1960 and his residence on the south edge of the town has become his permanent home in exile.

Tsuglagkhang: In front of the private enclosure of the residence of Dalai Lama is Dharamshala's main Buddhist temple, Tsuglagkhang. It has images of Sakyamuni, Padmasambhava, and

Avalokitesvara, all sitting in meditation and surrounded by offerings from devotees.

Gompa Dip Tse-Chok Ling: The small gonpa Dip Tse-Chok Ling is located on the bottom of a steep track. The main prayer hall has an image of the Sakyamuni. The monks who lived in the gonpa have made two huge drums covered in goatskin and painted around the rim. The butter sculptures, which are made during Losar, are destroyed in the next Losar festival. This gonpa is also famous for the fine and detailed mandalas.

Library of Tibetan Works and Archives: The Library of Tibetan Works and Archives stores almost 40 percent of the original Tibetan manuscripts and is a repository of the rich Tibetan culture. The library also has a photographic archive. At Gangchen Kyishong is the Tibetan Medical and Astrological Institute.

Namgyal Monastery: Namgyal Monastery is located in Dharamshala and is known by the name Namgyal Dratsang. It was founded by the third Dalai Lama, Sonam Gyatso, in 1575. The monastery was established to help the Dalai Lama carry on with his public religious activities as well as to perform prayers for the betterment of Tibet. Within the monastery premises, there is a monastery, an institute and a few temples.

The monastery is not open for public, and only His Holiness, the Dalai Lama and his students can enter it. The institute admits students for thirteen years of training in Tantra and Sutra. The admission is difficult, however, once in, the students can get to gain knowledge from the renowned spiritual teachers of Tibet as well as the Dalai Lama himself. The monastery is home to more than 180 monks.

Tilokpur

Location: 35 km below Dharamshala

It is a Mahayana Monastery for nuns.

Mandi District

Rewalsar Monastery

Location: 20 km south-west of Mandi

Rewalsar Monastery is a pagoda style monastery. Rewalsar is considered an extremely important place for Buddhists since it is from here that Padmasambhava set out to spread his religion in Tibet. This dharma which he spread came to be known as Lamaism.

The monastery stands on the edge of the Rewalsar Lake and the island in the lake is supposed to be inhabited by the spirit of Padmasambhava. Inside the monastery, murals in mixed Indo-Chinese style are attention grabbers.

Here, a fair called Sichu takes place every year in March-April in the Mani-Pani temple, an old shrine dedicated to Guru Padmasambhava who meditated here in AD 747 before going to Tibet.

Shimla District

There is only one ancient Buddhist temple in Shimla district. It is at Rampur built by Tikka Raghunath Singh of Bushahr in 1897. Recently, a large Tibetan monastery has been established at Sanjauli.

Another monastery has been built at Kusampati, near Shimla. This monastery is said to be a replica of the famous monastery at Dorjidak in south Lhasa, Tibet, which was destroyed by the Chinese in 1949. The newly built monastery was opened by His Holiness the XIV Dalai Lama on August 1, 1992.

Monasteries in Himachal Pradesh can be visited from Shimla or the district headquarters of Lahaul, Spiti, and Kinnaur valley.

Himachal Pradesh is famous as a tourist destination for natives as well as for foreigners. Tourists visit Himachal Pradesh for its hill stations, holy shrines, adventure sports like skiing, hiking, and other winter sports and to enjoy a variety of activities. For Buddhists, it is a place of pilgrimage, because Dharamshala is the abode of His Holiness Dalai Lama who is venerated today with equal fervour as was Lord Buddha. His fame around the world as the Nobel Prize winner for Peace is another reason why Dharamshala is flooded with foreign tourists around the year.

Buddhist Circuit of Himachal Pradesh

The itinerary starts from Shimla, the state capital of Himachal Pradesh and ends at Macleod Ganj.

Places Covered: Shimla, monasteries in Kinnaur, monasteries in Spiti, monasteries in Lahaul, monasteries in Rewalsar, monasteries in Kangra, Macleod Ganj.

Expected Duration: 13-15 days

General Information

Area: 56,673 sq. km

Capital: Shimla

Boundaries: Jammu & Kashmir, Punjab, Haryana, Uttaranchal;

Country – China

Chief Languages: Pahari, Hindi, Punjabi, Kinnuri

Main Towns: Shimla, Mandi, Dharamshala, Kullu, Manali, Bilaspur, Chamba, Key-long, Kalpa, Kangra

Air: *Airports* – Shimla, Gaggal, Bhuntar

Rail: There are two narrow gauge lines – Pathankot to Jogindernagar and Kalka to Shimla. The broad gauge line from Nangal to Talwara, is under construction. Main Railway stations – Pathankot, Jogindernagar

Road: Road length – 25,500 km. NH – 1,235 km.

8

JAMMU AND KASHMIR

Buddhism had reached Kashmir much before Ashoka, since Surendra, a native king of Kashmir, who ruled for a while after the Buddha (but before Ashoka), was also a Buddhist. He built two Buddha viharas. One of these, called Surendrabhavana, was in the city of Sauraka (present Suru, beyond Zojila) and another was at Saurasa (present Sowur) on the throne of Anchar lake near Srinagar.

Buddhism was established in Kashmir quite early with, as in many places in India, Emperor Ashoka, as its main promulgator. Around the time of the birth of Christ, the Third Buddhist Council took place in Kashmir and missionaries were sent to neighbouring regions of Central Asia, Tibet, and China. Buddhism was introduced by Madhyantika, the bhikuni who converted the Gandhara nation (Afghanistan).

Buddhism suffered at the hands of the anti-Buddhist Huna King Mihirakula (first half of the sixth century AD), but later the religion enjoyed prosperity. With the royal patronage of King Mihirakula and his Queen Amritaprabha, Queen Yukedevi, Queen Indradevi, several ministers of Yudhisthira and the zeal of the monks, Kashmir became an important center of Buddhist Sanskrit learning. Many subsequent rulers were also patrons of Buddhism.

Hiuen–Tsang, the seventh century Chinese traveller referred to it as Mo-lo-pho, the red land. It has also been known as Kachanpa, the land of snow and the land under the passes evolved into the current name 'Ladakh'. At the time of Hiuen–Tsang's visit, four stupas in Kashmir were believed to have been erected by Emperor Ashoka over the corporeal remains of Buddha. According to one account, recorded by Hiuen–Tsang and in some Tibetan books, the Fourth Buddhist Council under the Kushana King Kanishka

◀ The masked dances in Ladakh attract crowds of devotees and tourists

was held at Kashmir to reconcile the contradictory doctrines of the Sangha, then divided into 18 sects. It prepared a large number of treatises and commentaries of the *Tripitaka*, the copies of which were engraved on copper-plates, placed in stone boxes, and buried inside a stupa, on the orders of Kanishka.

In the eighth century AD, Kashmir was a major center of Buddhism. The founder of Toling monastery in west Tibet, Rin-Chen-Bzang-Po, in the interest of developing Buddhist art in west Tibet, went to Kashmir. When he returned from Kashmir he brought 32 Kashmiri artists, manuscripts, and teachers to translate sacred Buddhist texts.

The subsequent history of Kashmir also saw Buddhism flourishing side by side with Brahmanical cults, very often claiming the same persons as their patrons and votaries.

The Buddhists, with their notable way of life commanded respect even in the 12th century AD. But, Buddhism did not long survive the Muslim conquest of the valley in the 14th century AD.

Kashmir is known as paradise on earth because of its natural beauty. Jammu is known as an important pilgrimage site for those who worship goddess Vaishnodevi. And Srinagar is famous around the world for its houseboats.

Apart from its fame as 'heaven on the earth' Jammu and Srinagar are also well-known for the Buddhist sites here. Akhnoor, Gilgit, Harwan, Pandrethan, Paraspora, Ushkura and Mulbekh have yielded a number of Buddhism related items and antiquities during excavations. These sites need the attention of the archaeologists and historians from all over the world.

Ladakh

'Little Tibet' or the 'Moonland' or the 'Last Shangrila' are all names that have been applied to Ladakh. Ladakh has many historic monasteries called Gonpas, where Buddhist monks and nuns live, study, and practise their religion. The monasteries of Ladakh are situated in scenic locations, on hills and mountains and have a rich collection of Buddhist thangka paintings, art and artefacts.

Monasteries are the main centers for worship, isolated meditation, and religious teachings. These are the centers of cultural heritage and a spiritual hub for all social activities.

In the third century BC, the great Mauryan Emperor Ashoka sent Buddhist missionaries to Ladakh and Kashmir where they established their first town, Srinagar. Kashmir became the base from where the great work of Buddhism and scholarly Sanskrit literature spread and the region evolved as the crucible of a highly civilised cultural expression where Buddhism, Shaivism, and Sanskrit learning flourished.

Buddhism reached Tibet from India via Ladakh, and there are ancient Buddhist rock engravings all over the region, even in areas like Dras and the lower Suru Valley that today are inhabited exclusively by a Muslim population. The divide between Muslim and Buddhist Ladakh passes through Mulbekh (on the Kargil-Leh road) and between the villages of Parkachik and Rangdum in the Suru Valley, though there are pockets of Muslim population further east, in Padum (Zanskar), in Nubra Valley, and in and around Leh.

Many villages are crowned with a gonpa/gompa or monastery which may be anything from an imposing complex of temples, prayer halls, and monk's dwellings, to a tiny hermitage housing a single image and home to a solitary lama.

The living Buddhist heritage is manifest in the village where 'mani' walls are engraved with the mantra *'Om mani padme hum'* and stones are piled into commemorative mounds known as 'chorten'. The gonpas precariously perched on steep hillsides or rock faces seem an integral part of the rugged landscape.

Although the Islamic influences extends out the Kashmir valley, the predominant religion is the Tibetan, Lamaist form of Buddhism. Lamaism is a form of Buddhism influenced by the pre-Buddhist Bon religion of Tibet. This is especially noticeable on the stones and banners, which carry pictures and carvings of Bon demons and gods. Lamaism is the monastic side of the religion and the discipline requires long hours of meditation and years of study by the monks. Their religious observances are a part of everyday life.

In Leh, it is possible to find some families whose members are Muslims, Christians, and Buddhist since the Ladakhis are notably tolerant of other beliefs.

Monasteries in and Around Leh

Namgyal Tesmo Gonpa

Leh is the capital of Ladakh and there are many temples, castles, and stupas built by the ancestral Dharma Rajas who were patrons of Buddhism. Leh was the capital of King Takspa Bum-Ide, who ruled over the area of Stod that included Leh, from 1400-1430 AD. It was he who built the Red Chapel Namgyal Tesmo gonpa containing the statue of Buddha Maitreya, three-stories high. It stands atop the crag behind Leh Palace, having a full and splendid view of the town of Leh.

The Namgyal Tesmo gonpa was built during the time of King Tashi Namgyal, thereafter the temple of Namgyal Tesmo was named after him. It boasts a rich collection of some ancient manuscripts and wall paintings.

It houses a statue of Avalokitesvara and Manjushri, approximately one-storey high. Near the monastery is a fort, which now lies in ruins.

Also in the vicinity, are a number of temples. These temples are open only in the morning and evening. When the temples are opened up, a monk from the Sankar gonpa comes to light the butter-lamps in front of the images.

Sankar Gonpa

Sankar Gonpa, a subsidiary of the Sputik Gonpa, belongs to the Gelukpa or yellow hat sect of Tibetan Buddhism. It is a relatively modern monastery and serves as the residence of the head-priest Kushk Bakula.

To the right of the front yard of the monastery is a dukhang (assembly hall). Both the sides of the entrance are adorned with paintings of the guardian of the four directions. On the left wall of the entrance veranda is a 'Wheel of Life', held by Yama. As one enters the dukhang, one comes across some relatively new paintings of various Buddhas, along with the guardian deities. There is also a throne inside the dukhang reserved for the head Lama of the monastery. On the right side of the throne is an image of Avalokitesvara (Lord of All He Surveys) with 1,000 arms and 11 heads.

The central image inside the Sankar gonpa is that of Tsong-Kha-Pa, founder of the yellow hat sect of Buddhism, along with his two chief disciples. To the left of this image is another image of Avalokitesvara, again with 1,000 arms and 11 heads. And to the right is a case full of Tibetan bronzes. There are a number of other images like those of Sakyamuni, the present Buddha, Maitreya, the white guardian, and Amchi.

Diagonally opposite the door, in the small inner courtyard is a temple devoted to the deity Dukar. The main image is inset with turquoise and is shown with 1,000 arms, 1,000 heads and 10,000 eyes. To the right of the image is a statue of Maitreya Buddha. The walls are painted with mandalas, a Tibetan calendar and rules for the monks. Above the wooden stairs, one can see the residence rooms of the head Lama next to the guest rooms and the library.

Sankar Gonpa also possesses the *Kangyur* (scripture), the 108 volumes of Buddha's teachings. The icons here are made of pure gold and the wall paintings depict scenes from the *Panchatantra*.

The timing for visitors is between 7-10 am, or 5-7 pm. These restrictions have been placed because some of the monks of the yellow hat sect reside here permanently.

Stock Gonpa

Stock Gonpa dates back to the 14th century and was founded by Lama Lhawang Lotus. Stock is a subsidiary of the Sputik Gonpa and belongs to the yellow hat sect of Buddhism. As one enters the veranda of the monastery, one comes across bright friezes depicting the guardians of the four directions. The dukhang of the monastery displays a rich collection of banners and thangkas. The left side wall is adorned with the images of Vajrapani (Vajra in hand) and Avalokitesvara in his four-armed manifestation. The right side wall stands proud with the images of Sakyamuni and his two disciples, Amchi (the Buddha medicine), Tara (the Saviouress) and Nangyalma. There are two thrones inside the dukhang. The central one has been reserved for the Dalai Lama, while the one on its right is for the head Lama of Stock monastery.

As one exits the dukhang from the back, is one of the oldest small chapels. The central image inside the chapel is that of Tsong-Kha-Pa, the founder of the yellow hat sect of Tibetan Buddhism.

Inside the chapel, there are also images of Avalokitesvara in his four-armed manifestation, and Maitreya, the future Buddha or Buddha of Compassion. Another chapel to the right boasts of an array of Buddha images, depicting the gestures made by the Buddha with his right hand.

One of the major attractions in the Stock monastery is its own library. The library has a complete set of the *Kangyur*, the 108 volumes of the Buddha teachings. A new temple, dedicated to Avalokitesvara (displaying 1,000 arms and 11 heads), was added to the monastery. A ritual dance-mask takes place near the gonpa on the ninth and tenth day of the first month of the Tibetan calendar.

Stock Palace

About 15 km south of Leh on the west bank of Indus river is the royal palace, dating back to the 1840s when the invading Dogra forces deputed the King of Ladakh.

▲ Stock Palace

The Stock Palace is located on a glacier deposit of pebbles and overlooks a field of barley grown on terraces on the mountains. The palace is about 200 years old and is the only Ladakhi Royal Palace that is still inhabited. Standing four-stories high, the Stock Palace has 65 chambers, and the Queen of Ladakh occupies eight of them.

The small palace museum (with three rooms) is worth seeing. It has a fascinating collection of royal thangkas (400 years old), and some of the family's most precious heirlooms, including antique ritual objects, dresses, coins, head gear, religious objects, ceremonial tea paraphernalia, and exquisite 16th century thangkas illuminated with paint made from crushed rubies. The museum is also home to many treasured thangkas including a set of 35 representing the life of the Buddha.

Painted in the 16th century, each of them has the handprint of King Tashi Namgyal on the obverse, as if certifying their authenticity. The Chinese influence is predominant in the thangkas; the background shows clouds with a profusion of blue and white. The museum also has a volume of scriptures lettered in gold. Another attraction here is the archery contest, held in July. Stock monastery also has an oracle.

The last king, Raja Kunsang Namgyal, died in 1974 and, a chorten was erected in the village where he was cremated. The three-day trek from Stock to Spituk and the eight-day trek for Markha valley starts from here.

Shey Gonpa

Shey Gonpa was erected on the instructions of King Deldan Namgyal, in the memory of his late father, Singay Namgyal. Shey Gonpa was once the residence of the royal family and was built more than 550 years ago. According to tradition, it was the seat of power of the first King of Ladakh, Lhachen Palgyigon and of successive kings of Ladakh.

The main image inside the Shey monastery is that of Buddha

▲ The Shey Gonpa was built more than 500 years ago

Sakyamuni. About 34 feet high, the copper statue of Buddha, plated with gold, is installed inside this castle. It is a huge statue of the seated Buddha and is considered to be the highest metal statue and second largest Buddha statue in the Ladakh region. Copper sheets, gilded with gold, make up this amazing Buddha statue. It was made in 1633 by Deldan Namgyal as a funerary memorial to his father King Sengge Namgyal. There is also another image of the Lord Buddha about three stories high, to be seen at Dresthang, and made during the reign of Sengge Namgyal. The image also contains sacrificial offerings such as grain, jewels, holy signs, and mantras inside. On both the sidewalls of the Buddha statue, are displayed the 16 Arhats (worthy ones who have achieved Nirvana), eight on each side. The back wall of the statue is painted with the images of the two chief disciples of Buddha, Sariputta and Mudgalayana. There is hardly any space on the walls around the Buddha statue that does not have a painted image.

A large bowl of wax with a flame in the center, symbolising divinity and purity, is placed in front of the Buddha statue. This flame burns continuously for one year, before being replaced. Some exquisite murals adorn the second story of the Shey monastery. The lower story comprises a large library and is decorated with murals depicting Buddha's various hand gestures.

Shey monastery also has an oracle. During the Shey Shublas, the August harvest festival, the Shey oracle rides on a horse and stops at various places around Shey and makes prophecies. The oracle, a Shey layman, starts at the Tuba gonpa where he engages in a two- or three-day prayer while in a trance in order to be possessed and become an oracle.

The Shey oracle is held in the highest regard and viewed as a god who has achieved the highest level of existence. It is said that if one asks the oracle a question, but disbelieves the answers and goes to another oracle, no answer will be given.

An annual festival is also held in the Shey Monastery on the thirtieth day of the fourth month of the Tibetan calendar. In July, the Metukba festival takes place in the Shey Monastery.

Down the river from Indus are the monasteries of Spituk (7 km), Phyang (17 km), Likir (53 km), Alchi (69 km), Rizong (73 km) and Lamayuru (120 km).

Spituk Monastery

Standing majestically on top of a hilltop overlooking the Indus Valley, Spituk Monastery is from the Gelukpa/yellow hat sect.

Rin-Chen-Bzang-Po the great translator who helped spread Buddhism in Ladakh named the monastery. 'Spituk' means 'exemplary'. Three other monasteries in Ladakh, namely Stok, Sankar, and Saboo are considered to be branches of the Spituk Monastery.

The Spituk Monastery was founded during AD 1040-1050 by King Ol-de of Guge, and belongs to the Kadampa order. This order lost its importance in the 13th century and was taken over by the Kargyut-pa/Kangyupa order. In AD 1430 this monastery was influenced by the Gelung-pa/Gelukpa order.

> *Kangyukpa is a sect of Vajrayana Buddhism also known as the Red Hat sect. It lays stress on practical mysticism and direct transmission of esoteric teachings from Buddha to disciple. Gelukpa is a sect of Vajrayana Buddhism also known as Yellow Hat sect. The Dalai Lama belongs to this sect.*

Then during the lifetime of King Lha-chen Trakpa-Bum-Ide, the monastery was restored by Lama Chawang Lotos and the Gelukpa order of Jam-mgon Tsong-Kha-pa was introduced. After the Dogra wars, the Ladakhi royal dynasty ended its power in 1843 and the Gelukpa order could manifest itself as the supreme order in Ladakh.

The incumbents serving in all these monasteries are the successive reincarnations of Skyabsje Bakula Rinpoche. From Paldan Lhamo temple, a small path leads to the monastery where the built-in dukhang is worth seeing. There are wall paintings, thangkas, prayer flags, bookshelves and books, which are well illuminated. Near the dukhang are several other chapels; the new Chokhang is above a staircase.

Funeral ceremonies can be witnessed here. There are many small, old prayer rooms, the head Lama's room and the rooms of the monks. They contain some wonderful wall paintings, thangkas, silver chortens, Buddha figures, statues of other deities, and religious books. The principal statue is that of Lord Buddha. Within this statue is a sacred image of Amityyus, King Lha-chen Trakpa' Bum-Ide made by the great Tsomkha-pa.

The gonpa has three chapels of which the highest, Kali Mata or the Padlan Kamo Temple is more than 1,000 years old. Here one can see the 23 manifestations of Tara in addition to the many icons of the Buddha. The image of Mahakali is most awe-inspiring, it has 25 pairs of arms and eight pairs of legs. The face is covered with a scarf throughout the year, and is revealed only in January during the annual festival. The wall paintings featuring skulls and skeletons are very terrifying.

Every summer, on a date determined by a lunar calendar, ceremonies of the Heurka Shakrasambhava Mandala are held. From the hundred or so monks in residence, six gelongs (initiates) prepare themselves by undertaking a long fast, and carry out work under the supervision of the elders, and following to the letter the sacred texts. The mandala obeys very strict rules – colours, dimensions, proportions, creatures, and objects, everything that figures in this representation of a perfect universe must be true with wisdom, in harmony with the divine, worthy to be presented to the Enlightened Ones.

The object of the mandala rituals is to enable the seeker to free himself from appearances, to subdue his mind, master his creativity, to secure, for all those wandering in slumber for non-fulfillment – awakening and true happiness.

From the dukhang, 19 steps lead up to the inner courtyard where there is a flagpole around which, on the 28th and 29th days of the eleventh month of the Tibetan calendar, the Spituk Gu-stor is celebrated with mask dances.

From the highest point on the hill is a good view of the Indus valley, of the village Spituk, at the foot of the hill, of the mountains (usually snow-covered even in summer) that divide the Indus valley from Zanskar.

Phyang Monastery

Phyang Monastery belongs to the Drigyungpa order. It was the first monastery that introduced the Drigyungpa teaching of Skyobo Jigsten Gonbo in Ladakh that was founded by Chosje Danma Kunga during the reign of King Jamyang Namgyal in the 16th century AD.

According to local legend, while digging a canal near Hemis, the workers came across a strange looking lizard which they killed without any thought. The King immediately fell ill and none of the royal physicians could cure him. Finally, the King sent for Denma Kunga Trakpa, a mystic living in the Kailash-Mansarovar region. After much persuasion, he restored the King's health. Later when Denma expressed the desire to start a monastery at Phyang, the King gave him all the support he required.

▲ The Phyang Monastery

The site where the monastery stands today was once a part of the numerous monastic properties offered during the time of Dharmajara Jamyang Namgyal to Chosje Danma Kunga.

The gonpa today is the main center of the Drigyungpa sect in Ladakh. It has three temples rich with icons of Buddha in His various poses. One of the interesting features here is the flagstaff atop an elaborate pedestal; it is said that during the days of monarchy, if an offender managed to escape and reach this pole, he would be set free.

The pillars of the temple are covered with tiger skin, a gift by the Kalon (premier) to Jamyang Namgyal. Another attraction of Phyang Gonpa is its 900-year-old museum. Its rich collection boasts of numerous idols, thangkas, Chinese, Tibetan, and Mongolian firearms and weapons etc. Within the monastery, there are beautiful old royal period wall paintings and several old and small statues.

At present, the Phyang gonpa is under Apchi Choksi Dolma, the guardian deity. It has about 50 monks in residence. The monastery has had several renovations recently, including the addition of a large house for the head Lama and a new entrance hall with a large prayer wheel. The 665-year-old dukhang was renovated in the late 70s.

In 1979, one big thangka of Ratna Sri was inaugurated by Skyoba Rinpoche. This thangka is 50 feet tall and 36 feet long. There are many old thangkas brought from Tibet, China, Kashmir, Turkistan etc.

Phyang also celebrates a festival called Phyang Tseruk on the twelfth, thirteenth of the sixth month of the Tibetan calendar. The festival of Gang-Sgnon Tsedub is held every year from 17th-19th of the first month.

Likir-Gonpa

Likir means 'Naga Encircled'. Likir Gonpa stands surrounded by the bodies of the two great serpent spirits, the Naga-rajas, Nanda and Taksako. The fifth king of Ladakh, Lhachen Gyalpo, offered the site where the monastery stands today to Lama Duwang Chosje who was a great champion of meditation. The Lama blessed the site offered to him, after which the construction of the monastery was undertaken. It was built in the 11th century by the King of Ladakh, Lahchen Gyalpo. In the 15th century with the help of Khas-grub-j, the monastery was renovated and rededicated to a monastic order of the great Lama Tsong-kha-pa. This monastery still follows the rituals and observances according to the Tsong-kha-pa traditions. The old structure was destroyed in fire sometime after the 15th century. The present monastery building dates back to the 18th century. The new gonkhang was built in 1983.

The monastery consists of a number of shrines inside its complex. Presently, it serves as the residence of approximately 120 monks. The monastery also has a school, in which thirty students study.

Likir Gonpa came under the influence of Lodos Sangphu in the 15th century, under whose supervision this monastery flourished and prospered. The Monastery continues to be under the Tsong-kha-pa order till date. The ritual of the three basic Pratimoksa disciplines, the basic Buddhist teachings, are observed at the Likir monastery even in the present times.

The Likir Gonpa has been served by the succeeding reincarnations of Naris Rinpoche till date. Naris Rinpoche is the brother of His Holiness Dalai Lama. The monastery also houses a protective deity wearing golden armour, which stands inside. There are two dukhangs inside the monastery and it comprises six rows of seats for the Lamas. There are images of the Bodhisattva, Amitabha (Buddha of the west), Sakyamuni (the historic Buddha), Tsong-kha-pa (founder of the yellow hat sect) and Maitreya (the future Buddha), along with clay images of Buddha describing his life story and that of the 16 arhats (saints).

After the exit from this dukhang, one can see the new dukhang, diagonally across the courtyard's entrance. The main image in the new dukhang is that of Avalokitesvara with 1,000 arms and 11 heads.

The Gonpa also serves as the venue of an annual event called Dosmochey, the assembly of votive offerings. The event takes place from the 27th to 29th day of the twelfth month of the Tibetan calendar. During Dosmochey, sacred dances are also performed at the monastery. Most tourists purchase earthen pots from here, since Likir Gonpa is quite well-known for these souvenirs.

Alchi-Chos-Khor-Gonpa

Alchi-chos-Khor is the largest and most famous gonpa, with a widely renowned collection of paintings and massive lavishly carved and painted wooden statues (many of which are of the Buddha). Situated on the bank of the river Indus, dating back to 11th century, Alchi-chos–Khor is the only monastery in Ladakh on a flat ground, hence it is easily accessible.

The name Alchi–chos–Khor is derived from the language of the pre-Tibetan Dardic inhabitants. Chos–Khor, the Ladakhi version of this name, corresponds to the Sanskrit word 'Dharmachakra' or 'Dharma Mandala'.

The Alchi-chos–Khor Religious Enclave is the most famous and largest of all gonpas built by Rin-Chen–Bzang-Po. This Monastery has unique paintings probably made during the mid-late 11th century. One of the walls of the monastery features thousands of miniature paintings of the Buddha along with large images that are made of clay and have been painted brightly.

Rin-Chen–Bzang-Po appointed four families to look after Chos-Khor, as there was no monastic community introduced then. Then in the 15th century, Chos-Khor was taken over by the Likir Monastery, since then it is being looked after by the Likir monastery.

According to the inscriptions found at the dukhang, the Alchi–chos–Khor was built by Alchi pa skal–ldan Shes–rab of the Bro family, who had studied at Nyar-ma in Leh under the immediate followers of Rin–Chen–Bzang–Po. Later, he returned to Alchi and shared his experience of Buddhism and painting while constructing the Achi–Chos–Khor in early AD 1050. The design of the monastery is different from other monasteries. The architecture seems to have been influenced by a Persian from Kashmir. It is said that Rin-Chen-Bzang-Po invited artists from Kashmir to build the monastery.

Alchi–Chos–Khor consists of the following structures:

Dukhang: Built during the 11th century, it was constructed for the assembly of Buddhist monks for the performance of rituals. The square structure houses several idols of the main deity – four-headed Vairocana, arranged in two rows.

Sumtsek: It is a three-tier structure next to the Dukhang. It has a beautiful wooden porch supported by profusely carved wooden pillars. The three triangular wooden niches are occupied by the three wooden images of Buddhist deities probably of Avalokitesvara, Maitreya, and Manjushri. These wooden images have been replaced by the new massive clay images of Avalokitesvara, Maitreya, and Manjushri. The Sumtsek paintings are notable for the richness of their colours.

Temple of Manjushri: Built during the 11th century, there are four clay images of Manjushri in the temple, each facing the cardinal direction and painted with the appropriate directional colour – blue, yellow, red and dark green.

Lotsava Lhakhang: This was built during the 12th century. The Lotsava Lhakhang has an image of Buddha in the Bhumi-sparsha-mudra and has various mandalas painted on the interior walls.

Lhakhang Soma: It is a modest building known as the new temple bearing paintings displaying various styles.

Kanjur Lhakhang: This structure has Buddhist religious books and scriptures called Kanjur. It may be called the library of the Alchi–Chos–Khor.

Rizong Monastery

The Rizong Monastery, belonging to the Gelukpa order, was founded by the great Lama Tsultim Nima in 1831. The Rizong Monastery and its associated nunnery Julichen (Chulichen) are two interesting places in Ladakh.

Rizong is an active teaching gonpa, founded in 1829, and stands at a height of 3,450 meters. The gonpa is built on a sheer rock face and sprawls over seven levels. The approach up a twisting, narrow gorge of dry, crumbling shale, is spectacular.

The gonpa also has a rich collection of the painting blocks of Lama Tsultim Nima's biography as well as a number of objects made and books composed by the first Sras Rinpoche. The Monastery also consists of a number of shrines inside the complex. Serving as the incumbents of the Rizong Monastery, are the successive reincarnations of Lama Tuslim Nima and his son, Sras Rinpoche.

A nunnery, known as Chulichan (Chomoling) is located near the monastery, at a distance of 2 km. Comprising about 20 nuns, the nunnery is under the control of the governing body of Rizong Monastery. The nuns (Chomos) worship at the temple of the monastery itself. They also perform a number of chores for the monastery like spinning wool, milking, extracting oil for the temple lamps, etc.

The monastery serves as a residence for around 40 monks. This monastery is known for its well disciplined monastic order and abides by the teachings of Tsong-kha-pa. In the monastery, monks strictly follow *Vinaya* and do not observe sacred dances. All the monks reside at the monastery and get their dress and provisions from the governing body of the monastery. The inmates are not permitted to have anything on their person, except for religious robes and books.

Lamayuru Monastery

The Lamayuru Yung-drung Gonpa is built on a steep rock mountain. Lamayuru belongs to the Drigyungpa order of the Tibetan Buddhism and houses approximately 150 Buddhist monks.

It is said that the whole area of Lamayuru was under the sea in ancient times. Later, it was converted into a great lake. Probably in the 5th century BC. Arhat Nyi-ma-gong-pa came here and through his spiritual powers opened one side of the lake. The water flowed away. He threw corn into the lake. When the grains mixed with the earth, it looked like a beautiful Swastika in the lake. Therefore, when this monastery was founded it was named after the Swastika and called 'yung-drung'.

The Lamayuru Monastery is made up of a number of shrines and also has a very rich collection of thangkas and magnificent wall paintings. The murals at Lamayuru are not very impressive, though there is a mandala of fierce divinities in the Yab–yum (cosmic union) posture. The gonpa has an impressive 11-headed 1,000-eyed image of Cherezing. In the inner shrine are 21 manifestations of Tara made in copper, crafted in Aligarh. Here is also a chorten moulded in coloured butter, which is a special art practised by the lamas. This ancient art survives even today, and butter sculptures are made during the annual festival held in March.

This is one of the highest places in Ladakh, created in the 11th century by Rin-Chen-Bzang-Po. The great translator had been sent out by King Yeshe-O of Tibet to study Buddhism in Kashmir. While he was there he became a master of esoteric practices, and on his way home established a large number of monasteries – 108 in all. Though tradition has it that Lamayuru Monastery was founded by Rin-Chen-Bzang-Po, according to some historians, this was earlier a place of Bon-chos or animistic practices.

In one of them, the great Indian yogi, Naropa, founder of the Kargyugpa school, passed several years meditating in a cave, a statue representing this event is on view in the Dukang Chenmo Temple, which was built around the cave sanctified by the venerable Mahasiddha (yogi possessing the great power).

Lamayuru adheres to the traditional mandala plan of a central temple surrounded by four temples in the four cardinal points. However, only the main temple survives today.

Lamayuru also belongs to the Drigyungpa sect and owes its wealth to King Jamyang Namgyal who donated vast tracts of land to it. There is an area called thama ling (freedom land) where people convicted of crimes would not be punished.

At Lamayuru, the mani-walls, or prayer walls made with stones that have been intricately carved with sacred words (such as *'Om-mani-padme-hum'*) and decorations, are piled up by devout pilgrims, stone by stone (often dragged there from many kilometers away). These walls have more than just religious significance. These stone walls protect the fields in the valley's bottom from avalanches.

The Yuru Kabgyad festival is held here annually in the summer on the 28th and 29th days of the second Tibetan month.

Every year, the Lamayuru Gonpa plays host to a masked dance, which takes place on the 17th and 18th day of the fifth month of the Tibetan lunar calendar.

Wanala Gonpa

Wanala is on the trekking route from Lamayuru to Padum. Slightly south-west of Lamayuru, this gonpa is reached by a climb of several kilometers to the top of a pass. The old monastery was built about a thousand years ago during the time of Rin-Chen-Bzang-Po. Its main image is the 11-headed Mahakaruna, or Avalokitesvara, which stands more than two-stories high. The wall paintings are of the Buddhas, Bodhisattvas, mandalas, and other religious icons. There is also a sacred image of Atisha.

Monasteries – Zanskar Region

Karsha Monastery

The full name of the Karsha Monastery is Karsha dkar-cha-Byams-pa-gling, and it was established by Phagspa sherab. The monastery as it stands today, was the result of the efforts of the teacher, Dorje Shesrab. Shesrab Zangpo of Stod was the one to introduce the Gelukpa order in the Karsha Gonpa.

The monastery consists of a number of shrines and boasts of some of the most exquisite wall paintings by the Lama Dzodpa Dorje. The collection also includes the bone relics of Dorje Rinchen.

The temples built by Rin-Chen-Bzang-Po, known as the Tugs-rje-chen-po Lg and the L-khra-bo, are situated near the Karsha Monastery. Also close by are the monasteries of Khagsar, Purang and Phagspa, and a nunnery called Dorjezong, at the top of the valley. The ruins around the nunnery are believed to be the original foundation of Karsha. Near the ruins is the old temple of Chukshik-Ja that houses an exquisite central figure of Avalokitesvara, the patron deity of Tibet. The present complex was founded during the 14th century. An old stupa surviving among the ruins is still adorned with the original murals reflecting Indian artistic influence.

The Gustor festival is celebrated in Karsha every year, on the 28th and 29th day of the sixth month of the Tibetan calendar. The celebrations also include the performance of the sacred dances.

Phugtal Gonpa

One of the most isolated monasteries of the region, the Phugtal Gonpa dates back to the early 12th century, and stands at the opening of a huge cave in the Zanskar region. The cave is located in front of a huge gorge, which also serves as a passageway for a major tributary of the southern Lungnak River (Lungti-Tsarap). To reach the Phugtal gonpa, one can also go via the Padam-Manali trekking route.

A number of chapels are situated inside the premises of the Phugtal Gonpa. This monastery consists of an old collection of statues and wall paintings. The frescoes as well as the decorations on the ceiling, adorning the chapel, bear the marks of artistic and iconographic influence of India. The Monastery also serves as the residence for about 40 monks.

Every year on the 18th and 19th day of the twelfth Tibetan month, the Monastery organises the Gustor festival in which the Lamas perform sacred dances.

Rangdum Gonpa

The Rangdum Gonpa was founded by Lobzang Gelek Yeshas Gragpa of Ngris-thang during King Tshewang Namgyal's reign of Leh in the 17th century.

The monastery rises over a centrally ascending mound, entrenched by the bifurcated route of a mountain stream. It gives it the appearance of an age-old fortification, which stands as the protector of a mystical mountain valley.

One of the major attractions in the monastery is its small museum, which has a rich collection of fascinating Tibetan as well as other relics. The Monastery owns the entire valley around it, including the fields tilled by the villagers, the pastures, hills and even the streams. The villagers staying around the monastery are the descendants of the self-tenants of the monastery and do not have any land of their own.

Zonhkul Monastery

A cave monastery of Zanskar, Zonhkul stands perched on the face of the Atling Gorge. As per the legend, it is said to be connected with Naropa, the famous Indian Yogi from Vikramshila. In fact, it is believed that he even used the two caves of the monastery for the purpose of his solitary meditation. Even today, one can see Naropa's footprint embedded in the rock and a sacred spring, inside the meditation cave.

After Naropa meditated here, the monastery became the sacred place for meditation for all the mahasiddhas of Zanskar.

Enlightened people like Dubchen Kunga Gyatso, Dubchen Nawang Tsering, Dzadpa Dorje, Karmapa and others have gone into the Zonhkul for meditation. The Zonhkul gonpa consists of a number of blessed shrines.

It also boasts of a rich collection of precious artefacts, like the ivory image of Samvara, a crystal stupa, texts containing the spiritual songs and biographies composed by the successive mahasiddhas, etc. Not to be missed are the splendid murals, made by Zhadpa Dorje almost 300 years ago.

There is a Zonhkul Hutchot festival on the 16th and 17th days of the fourth month of the Tibetan calendar, but there are no mask dances.

Monasteries – Padum Region

Bardan Monastery

The Bardan Monastery, standing atop a rocky crag, dates back to the 11th century. It was founded by the Dewa Gyatsho. It belongs to the Dungpa-Kargyud monastic order. In fact, it was one of the first centers of the Dungpa-Kargyud monastic order to be set up in Zanskar. A number of smaller monasteries in the region come under the management of Bardan. One such monastery is the Sani Gonpa.

Bardan Gonpa consists of a large assembly hall. All the other structures within the monastery are structures around the dukhang only. The hall boasts of some of the most magnificent statues of Buddhist divinities, along with some small stupas in clay, bronze, wood and copper. The Buddha Maitreya statue (two feet high) is the principal image and was brought from Kashmir.

The monastery was previously built at the top of the mountain called Thar-lha. Near the Bardan monastery lies the monastery of Muney, famous for its splendid art treasures.

The Gertsa festival is organised by the Monastery every year on the 15th day of the fourth month according to the Tibetan calendar. During the festival, Lamas perform mask dances.

Sani Monastery

The Sani Monastery belongs to the southern branch of the Drukpa Kangyupa School. This monastery was built in different stages, each dating to a different century. The chorten inside is believed to have been erected in the second century AD, while the dukhang (assembly hall) is said to be constructed in the early 17th century.

The monastery is built in the form of a castle and has the Kanika stupa in the backyard of its walled complex. Because of the existence of this stupa, it is believed that the monastery was associated with Kanishka, the Kushan ruler of second century AD. The central praying hall is situated in the main building of the monastery and stands ornamented with a rich collection of the statues of popular Buddhist divinities and Kangyupa high lamas. The walls and the praying hall are adorned with frescoes and thangkas. A small chapel at the back, houses some of the most beautiful stucco murals depicting landscapes and floral designs, based on the life of Guru Padmasambhava.

Outside the complex is one of the eight important cremation grounds for Tibetan Buddhists. The cemetery is encircled by a ring of ancient rock-carvings, which reveal a touch of Indian art.

The Sani Gonpa is said to be connected with the famous Indian yogi Naropa. It is believed that the yogi meditated under the Kanika stupa, in the monastery's backyard. The same spot, where the yogi sat and meditated, is a small room with a veiled bronze statue of the yogi.

Every year, the statue is unveiled in late July, i.e. on the eve of the masked-dance festival, Naro-Nasjall. During this festival, the Lamas from Bardan monastery perform masked dances as ritual offerings.

It is said that Guru Nyima Ozer stayed in Sani monastery and practised meditation for many years.

Stongdey Monastery

Stongdey Monastery is considered to be the second largest monastic institution in the Zanskar region, situated on the road to Zangla. Founded in 1052, by Lama Lhodak Marpa Choski Lodos, it comes under the Tsongkhapa order. The incumbents serving at Stongdey are the reincarnations of Nan Tulku.

The main prosperity of the Stongdey monastery came while under the influence of Shakya Zangpo. There are a number of beautiful temples situated inside the complex. Another major attraction in the monastery consists of the gorgeous wall painting adorning its interiors.

Stongdey also serves as the venue of the Gustor festival, an annual festival that takes place on the 28th and 29th day in the eleventh month of the Tibetan calendar.

There are about a dozen Buddhist monasteries, situated on or near the Indus, and a treasure trove of images and artefacts. Upstream of Leh are the monasteries of Thicksey (17 km), Stanka (25 km), Hemis (40 km), Chemrey (47 km), Takhtok (50 km), and Matho (26 km).

Thiksey Monastery

Thiksey is one of the most frequently visited and most photogenic monasteries in Ladakh. Situated at an altitude of 11,500 feet above sea level, built some 600 years ago, Thiksey Monastery is the most beautiful monastery in Ladakh. It has 12 levels ascending a hillside, culminating in the private abode of the incarnation of the Lama. It is the seat of Rin-Chen-Bzang-Po, the main leader of the Gelukpa school of Buddhism, and is the main monastery in Ladakh. It is believed that in the early 15th century, Tsongkhapa, the founder of the reformed Gelukpa school, sent six of his disciples to remote regions of Tibet to spread the teachings of the new school. One of these six disciples was known as Sherab Sangpo. He went to Ladakh and was the founder of a small monastery at the end of a valley in the village called Stagmo. Palden Sangpo, Sherab's disciple, carried on with the work of his teacher and he was the one who founded Thiksey monastery a few miles away from Stagmo near the river Indus, on a sacred hill above a village of the same name.

The outside of the gonpa is painted red and is visible from far away. The gonpa contains 10 temples, below the monastery itself are chapels and houses of monks stretching down the hillside. After entering the main courtyard, to the immediate right and up several steps is a new temple containing a large Buddha statue. In 1980 the Dalai Lama constructed this 48 feet tall Buddha statue. The statue was made under the guidance, supervision and direction of Kushok Nawang Chamba Stanzin, the present head Lama of Thiksey monastery.

The statue is the largest Buddha figure in Ladakh. It took four years to construct and is made of clay and covered in gold paint. The statue houses the sacred *Kangyur* and *Stangyur* texts. The statue was made entirely by local craftsmen and represents Maitreya – the Buddha of future. The prophecy made of the Buddha is that the world will undergo such chaos that the future Buddha will teach compassion to the people. About a hundred monks live here.

Located directly above this temple is a small narrow room used as a schoolroom for the local boys. Here the Lamas instruct the children; some of them are later selected to become Lamas.

Traditionally, Ladakhi families donated one son to become Lamas, although this practice is gradually disappearing.

Returning to the main courtyard and going up the steep steps directly across from the new temple, on the far wall are murals of two Tibetan calendars, with a Wheel of Life. To the right of these murals is the main prayer room, which contains racks of books along the left wall. Many of these books are handwritten or painted. New books are block printed. In a small room behind the main prayer room is a large image of

▲ The Thiksey monastery has some of the most breathtaking Buddhist artefacts in India

Sakyamuni flanked by two smaller Bodhisattva images. On the left is the 11-headed Avalokitesvara. On the rooftop is the Lamokhang temple where only men may enter. Also on the top is Thiksey library, which women can also enter, it contains numerous volumes, including *Kangyur* and *Stangyur*.

The small temple of Zan-la is beside the car parking area. In the gonpa courtyard there are some interesting wall paintings. In the chapel there is a picture of Tsangkhapa the founder of the Gelukpa sect. On the roof balcony there are rooms for the head Lama.

Thiksey monastery is known for its annual festival held from the 17th to 19th day of the twelfth month of the Tibetan calendar. Sacred dances also form a part of this ritual, which take place every year.

Stanka Gonpa

Stanka Gonpa is situated on the right bank of the river Indus. The name 'Stanka' literally means 'Tiger's Nose'. The monastery was so named because it was built on a hill, which is shaped like a tiger's nose. The Monastery owes its inception to Chosje Jamyang Palkar, the great scholar and saint of Bhutan. It formed a part of the many religious estates offered by the Dharmaraja Jamyang Namgyal's to the saint, around AD 1580.

The most important image in the monastery is one of the Avalokitesvara, which is said to have come from Assam. In the chapel are three paintings – a large picture of Choshikzal, and the red and blue figures of Dorje Chang.

In the wooden cupboard is a large standing figure of Dorje Phakma, besides eight Sashan Gyat. Under this main chapel is another chapel which may only be entered by Lamas.

The successive reincarnations of the Stanka Tulku continue to serve as the incumbents of the monastery, preserving the teachings of the Drugpa order.

On entering the capital courtyard, one comes across the dukhang (main assembly hall). The head Lama had silver chorten, seven feet high, erected inside the dukhang in the 1950s. The chorten comprises a statue of Buddha as well as numerous Buddhist texts. The left wall is adorned with three new paintings, those of the Tsephakmad (a Buddhist deity), Sakyamuni (the Historical Buddha), and Amchi (the Medical Buddha).

The wall opposite the dukhang entrance is also painted with three images, those of a Bodhisattva, Padmasambhava (eighth century Indian Buddhist scholar and translator of Buddhist texts into Tibetan), the present Buddha and Maitreya (future Buddha). The throne of the head of Stanka lies on the left side of the dukhang.

There are five monasteries under Stanka. They are:

1. Munth (in Leh district)
2. Karu (in Leh district)
3. Stakrima (in Leh district)
4. Bardan (in Zanskar Kargil district)
5. Sani (in Zanskar Kargil district)

Hemis Monastery

Hemis Monastery holds the distinction of being the biggest as well as the wealthiest monastery in Ladakh. Hemis is also known as the Chang-Chub-Samling (The Lone Place of the Compassionate Person).

Belonging to the Duppa or Drugpa order, the Kar-gyut-pa (red hat) or Kangyupa sect of the Tibetan monasticism, Hemis Monastery was built in the 17th century by Chapgon Gyalshas, and stands on the western bank of the Indus river. It dates back to 1630 and was founded by the first incarnation of Stagsang Raspa Nawang Gyatso, who was invited to Ladakh by King Singey Namgyal who offered him a religious estate throughout the region.

The youngest son, Nawang Namgyal became a monk and his name was changed to Zamling Drags. The monastery was named Chang-Chub-Samling.

Hemis Monastery also has a gigantic thangka. This thangka is one of the largest in the world, which is unfurled once in 12 years. The monastery is divided into two, the assembly hall on the right and

▲ Monks at Hemis, the biggest monastery in Ladakh

the main temple on the left. The hall or dukhang is also used as a green room by the dancers during the festival. In the dukhang, the general assembly room, the throne of the Rinpoche dominates the sitting place of the monks. Near the dukhang is the lakhang which is the first chapel after a small set of steps from the yard. The side walls of its front room are covered with (partially damaged) frescoes of the watchers of the heavenly directions. In the lakhang is a large gilded statue of the Buddha Sakyamuni with blue hair, surrounded by several silver chortens decorated with semi precious stones.

Hemis has a valuable collection of thangkas of which that of Guru Padmasambhava is noteworthy. Huge, over 44 feet long embroidered thangkas, embellished with pearls, is open for viewing only once in twelve years. The last time it was allowed for viewing was in 2004.

Hemis also has an excellent library, some particularly well preserved wall paintings and various images of Buddha and frescoes including the famous 'Wheel of Life'.

On the second and third stories, near the Zankhang chapels are the Kharrabgysal, the rooms of Rinpoche.

Hemis Monastery is famous worldwide and is the main attraction for tourists and researchers.

This Monastery is known the world over for its two-day annual festival, which is held in summer. Hemis festival is celebrated for two days and a portrait of Dadmokarpo or Rygyalsras is displayed for people to worship. The highlight of the festival is the sacred mask dances, called Chham, that are performed by the monks. The beating of drums, clashing of cymbals and the spiritual wail of pipes add a mystic touch to the festival.

Some 500 monks are attached to the gonpa, members of the Drugpa-Kargyud school. Some of the festival dancers celebrate the birth and achievements of Padmasambhava, alongwith the recitals of the saga in which facts and mythology are inextricably intertwined. Banners flutter on long poles erected in the courtyard and Lamas dressed in richly brocaded gowns and sporting grotesque masks dance around them.

As his (Padmasambhava) activities in diffusing the wisdom of Buddha were deployed in every direction, these ritual dancers (chham) depict him appearing simultaneously in eight guises, wearing masks of the Buddha both angry and serene.

The umbrella carried in some of the manifestations is a symbol of royalty emphasing that this ascetic yogi was both king and monk, as is the Dalai Lama today.

The sacred mask dance takes place on ninth and tenth day of the fifth month of the Tibetan calendar.

There is a sacred hermitage called Gotsang about an hour's journey from Hemis Monastery on the side of the mountain 3200 feet higher than Hemis. This hermitage was built by Gyalwa Gotsang–pa before the main Hemis Monastery in the 13th century. He meditated in a nearby cave, where you can see his foot and hand print in the rock.

Chemrey or Chmde Gonpa

Chemrey Gonpa was founded by Lama Tagsang Raschen and dates back to the 17th century; it belongs to the Drugpa Order. It serves as the residence of approximately 20 monks of the diminishing Drugpa community, and also their young apprentices. Chemrey Gonpa was initially built to serve as a funeral memorial to King Sengge Namgyal. There are also a number of shrines inside the monastery.

One of the major attractions of the Chemrey Monastery is the one-story high image of Padmasambhava. Other than that, the monastery boasts of a precious collection of scriptures – the title pages are in silver and the text uses gold letters. The successive reincarnations of Lama Tagsang Raschen have been serving as the incumbent of the Chemrey Gonpa, since quite a long time.

The monastery also serves as the venue for the festival of sacred dances. The festival takes place on the 28th and 29th day of the ninth month of the Tibetan calendar.

Close by is a cave of Padmasambhava. It is said that Padmasambhava meditated here for some time.

Takthok Monastery

Takthok Monastery, situated in Sakti village, once served as the meditation cave of Mahasiddha Kungpa Phuntsong. The name 'Takthok' literally means 'rock roof'. This is the only monastery belonging to the living Nying-ma-pa/Nyingmapa order. Guru Rinpoche (Padmasambhava) is said to have founded this monastery. The temple where he meditated is still to be seen at the Takthok Monastery.

It is the only gonpa in Ladakh that follows this order. To the left of the central courtyard is the cave chapel of the monastery. The cave hall is the oldest and from time to time sacred water drops from the cave's ceiling. Opposite the chapel are the images of Padmasambhava and Avalokitesvara. There is a small cave behind these images, which is why people believe this is the place where Padmasambhava lived and meditated for three years.

On the right of the central courtyard, lies the dukhang or the main assembly hall. Murals of guardian divinities adorn the verandah entrance to the dukhang. But they are displayed only at the time of the annual festival of the monastery. There is a throne inside the dukhang, reserved solely for the Dalai Lama. It is situated just opposite the dukhang entrance. The wall to the left of the throne stands decorated with the mural of Padmasambhava, while the one on the right has a painting of Sakyamuni.

Also inside the dukhang are the statues of Maitreya, Padmasambhava, and Dorje Takposal (a manifestation of Padmasambhava). The statues in this temple are different forms of Padmasambhava and the frescoes are images of renowned spiritual personalities of the various schools of Buddhism. Takthok monastery also houses the *Kanghur/ Kangyur* – the 108 volumes of Buddha's teachings.

The new museum is built on ground level and contains the image of Guru Nang Sroth Zilon in the center; to its right is an image of Guru Dorje Dolo and to its left is an image of Guru Padma Gyalpo. There is a seat of Taklung Rinpoche, the incarnate Lama of the monastery.

Every year a festival is held at the Takthok Gonpa on the ninth and tenth day of the sixth month of the Tibetan calendar. The celebrations include sacred dances and the ceremony of hurling votive offerings.

Matho Gonpa

Matho Gonpa is located on the opposite bank of the Indus River across the Thiksey monastery. The gonpa was founded in the 16th century by Tubgpa Dorje but was almost destroyed during the war between Muslim invaders and the Ladakhis in the late 16th century. After a few years, the Lama Chokyi Lodo renovated the monastery and restored its activities. The Matho Monastery boasts of an amazing array of ancient and very beautiful thangkas, some are even in the form of Mandalas.

> *The two-day Nagrang festival (for the Tibetan New Year in February) and a one-day festival on the eighth day of the second Tibetan month (usually in March) called the Nispetsergyat are celebrated here. During these two festivals, two special monks (called Rongzam) go into a trance and then adorned with gold weapons, run over the mountain ridges in the area and over the roofs of the monastery.*
>
> *During the Nagrang festival, the Lamas are said to be evil-minded on the first day (they hit spectators) but are very peaceful on the second day. At the Nispetsergyat, the two Rongzam ride the stretch, which they went over on foot at the beginning of the Tibetan year.*
>
> *Both of these festivals are accompanied by mask dances.*

> *High in the mountains there are two Lathos, special red chortens from which prayer flags flutter, dedicated to these two monks. They are about 5-6 km from the monastery, close to a glacier. The monks, also known as Luyar, are like other monks at other times of the year, but if someone in the village doesn't believe in or has lost faith in the powers of Buddhism, these two monks batter themselves on arms, feet, and tongue with their old weapons. The wounds do not bleed and their injuries are said to heal so quickly that they are able to dance a short time later. They do this in order to show that they possess divine powers. This ritual is still practised on the 14th and 15th days of the first month of the Tibetan calendar.*

In front of the door to the gonkhang room is a prayer mill made out of oil cans – a sign of the times – but still adorned with the mantra *'om mani padme hum'* in addition to the prayers. These are written on paper rolls. The gokhang room, in which one can meditate, is ascribed with its own spiritual power.

Matho is quite famous amongst Ladakhis because of its oracle. The Lhaba of Matho lives in the monastery. On special days (in winter on the eighth day of the second month of the Tibetan calendar) the oracle runs over the mountain near Matho. He is blindfolded and 'sees' only with a painting on his breast and back. The oracle speaks to the audience of village dwellers by a small spring at the foot of the monastery.

The hidden monasteries of Ladakh are the most popular and preferred destinations for Buddhists from all over the world. Many monasteries of the state are World Heritage Sites. Buddhism is the religion of this region and the monasteries are busy with monks dressed in yellow/red coloured robes, the colourful flags, chortens, and the chanting of the mantras by the monks and devotees.

The way the festivals are celebrated here by the monks is also a draw for tourists. Needless to say the calm and scenic atmosphere is a perfect place for meditation. The nearest airport one can come to, to visit the monasteries is Leh and a convenient base to start the journey by road is Srinagar. Monasteries are generally located far away from where people live, and the road to some of them is not motorable.

There are state transport buses operating within the state, or from Jammu and Srinagar to certain districts. But hiring private vehicles saves time and energy for the tourists. Foreigners are required to check about inner line permits to visit Ladakh, the rules keep changing from time to time.

Jammu & Kashmir government and the Tourism Department announces various programmes to attract tourists.

Shanti Stupa

The Shanti Stupa was constructed by a Japanese Buddhist organisation, known as 'The Japanese for World Peace'.

The aim behind the construction of the stupa was to commemorate 2,500 years of Buddhism and to promote World Peace. His Holiness Dalai Lama inaugurated the Shanti Stupa in 1995.

A magnificent white-domed structure, the Shanti stupa of Leh offers spectacular views of the sunrise and sunset. The stupa looks best at night, when it is beautifully illuminated with glittering lights. A large number of tourists come to Ladakh every year to visit this amazing stupa.

Bazgo/Basgo Monastery

Bazgo Monastery is worth a visit for just seeing the Buddha figures. There is a copper-guild of the Buddha Maitreya two-stories high. It was built by the King of Ladakh Sengge-Namgyal as a funerary memorial of his father King Jamyang-Namgyal. The ruins of a temple and a stupa built by Rin-Chen-Bzang-Po, the translator, can also be seen. The Buddha Maitreya image made of clay and three-stories high can be seen at the top of the castle.

The Bazgo Monastery was the seat of power for a branch of the

Namgyal family. It was here in AD 1680 that invading Mongol and Tibetan armies were held in check over a three-year long siege.

There are original 16th century murals and other art objects in the monastery. Besides huge Buddha images, small Chamba statues stand in front of the figure of white-clothed Chamunda. Monks live below the monastery in a small house.

General Information

Area: 2,22,236 sq. km

Capital: Srinagar (summer), Jammu (winter)

Boundaries: Himachal Pradesh, Punjab;

Countries – Pakistan, Afghanistan, China;

Mountain – Himalaya

Chief Languages: Urdu, Kashmiri, Dongri, Pahari, Balti, Ladakhi, Puring, Punjabi, Gurji, Dadrir

Major Towns: Srinagar, Jammu, Leh, Anantnag, Baramula, Pulwama, Punch, Doda, Udhampur

Air: Srinagar, Jammu, Leh

Rail: Jammu

Road: length – 15,012 km

9

KARNATAKA

The home of Buddhism was evidentially north India, from where it spread to different parts of the world. But, Buddhism does seem to have travelled from north to south during the lifetime of the Buddha. *Suttanipata*, assignable to the close of the sixth century BC or the early part of the fifth century BC refers to Dakshinapatha and vouchsafes for the existence of Buddhism on the banks of the river Godavari and was also the center of Buddhism. Mulika and Assaka (Asmaka) were two of the 16 Mahajanapadas, kingdoms, along the Dakshinapatha, the route taken to spread Dhamma from north to south. Buddhism spread there intensively before Ashoka's influence (third century BC).

Buddhism entered Karnataka before Emperor Ashoka's time (274-235 BC). It is a fact that the southward expansion of the Magadha Empire was mainly responsible for transforming the pastoral communities into a network of state-governed societies. By the time Ashoka conquered Kalinga, most of the well-populated Buddhist centers in Karnataka had already developed into vibrant urban centers and established commercial and cultural links with the rest of the south India. That is why, Ashoka sent his Buddhist missionaries to Vanavasa (Banavasi) and Mahishamandala (north-north-eastern Karnataka) to propagate the message of Buddha, as recorded in *Mahavamsa*.

Cullavagga of Vinaya Pitaka, written in 383 BC discusses variations to the monastic codes that were introduced under pressure from the community's regional expansion. It gives an account of the second Buddhist Council held at Vaishali which mentions that bhikkus/bhikshus from Dakshinapatha attended this conference. This shows that during the fourth century BC,

◀ Aihole was a workshop for temple sculptors and artisans

Buddhism had flourished in Karnataka.

Four stages are noticed in the growth and spread of Buddhism in Karnataka. The first stage is that of the Mahishasana branch of the earliest Buddhism (Hinayana) stepping into Karnataka in the period between the First and Second Councils of Buddhism. The second stage is during the Mauryan period, this is when Buddhism put forth deep roots in Karnataka. The third stage falls during the period of Satavahana (100 BC-AD 100). The period of the Ganga, Kadamba, Chalukya, and Rashtrakuta is the last stage. The Ganga dynasty ruled from about AD 350-1000, Kadamba ruled from AD 345-525, Chalukyas ruled from AD 636-740, Rashtrakutas ruled from AD 753-982. Afterwards Buddhism began to lose ground.

After the Kalinga war, Ashoka accepted Buddhism and desired that the message of the Lord Buddha should reach the common man. He carved a number of inscriptions, which are known as the Edicts of Ashoka.

The largest concentration of Ashokan inscriptions, south of Vindhya, are found only in Karnataka. Perhaps, no other state in India can boast of having Ashokan inscriptions in such large numbers. Naturally, all these places where the Ashokan edicts are found, have been well populated cultural and commercial centers of the Mauryan Emperor. Ashoka himself is stated to have camped at Suvarbagiri (identified differently with many places).

Rock Edicts in Karnataka are found at Maski, Koppala Gavimath, Koppala Palkigunda (District Raichur), Brahmagiri, Siddhapur, Jatia Ramesvara (Chitradurga District), Nittur, Udagol (Bellary District), Sannati (District Gulbarga).

Buddhist sites

Aihole

Art historians say that Aihole was a workshop for temple architects and sculptors patronised by the early Chalukyan monarchs. The hillock in Aihole, Meguti, has the most important surviving Buddhist temple in Karnataka.

The chaitya, a double-story structure, is half-structural and half-carved in rock. The sanctum sanctorum is in the upper story. It has a rectangular verandah (28 feet x 7 feet). In the center of the verandah's ceiling is a relief of Buddha, who has assumed a preaching posture. Of the three Buddha sculptures at Aihole, this is the best preserved and is 61 cm in height. He is seated on the Padmapitha, his right hand is placed against his chest in the Vyakhyana-mudra while the left is placed on the right foot with the palm facing upwards. His right shoulder and right breast are uncovered. There is a triple umbrella above him and his attendants are nearby. Stylistically it is dated to the post Gupta era (sixth century AD).

Banavasi

The Kadambas were also tolerant towards Buddhism as epigraphic evidence shows. The Kadamba capital was also Banavasi (known as Vaijayanti) and their country was a prominent one for Buddhism in Karnataka.

Chinese pilgrim Hiuen–Tsang, visited Banvasi in the seventh century AD and saw 1,000 sangharamas and three stupas. He says, 'By the side of the royal palace is a great sangharama with 300 priests, all men of distinction. This convent has a great vihara 100 in height.'

Foundations comprising two large brick structures, apsidal in nature, were exposed during the course of an excavation by the Department of Archaeology of Mysore. The structures datable to the early centuries of the Christian era may be identified as a Buddhist chaitya hall.

Belagami

A mutilated sculpture of Tara-Bhagwati was reported from this village, located in Shikrapur taluka, Shimoga district. One of the inscriptions from this place mentions the construction of the Jayanti Prabha Buddha Vihara by a Maha Pradhana called Rupabhattayya. The inscriptions also note donations of land to the vihara for not only the worship of idols, but also for feeding the yoginis, kusalis, and sanyasis residing in the vihara.

Dambal

A place named Dambal in Dharwar district seems to have become important as a Buddhist center in the eleventh century AD as seen from an inscription ascribed to AD 1095, according to which a temple of the Buddhist deity Tara, and a Buddhist vihara were built by the 16 settis or merchants of Dambal during the reign of Lakshmidevi, the Queen of Vikramaditya VI, over the district of 18 agraharas. It is believed that another Temple of Tara was built at the same place by Setti Sangramaya of Lokkigundi.

Kaganahalli

At Kaganahalli district, Gulbarga, a stupa has been found. The excavation has brought to light off-set entrances provided with chandrasila. At the western and southern entrances is a pedestal. The pradakshinapatha all along the stupas is disturbed at places. The stupa had huge sculptural panels depicting the dharmachakra stupa models, and Simhasana, Bodhi-vriksha and Muchilinda naga as encasing members. Some of these sculptural panels are inscribed in Brahmi characters from the first to the third century AD, and record the donations made from traders and even commoners. During excavations, many Buddha-padas, fragments of chhatras, cornice slabs, coping members, animal friezes, three-seated sculptures of Buddha and many sculptural friezes were recovered. Apart from the inscriptions and architectural members, 18 lead coins, all of Satavahana period were retrieved. Most of them belong to the reign of Sri Satakarni.

Kolivada

From the village Kolivada in Hubli taluka of Dharwar district, an image of Tara with an inscription on the pedestal was reported to be belonging to about 13th century AD. It is a fairly well-preserved image seated in the lalitasana with two hands carved in granite stone. This is the last such vestige reported in Karnataka region.

Mangalore

Scholars are of the opinion that the famous temple Mangalambika at Mangalore and Mukambika near Coondapur might have been originally Buddhist in character. Same is the case with the famous Manjunatha temple at Kadri near Mangalore.

The discovery of bronze icons of Buddha, Lokeswara, Halahala Lokesvara in the Manjunatha temple complex, obviously suggests that the present temple dedicated to Shiva as Manjunatha was originally a temple dedicated to Manjushri, a familiar deity in Mahayana or in the Vajrayana pantheon of Buddhism. The three bronzes, the six-armed Halahala Lokesvara stands as a masterpiece in Chola art tradition prevalent in the area.

Sannati

At Sannati, (Chitrapur taluk, Gulbarga district), on both banks of the river Bhima, there are many Buddhist stupas from the Satavahana era that have been found. By the first century BC a flourishing center was established at Sannati on the banks of the Bhima. It resembles Amaravati and was the Buddhist center of the

▲ The remains of stupas at Sannati in Gulbarga

Satavahana period of the pre-Christian era and is spread over a 3 sq km area. Fine sculptures can be seen all along and the Buddhist ruins found there are in large numbers. They include remnants of stupas, stone pottery for holy bones and an ayaka stambha, which symbolises the birth, parinishkramana, enlightenment, preaching, and Buddha's nirvana. Inscriptions in the Brahmi script contain the names of those who gave grants to the sangharama, stupas and viharas. The words *'visiriputta sirisata mahasataraha'* indicates the beginning of the Christian era and refers to Banavasi. There are stupas carved in stone, and another stupa (first to third century AD) has Buddha's feet engraved in stone.

Karnataka is made up of 29 districts. All the districts are well connected by the Karnataka State Road Transport system. Maharashtra, Karnataka, Andhra Pradesh, Tamil Nadu are also connected by private transport operators with comfortable sleeper coaches and Volvo buses. Private taxis and local three-wheelers operate within city limits.

Major cities offer best facilities for accommodation ranging from star hotels to guest-houses, and dharamshalas in the cities of pilgrimages.

There are Government of India tourist offices in major cities and Karnataka State Tourism Corporation's offices in all major cities of the state. Guides who are conversant in several languages can be found in certain cities.

General Information

Area: 1,91,791 sq. km

Capital: Bengaluru

Boundaries: Kerala, Goa, Maharashtra, Andhra Pradesh, Tamil Nadu

Sea: Arabian Sea

Chief Languages: Kannada, English

Main Towns: Bidar, Gulbarga, Bijapur, Belgaum, Dharwad, Hubli, Raichur, Bellary, Shimoga, Mangalore, Madikeri, Mysore, Bangalore, Kolur, Hassan, Devangere

Air: Bengaluru, Belgaum, Mangalore, Hubli, Devenahalli

Rail: Bengaluru, Mysore, Tumkur, Hassan, Bellary, Hubli, Bijapur, Dharwad, Gulbarga, Belgaum. Railway length – 3,172 km

Road: Length – 1,17,972 km; NH – 3,967 km; SH – 9590 km

10

KERALA

Though not currently prevalent, Buddhism in this land of splendorous plenty has left behind an unbelievable collection of relics and traces. The centuries-old Buddhist practices and customs have had a significant influence on Kerala's culture, literature, and art forms.

The emergence of Buddhism in Kerala is shrouded in mystery. But a new school of thought traces Buddhism back to the reign of Emperor Ashoka, whose literary work titled *Keraputhra* delves into the depths of this ancient religion in Kerala. The important Buddhist rulers of Kerala (or 'Cheradesa') were King Jayasimha Perumal who ruled the region of Quilon in Travancore in the first century BC and the other monarch was King Bana Perumal (Baudh Perumal) in the third century AD. The great ruler of the Cheradesa during the medieval period was the King Vikramaditya Varugunan (ninth century AD) who ruled the territory when the capital was Sramulavasam (Alwaye). He was instrumental not only in propagating Buddhism in his kingdom, but also in other regions of the sub-continent. This was clearly confirmed by the discovery of an inscribed bronze image by archaeologist A. Foucher. A label inscription reads *'Daksinapatte Mulavamsa Lokanathe'*, which is translated as 'the ruler of Srimulavasam (of Cheradesa)'.

Other evidence that proves the existence of Buddhism in Kerala is

▲ There are several precious relics in Kerala such as the Karumadi-kuttan stupa

◀ Black granite statue of the Buddha, believed to be as old as the 9-11 century

quite meager, except for the lone epigraphical reference in Paliyam plates (written in 868 AD) of Varajuna of the Vrishnikula, in which was found an invocation of Sauddhodani (Buddha), Dhamma, and Sangha and the discovery of a few images of Buddha at Karumadi, Bharanikkam, Marudukulangrai, Pallikkal, and Mavelikkara. Other evidence such as habitation sites and structural remains are yet to be reported. Of the five images so far reported, two have been taken up for study and the remaining images though mutilated, were found to be more developed than that of the Karumadi figure. On stylistic grounds, they have been dated to the ninth century AD.

South Travancore seems to have been a stronghold of Buddhism, even as late as the ninth century AD. By that time, the decline of Buddhism had accelerated throughout south India, but there is some strong evidence to prove its popularity in south Travancore.

An inscription, made by the King Varajuna in south Travancore has been discovered (AD 868); this inscription is the only one in the whole region of Kerala, which makes a direct and clear reference to the prevalence of Buddhism.

Some evidence of the prevalence of Buddhism in the districts of Alappuzha, Kottayam and Kollam in Kerala, has been found.

For further information about Buddhism in Kerala, please contact Mr. KP Ramesh who has written the book *Buddhism in Kerala* in Malayalam (Zorba Publication). He can be reached on: rameshzorba@gmail.com

General Information

Area: 38,863 sq. km

Capital: Thiruvananthapuram

Boundaries: Tamil Nadu, Karnataka, and Lakshadweep Island

Main Towns: Thiruvananthapuram, Kochi, Kozhikode, Trissur, Kannur, Kottayam, Kollam, Allapuzha, Palakkad, Pathanamthitta

Air: Thiruvananthapuram, Nedumbassery (Kochi – India's first private airport opened in June 1999), and Karipur Port (Kochi)

Rail: Main Railway Stations – Thiruvananthapuram, Kollam, Chenganur, Kottayam, Ernakulam, Trissur, Palakkad, Kozhikode, Kannur, Kasargod

Road: 1.61 lakh km

11

MADHYA PRADESH AND CHHATTISGARH

Buddhism appears to have been firmly established in Madhya Pradesh since the days of Emperor Ashoka who erected a stupa and a pillar in Sanchi. Since then, Buddhism has had a long life in this part of the country.

Of the several known Buddhist sites that had existence from the third century BC to the 12th century AD in 26 of the 45 districts of the erstwhile Madhya Pradesh (now divided into Madhya Pradesh and Chhattisgarh), a large percentage had their roots in the Mauryan period. During the Gupta period, a marked lull in activities is noticed. From the seventh century AD onwards, a conspicuous rise in structural and other activities is observed, which reached its zenith in the ninth century AD. Following which, the graphline moves downward with increasing rapidity and reaches the nadir by the end of 12th century AD.

The use of trade routes for the propagation of Dhamma has been established, on the basis of inscriptional and literary artefacts as evidence, such as NBP ware, extraneous sculptures, and influence on art. The numerous brick, stone, and monolithic structures indicate a symbiotic relationship existed between the master craftsmen and the Buddhist socio-religious setup. The presence of lime plaster on stupas and other structures shows that this technology was by and large sustained by the Buddhist establishments. In the field of art also the congregation helped several art forms flourish and in the process aided the assimilation and diffusion of various techniques. So, it can be concluded that the need to spread Dhamma and the new techniques of art and building combined with the constant plying along trade routes resulted in national integration and unity to some extent.

The two centuries immediately preceding the Christian era

◀ Madhya Pradesh is home to several important Buddhist monuments such as the stupa and pillar in Sanchi.

witnessed a tremendous outburst of creative activity in Akara (eastern Malwa). The economic prosperity of its populous capital, Vidisha (modern Besnagar, near Vidisha), at the confluence of the Betwa and the Bes, gave a great stimulus to these vast building schemes. Apart from Sanchi, where monumental edifices were added to the already existing ones, there sprang forth several important groups of Buddhist establishments in quiet spots on sandstone hills within a radius of 20 km from the capital.

The actual impact of Buddhism was felt in Central India during the visit of Ashoka the Great (circa 273-236 BC) on the way to Ujjain via Sanchi where he married a lady from Vidisha and built a stupa and erected a monolithic pillar there. The route followed by Ashoka starts from Rajgir (Rajagriha, eastern terminus) to Sravasti, Saket, Kaushambi, Tumabvana, Vidihsa, and Ujjaini. This route goes further to Mahismati and Pratishathana in Maharashtra. Buddhism in Malwa has been a great cultural force and affected various other cultures.

It appears that the spread of Buddhism has been through Buddhist disciples. Innumerable brahmanas and businessmen were converted in the course of time. The most effective factor for spreading Buddhism was most probably the trader. The visit of Ashoka's son Mahendra and daughter Sanghamitra to Sri Lanka from Sanchi for the propagation of Dhamma must also have been an important event in Madhya Pradesh.

Buddhism received an initial setback during the reign of Pushyamitra Sunga. Buddhism flourished again in the Sunga, Satavahana period in Central India. Places like Sanchi, Satdhara, Bharhut, Talpura, Panguraria, Ujjain, and others stand witness to this. Buddhism was also prosperous in the region in the days of the Guptas. It is proved not only by the structural remains and sculptures of Sanchi, but by monuments, sculptures, and inscriptions in other places too. Pawaya, Bagh, Dhamnar, Mandasur are the prominent Buddhist centers that flourished during the Gupta period.

Buddhism continued to flourish in the post-Gupta period as well. The existence of a prosperous Buddhist establishment during the reign of the Panduvamisis of South Kosala at Sirpur, shows that it was a flourishing center of Buddhism in the eighth-ninth centuries AD. The other important centers that flourished in the post-Gupta period are Gyaraspur, Suvasra, Nandapur, Khurd, Mather, and Arang. Mather and Arang both are now in Chhattisgarh.

Buddhist Sites

Bagh

Location: 145 km south-west of Mhow railway station

On a solitary cliff in the otherwise basaltic region of the Vindhyan slopes, with a tributary of the Narmada at its feet, Bagh flourished in the fifth and sixth centuries AD. It was a small Buddhist colony comprising nine caves.

Nature has dealt relentlessly with these caves, their soft friable texture precipitating the wreckage. This has caused irreparable loss to our heritage, as the walls and ceilings of these caves were once a repository of a splendid array of classical paintings, parallels of which alone survive in India, the contemporary murals of Ajanta, both belong to one cognate group. The remnants of the paintings, though extremely scanty, are of such compelling quality that the place, notwithstanding its remote location, is a pilgrimage to artists who aspire to catch something of its sacred fire.

Cave 1 is a four-pillared chamber by a portico, the latter utterly ruined. Cave 2 is the usual quadrangular cave, but on an elaborate scale. It is probably known as *Pandavonki Gumpha* besides being one of the most elaborate caves, and is also best preserved in the whole group. Its façade was originally relieved with chaitya windows having insets of tiger-heads and lotuses.

The cave has a court with niches for an image at either side, a pillared verandah with a cell at either side, a hall with eighteen cells arrayed on three sides and a pillared antechamber leading to a shrine at the back of the hall. The side-walls of the antechamber each have a bold relief of a standing Buddha in vara-mudra flanked by two attendants. The door to the shrines is guarded by two Bodhisattvas, of which the one bereft of ornaments and with a water-flask in the left, stands for Avalokitesvara. The stupa in the shrine has a high-moulded octagonal base, a corbelled harmika, and a chhatra reaching up to the ceiling.

Cave 3 is locally known as the 'Hathi Khana' and is also a vihara. It consists of a hall, octagonal pillars, and a complex of cells leading to a rear chamber, with painted figures of Buddha on the walls.

Cave 4 is locally known as 'Rangmahal', on account of the paintings in it, and is the most ornamental of the caves. The frame of the central doorway is sculptured elegantly with bands of scroll-work, floral motifs and cable-patterns, besides seated figures of Buddha and chaitya-windows inset with heads on the upper facets of the lint supported by pilasters and the figure of Ganga on the consoles at either end. This cave was once lavishly painted, the ancient brushwork surviving only in patches. The walls, ceilings and some of the pillars of the hall are embellished with a great variety of floral and plant compositions and animal figures, all rendered with consummate skill.

The pillared verandah of Cave 5 is a continuation of Cave 4. Connected with a passage to the hall of Cave 5 is Cave 6, a small monastery with a hall and three cells at the back, and two on the right.

The remaining three caves are badly dilapidated. Among them, Cave 7 has a fairly large monastery with a stupa in the chapel.

Bharhut

The Bharhut monument flowered during the rule of the Sungas, who supplemented the Mauryas. The Bharhut monument was considered to be magnificent in terms of its supreme beauty and aura of peace, not only in the Buddhist world, but in the history of Indian art. The monuments at Bharhut were completely razed to the ground; the materials of the foundations were utilised by the villagers to make their houses. Some of the pieces from the edifices are now in Allahabad and National Museum, New Delhi, Kolkata, Ramvan, and other places. Practically nothing at present exists here except for a few remains of stupas, architectural fragments, etc.

Sanchi

Location: 45 km north-east of Bhopal

Vidisha, originally the capital of ancient Akara region, is about 10 km from the Buddhist site of Sanchi.

Sanchi is the site of the most extensive Buddhist remains now known to the entire world. Crowning the hilltop of Sanchi, nearly 290 feet in height, is a group of Buddhist establishments that commands a grand view.

It is unique not only in its having the most perfect and well preserved stupas but also

▲ The *toran* on the gateway a form of Buddhist art

in offering a wide and educational field for the study of the genesis, efflorescence, and decay of Buddhist art and architecture for a period of about 1300 years, from the third century BC to the 12th century AD, almost covering the whole range of the history of Indian Buddhism.

Sanchi, variously known as Kakanaya, Kakanava, Kakanadabota and Bota Sri Parvata in ancient times, has a singular example of remarkable Buddhist art and architecture, right from the early Mauryan period (circa 3 BC-12 centuries AD).

The site had no apparent connection with the traditional history of Gautam Buddha; nor is it known to have been the focus of any Buddhist philosophy. Even the itineraries of the Chinese pilgrims, do not refer to this site at all. It is surprising therefore that the monuments at Sanchi should now form the most magnificent and perfect examples of early Buddhist art in India.

Most of the monuments are situated on a plateau on a hilltop which was enclosed by a wall of solid stone in about AD 1100. The monuments vary in size, ranging from the great stupa that measures 100 feet in diameter at the base and has a vast, imposing dome barely 50 feet in height and miniature ones no more than a foot high.

Originally built of brick in the time of Ashoka during the Sunga era, several edifices were raised at Sanchi and its surrounding hills, which included the enlargement of the Ashoka stupa with stone veneer and the addition of balustrades along with a staircase and harmika on the top, as well as four imposing gateways.

▲ The Jataka tales are meticulously represented in panels such as this in Sanchi

These gateways (toranas) on the four cardinal faces constitute, with their richly carved decorations, a most striking contrast with the simplicity of the structure itself. All the four gateways are similar with columns and superstructures, richly carved with bas-reliefs illustrating the *Jataka* tales, scenes from the life of the Master, and important events in the history of the faith. The reconstruction of Temple 40 and erection of Stupa 2 and Stupa 3 also seems to have taken place in the same period.

In the first century BC, the Andhra Satavahanas, who extended their sway over the eastern Malwa area, made the elaborately carved gateway to Stupa 1. From the second to fourth century AD, Sanchi and Vidisha were under the Kushans and Kshatrapas and subsequently passed on to the Guptas. During this period, some of the finest temples were added at Sanchi and Udayagiri near Vidisha. Shrines and monasteries were also constructed at this site during the rule of Harsh, Pratihara, and Parmara dynasty (circa 700 to 1200 AD).

Since the 14th century AD, Sanchi remained deserted and uncared for till 1818 when General Taylor rediscovered the site. General Alexander Cunnigham, Captain FC Maisey (1851), Major Cole

(1881), and Sir John Marshall (1912-1919) explored, excavated and conserved the monuments. In 1936, Mohammed Hamid brought to light a well preserved monastery, probably assignable to Mauryan period.

Stupa 1: The largest among the stupas at Sanchi is Stupa 1 which still has a ground railing, four entrances, and a flight of steps leading to the upper terraced railing, the members of which bear donatory inscriptions datable to the first century BC and later to the second century BC. Four richly carved gateways, depicting Buddhist *Jatakas,* scenes from the Buddha's life and other themes, were symbolically added at the four cardinal entrances of the round railing in the first century BC. In the fifth and sixth centuries AD, coeval with the Gupta period, four Buddha images were installed each facing the gateway. The extant remains of this stupa include the Anda (dome), the Bhu Vedika (ground railing), and two Sopana (staircases). About a half kilometre from Stupa 1, the pathway by the front of the western gateway leads to Stupa 2.

Stupa 2: It is situated on the western slope of the hill. At present only its dome and ground railing with two fine entrances are still standing. On the basis of the paleographic record of the railing and style of bas-reliefs, construction is assigned to the last quarter of second century BC. The ground railing is richly carved with gateways constructed during the first century BC.

Stupa 3: It is to the north-east of the great stupa, and was built during the Sunga rule in second century BC. In the relic chamber of this Stupa, General A Cunningham discovered the relics of Sariputa and Mahamongalayana, two famous disciples. In addition, there are several smaller circular stupas, scattered around the site. Only the ground plan and a few stone courses have remained at present. These smaller stupas were meant for acharyas and disciples. It is believed that those devotees whose wishes were fulfilled used to construct these votive stupas. The votive stupas are numerous.

Monolithic Pillars: There are several monolithic pillars, such as the one set up by Ashoka (Pillar 10), at the south gateway of Stupa 1. It is outstanding because of its mirror-like polish and is inscribed with a message of excommunication from the Buddhist fold if any monk or nun attempts to create a schism in the sangha. Its magnificent lion-capital is now preserved in the site museum.

Temples: Among several temples at this site, the most important ones are an apsidal chaitya-hall (circa second or third century BC) buried within the plinth of the pillared pavilion (Temple 40); Temple 17 (circa fifth century AD) comprising a flat-roofed square sanctum and pillared portico supported on four pillars is the best preserved example of the earliest form and represents an important phase in the development of Indian temple architecture.

Chaityas: Located in front of Stupa 1, the chaitya was used to impart education to the Buddhist monks. The upper portion of the chaitya stands destroyed, and only pillars are seen at present.

Monasteries: Sanchi preserves the remains of several monasteries on the top of the hill. Each monastery comprises a central courtyard surrounded by cells. Monastery 51 is the most impressive structure unearthed at Sanchi, measuring 105 feet from east to west and 102 feet long from north to south. On the basis of the typical Maurya brick size, it may be inferred that it was built by Devi.

Deorkothar

▲ The Abacus of a fragmented Mauryan Pillar was recently brought to light

Location: 4 km north-west of Katra on the Rewa-Allahabad road

These monastic complexes are dated to the third or second century BC. Some have cells and steps to the entrance from either side.

The discovery of this site in 1982 brought to light a cornucopia of four Mauryan brick stupas, several inscriptions in

Brahmi script, Mauryan pillar pieces, railings, 30 stone stupas and many monasteries spread over a half kilometer wide area.

Mauryan Pillar: The art at Deorkothar receives corroboration as the earliest art works of the type that were executed well in the Mauryan period. The outstanding discovery of the colossal Mauryan pillar which alludes to Ashoka, has a chakra on the abacus and many letters of the inscription carried over from his time. This Mauryan pillar lay in several pieces directly on the flagstone flooring along with the balustrades broken into smithereens. A host of interesting antiquities came to light on and around this structure. Amongst these, towards the eastern part of the structure were found several pieces of Mauryan polished chhatra, some other stone pieces from caskets and bangles with exquisite polish, some copper objects and copper pieces, several iron slags and an iron ore lamp.

Other antiquities include legs of terracotta animals, a lead strip coiled ear stud, two score iron nails, and a few coins. All these findings indicate that the site was an active center of trade. Perhaps, the genesis of this pilgrimage site occurred amidst a vibrant mercantile community.

One of the most extraordinary discoveries within the stupa complex is that of a well-developed water canal system, dug into the bedrock which ensured that the water, percolating through the stupas in the rainy season, was properly drained away from the structure, thus protecting the monuments. The water channels are very prominent and can be seen even today.

About 63 rock shelters have been discovered at the site. Some of these also bear red coloured prehistoric paintings on the surface of the rocks. In all likelihood, these rock shelters were used by the Buddhist monks for meditation, as is seen in many other Buddhist sites and places in Bihar and central India. Perhaps, some of the rock paintings were done by the Buddhist monks who lived here, in the vicinity of the stupa. In a few rock shelters, Buddhist paintings, besides a painted Brahmi inscription, have also been discovered.

Sirpur (now in Chhattisgarh)

Location: 84 km from Raipur

Sirpur is well known for its archaeological monuments. Situated on the bank of Mahanadi, it has a rich background of traditional cultural heritage and architecture.

The Buddhist remains were excavated here in 1954-56. Till date, Sirpur has revealed eight viharas, of which the earliest to be discovered was the Anandaprabha Kutir vihara and the Swastika vihara that date back to the latter half of the first century AD.

Anandaprabha Kutir Vihara: Epigraphic evidence indicates that this vihara was built by Anandaprabha who was an ardent follower of the Buddha. The Complex is rich in carvings and ornamentation. The main gate is flanked by two stone statues of dwarpalas, while the side walls of the porch are linked with the images of yakshas. The garbhagriha contains an almost 2 metre high image of Buddha in the bhumi-sparsha-mudra.

Swastika Vihara: The garbhagriha houses a colossal 2.5 metre high statue of Buddha in the bhumi-sparsha-mudra. A very fine image of Padmapani on a pedestal also adorns the shrine. A red sandstone sculpture of Hariti was discovered in the south-west corner of the courtyard.

Tivaradeva Mahavihara: Named after the King Tivaradeva, it is the largest and most ornate amongst all the viharas. The lintel of the main doorjamb has carvings of a naga couple, and Buddhist figures. The outermost band depicts two yakshis whereas the two inner bands are composed of sculptures of nayak-nayikas, couples in erotic poses, and vamanas (dwarfs). The sanctum sanctorum of the vihara houses Buddha in the bhumi-sparsha-mudra. To the left of the main vihara, archaeologists have unearthed two other mandapas with residential cells around them.

Madhya Pradesh is dotted with several villages and towns from where a number of remains of stupas with burnt bricks, plans of stupas, stone images of Buddha and Buddhist deities, Buddhist related items and antiquities have been found.

The Buddhist centers in Madhya Pradesh and Chhattisgarh are as follows, Bhongapal, Gubrahin, Jaitagiri (Bastar District); Nadur Khurd, Mather (Bilaspur District, now in Chhattisgarh); Khajuraho (Chhattarpur District); Badoni, Barauni (Datia District); Atud-Khas, Phophnar (East Nimar District); Tumain (Ashoknagar District); Pawaya (Gwalior District); Bagrol, Hirapur, Khirki (Hoshangabad District); Azad Nagar (Indore District); Bilhari, Gaurighat, Tripuri (Jabalpur District); Dhamnar, Indragarh, Mandsur, Poladonger, Suvasra, Khejadia Bhup (Mandasur District); Mawai (Mandala District); Arang (Raipur District, now in Chhattisgarh); Katra Bihar, Sarangpur – Rajgarh District Andher, Besar, Bhagwanpur, Bhimbekta, Bidar, Bineka, Gulgaon, Hakimkhedi, Lakhajuar, Kharwai, Manchi, Murel Khurd, Nandur, Patandeo, Raisen, Sakasen, Sonari (Raisen District) Bhatanwara, Ramvan (Satna District); Singhpur (Shahdol District); Bayan, Pangoraria, Talpura (Sehore District); Gyaraspur, Jamil Khurd, Pathari (Vidisha District); Dangwada, Kayatha, Ujjain (Ujjain District); Kasarvad, Navdatoli (West Nimar District).

Madhya Pradesh has 48 districts and they are all connected by the transport organisation operated by the Madhya Pradesh State Government.

The Sanchi monuments symbolise art, architecture, beauty, grandeur, history, legacy – which are all unforgettable. These monuments are magnificent and instructive. Sanchi has won international fame through its well-preserved monuments and attracts thousands of visitors, including pilgrims and students of art and archaeology. The museum run by the ASI is also a must visit; every passionate visitor will feel proud of our history.

The monuments are within a kilometer of the railway station at Sanchi. The place is also accessible by road from Vidisha, the headquarters of the district of that name and Bhopal, the capital of Madhya Pradesh, 10 and 70 km away respectively. Accommodation facilities are available at government guesthouses and dharamshalas.

During my visit to Madhya Pradesh, I visited the Archaeological

Survey of India, office of the Bhopal circle, in Bhopal. I met Mr. Joseph Manuel, historian, archaeologist and researcher in the ASI. He was compassionate and exceptionally helpful and the credit for the captioned information has been entirely provided by him. The research and archaeological excavations in Buddhist sites were also carried out by the Department of Archaeology, Government of Madhya Pradesh.

General Information

Area: 3,08,000 sq. km

Capital: Bhopal (Madhya Pradesh) and Raipur (Chhattisgarh)

Boundaries: Gujarat, Maharashtra, Rajasthan, Uttar Pradesh, Chhattisgarh

Chief Language: Hindi

Main Towns: Indore, Bhopal, Gwalior, Sagar, Rewa, Jabalpur, Ujjain, Ratlam, Sagar, Una, Katni, Vidisha, Khajuraho

Air: Bhopal, Gwalior, Indore, Khajuraho

Rail: Bhopal, Bina, Gwalior, Indore, Jabalpur, Katni, Ratlam, Ujjain

Road: Length – 67,600 km, NH –3700 km; SH – 7,300 km

12

MAHARASHTRA

In Maharashtra, Buddhism has had a history of some thousand years. This is based on evidence found in various monastic settlements or clusters in Maharashtra.

The Buddhists were pioneers in the art of excavating and making rock-cut temples in India. The Deccan trap has revealed the existence of several excavated Buddhist monuments. Out of some 1,200 excavated rock monuments in India, 800 or over 60 percent are located in Western India, mostly in Maharashtra. These chaityagrihas (shrines) and viharas (monasteries) encapsulate the history of Buddhism in Maharashtra from about 200 BC until AD 1000 – a span of 1,200 years. The evolution of their architectural, sculptural, and painting styles and the inscriptions on their walls and pillars contain a wealth of information about the vicissitudes of fortune to which Buddhism was subjected to, through more than a millennium. Royal support was an important element in the spread of Buddhism and its prosperity.

The panorama of life in Maharashtra reveals that the state had become a well-organised regional, political, and cultural unit at least by 200 BC. Its connection with land and sea trade routes led to its integration with the large economic unit of the country; it formed a valuable link between the north and south, as well as the east and west. Buddhism underwent a transformation in the region from Theravada to Mahayana and finally to Vajrayana and Tantrayana. The excavations at Pauni have strengthened the case for arguing that Buddhism existed before the Ashokan period in Maharashtra.

The story of Bavari and his disciples, narrated in the preamble of *Parayanavagga*, part of a text called *Sutta Nipata*, one of the oldest texts (on grounds of antiquity) both of ideas and language,

◀ This Lion Pillar at Karle is one of several important Buddhist monuments in Maharashtra

is of great significance to understand the beginnings of Buddhism in Maharashtra. Bavari was a Brahmana acolyte whose ashrama was near Alaka in the Assaka country. Assaka has been identified with the area now covered by the Nanded–Nizamabad–Aurangabad region of Maharashtra and Andhra Pradesh. Bavari came to hear about the Buddha and his mission in somewhat miraculous circumstances and sent his 16 Brahmana disciples to meet the Buddha in a place identified with present day Saravasti/Sravasti. According to some accounts, a few of Bavari's disciples met the Buddha and posed before him some philosophical questions. They are said to have returned to Deccan after their conversation and probably founded the first monastic settlement there. The route they followed is of great relevance in determining the spread of Buddhism from the north and east to south and west. If the evidence is accepted as historical fact, the beginning of Buddhism in Maharashtra may be placed before 486 BC i.e. before the passing away of Buddha. This is similar to the story of Buddhism's history in Andhra Pradesh and Karnataka also. The account of the Second Buddhist Council shows that Maharashtra played an important part in the events associated with the Council.

In the fifth century AD, Buddhism once again emerges on the horizon of history. The hills around Aurangabad begin to resonate with the hammerings of gifted artisans who carved out of the inert rock some of the most beautiful shrines and monasteries, which inspired artists to decorate them with murals of indescribable beauty. These monastic communities belonged to the Mahayana faith, which in its final phase turns into Vajrayana and Tantrayana at Ellora and Kanheri.

The travels of Hiuen–Tsang brought him also to Kung-kan-na-pu-lo (Konkan) and Mo-ha-la-cha (Maharashtra). He visited two areas, one of which is identified as Konkanapura and the other Maharashtra. Kung-kan-na-pu-lo has been variously identified as Banavasi or Annagundhi on the northern bank of the Tungabhadra river. His visit and descriptions give us some idea of the state of Buddhism in Maharashtra and adjoining regions in the first half of the seventh century AD.

That Buddhism was yet a vital faith in the eighth and ninth centuries AD during the rule of Rashtrakuta, who had overthrown the Chalukyas, is proved by an inscription in Kanheri, recording the gifts of the Shilahara feudatories of the Rashtrakutas. Lingering traces of Buddhism in Maharashtra are available from as late as the 12th century AD.

To summarise, it is highly probable that Buddhism had arrived in Maharashtra (Paithan and Sopara) by 450 BC if not earlier. The expansion of Buddhism may have taken place along three distinct routes, along Ujjaeni-Mahisasati-Bodhan-Paithan route; through Nagpur region; and through the Baurat-Broach-Sopara route. Before 250 BC, the Buddhist communities in the regions of Maharashtra must have been very small, possibly scattered monastic settlements housed in buildings of brick, wattle, and daub, supported by a small lay community. With the reign of Ashoka and his patronage and the missionary efforts made by the Theravada Sangha after the Pataliputra Council, Buddhism must have spread rather extensively, and by 200 BC the Buddhist communities began to use excavated dwellings in the Bhor Ghat, Nasik region, and Ajanta. Buddhism had secured the support of a lay community engaged in diverse occupations such as farming, industrial arts, trade, commerce, and banking. It had also secured royal support from the Satavahanas, the Kshatrapas, Vakatakas, Chalukyas, Rashtrakutas, and the Shilaharas. The long and peaceful reign under the powerful Yadavas ended in AD 1294, and it was followed by a series of Muslim dynasties.

Buddhist Sites in Maharashtra

Ajanta – Aurangabad – Ellora – Pitalkhora Group

Ajanta Caves

Location: 106 km from Aurangabad

The Ajanta and Ellora caves are very famous in the Buddhist world as they were created by skilled Buddhist craftsmen and were also the abode of Buddhist monks. These caves, which are famous for their wonderful mural painting and sculptures, are cut out on the scrapped side of a huge semi-circular rock about 600 yards

▲ General view of Ajanta Caves

long in the mountain gorge in the Sahyadri ranges.

At the end of the seventh century AD, Buddhism began to decline in the country of its origin and its shrines fell into desolation and ruin. Occupied for almost 700 years, the caves of Ajanta seem to have been abandoned rather abruptly. They lay covered in natural growth and lay buried in the jungle-clad slopes for more than a thousand years. They were accidentally discovered in 1819 by John Smith, a British army officer. The 'view point' from where John Smith first glimpsed the caves, provides a magnificent sight of the U-shaped gorge and its scenic surroundings. Cascading down the cliff is a spectacular waterfall, which at the bottom feeds a natural pool called the Saptakunda.

Although the exact date when these caves were first used is not known, it is generally accepted that the earliest ones go back to the second century BC, while the latest are assigned to the seventh century AD. The caves of Ajanta date from the later centuries of the pre-Christian era, and taken in chronological order, they constitute a complete record of the development of these artistically carved monuments.

In Ajanta, there are 30 caves that have been excavated in the picturesque horseshoe-shaped valley with a magnificent vertical scarp, more than 225 feet high, from the river bed of Waghora that meanders through the valley. This retreat also provided the monks with enough time for furthering their religious pursuits through intellectual discourses for a considerably longer period particularly during the rainy season 'Versavasa'. A fragmentary inscription from the eighth–ninth centuries AD in front of Cave No. 26 indicates that these caves were occupied during that period.

The caves belong to two different Buddhist sects, viz. Hinayana (the lesser vehicle, in which Buddha was represented in symbolic form) and Mahayana (the greater vehicle, when the image of Buddha was conceived and worshipped). The Hinayana caves (Caves No. 8-10, 12-13 and 15A) were excavated between circa second century BC and second to third centuries AD while the Mahayana caves (Caves No.1-7, 11, 14 and 15-30) were excavated between circa fourth and seventh centuries AD.

Architecturally, the caves at Ajanta can be classified into a vihara (monastery, the residing place of the Buddhist monks combined with a shrine for Buddha in some cases), chaityagriha (the worshipping place of chaitya, the symbolic representation of Buddha), podhis (water cisterns for the monks) and rock-cut steps (which once connected the individual caves to the river Waghora). Of these, five (Cave No. 9, 10, 19, 26, and 29) are chaityagrihas and the rest are viharas.

Ajanta is famous all over the world today, for not only the caves, but for the immense wealth of the most delectable mural paintings which are retained in more than half a dozen caves. The beginning of the paintings date back to pre-Christian era, examples of which can be seen in Caves 9 and 10. The artists' brush attained the zenith of creativity and beauty during the fifth to seventh centuries AD when most of the caves were painted, some of which can still be seen in Caves 1, 2, 16 and 17. These paintings are richly embellished, colourful, most exquisite, exhibit harmony of forms and colour that are vividly portrayed, communicative, expressive, with multiple perspectives, and attract everyone's attention – the result of the extreme faith the monks had in Buddha.

▲ Sculptural panels adorn the caves and depict important events from Buddha's life

The subject matter of the paintings deals with various *Jataka* tales (stories related to previous births of Buddha as Bodhisattva).The important painting associated with the Buddha can be seen in Cave 1 (Miracle of Saravasti and the manifestation of Buddha into a thousand forms), Cave 2 (Birth of Buddha), Cave 16 (Conversion of Nanda), Cave 17 (Subjugation of Nalagiri, the Instigated Elephant; Buddha preaching in Tusita heaven; Buddha's visit to Kapilavastu and meeting his wife Yasodhara and son Rahula). The important *Jataka* stories can be seen in Cave 1 (Sibi, Hamsa, Mahajanaka Jataka); Cave 2 (Vidhurapandita Jataka), Cave 10 (Sibi, Chhaddanta Jataka); Cave 17 (Chhaddanta, Mahakapi, Hamsa, Vessantra, Mahaummaga, Matriposaka, Mahisa, Matsya, Mriga Jatakas).

Apart from the painted representations of events from Buddha's life, sculptural panels of the Great Departure (Buddha leaving Kapilavastu in Cave 1), Miracle of Saravasti (Cave 7), Buddha visiting Kapilavatsu (Cave 19), and Subjugation of Mara, Mahaparinirvana (Cave 26) are also well represented. The most famous paintings, however, are the representations of Bodhisattva Padmapani and Vajrapani (Cave 1), and the flying apsara (Cave 17). The inscriptions are found in Caves 9, 10, 12, 16, 17, and 26.

The paintings were executed after elaborate preparations of the rock surface followed by two layers of carrier surface to hold the paintings. Over this a plain and smooth layer of lime was applied and the paintings were executed over it. The colours and shades provided vary from red and yellow ochre, terra verde (for green), lime, kaolin, and gypsum (white), lamp black (black) and lapis lazuli (blue). The Ajanta paintings can be defined as tempera, and they are not frescoes as it is widely believed.

Thus, we can see that Ajanta is a monument of many facets and a wealth that cannot be measured by any parameter. Its immense quality and character has been recognised by the UNESCO when in its declaration in 1983 it included Ajanta as a World Heritage Monument, one among 732 such monuments all over the world.

Aurangabad Caves

Location: Near Aurangabad city

The rock-cut caves of Aurangabad are at a height of nearly 325 feet from ground level, and are hewn out of the Deccan trap formation. These caves were not natural. The solid rock-face was hewn and carved with primitive tools. The method employed was to make a plan and then start work from the top. Proceeding downward, the rock-cutters left solid blocks for pillars. The carving with hammer and chisel was carried out simultaneously with the excavation which was carried out with pick-axes. The facade and the verandah were first completed and then the hall, antechamber and cells of the shrine were taken up. The procedure was the same in all the caves.

There are 12 caves in all, categorised into three groups. The first group consists of Caves 1-5, the second from Caves 6-9, and the third from Caves 10-12. These caves are dedicated to different sects of Buddhism, viz. Hinayana, Mahayana, and Vajrayana, and are datable from third century AD to seventh century AD.

First Group (Caves 1-5): Cave 1 is an incomplete cave and only the portico and the pillars are finished. Caves 2 and 5 resemble contemporary structural temples, which are rare in rock-cut examples. Cave 3 is the most prominent and also the largest cave in the first group. This is a huge monastery with a sanctum and circumambulatory passage. The pillars are richly carved with foliage, caryatid figures, mithunas, and also scenes from the *Jataka* tales. Cave 4 is the only chaityagriha, which belongs to the early phase, i.e. Hinayana. The other caves in this group are dedicated to the Mahayana sect and are datable to circa fifth century AD.

▲ Not only are the idols here created by meticulous artists, but the caves themselves were chiselled by hand

Second Group (Caves 6-9): The second group is located nearly 1 km to the north-east of the first group and is dedicated mostly to the Vajrayana faith. This group has clusters of sculptures, which are the best specimens of such sculptures in the Aurangabad caves.

The small cave, Cave 6-A, a later addition is dedicated to Lord Ganesha. Caves 6 and 7 are monasteries, which are important for their rich sculptures that have great artistic value. The pillars are beautifully carved with foliage, geometrical designs, dwarf figures in the corner, and mithunas in medallions. Cave 7 has a most unusual design. It includes a number of beautiful sculptures that may be regarded as among the most significant products of Buddhist India. It also contains a dance panel comprising sculptures of exquisite beauty, representing a group of seven artists among whom the one in the middle is a dancer; the others are musicians.

Caves 8 and 9 are unfinished excavations, but give us an idea of the process of excavation. The important sculptures in the second group are gigantic figures of Bodhisattvas, Ashtamahabhaya Avalokitesvara, Buddha Bodhisattvas with six Prajna deities, Hariti-Panchika, a dancing panel, Buddha's Mahaparinirvana, etc.

▲ Unnoticed idol of sleeping Buddha

Third Group (Caves 10-12): The third group of caves is located at the far end of the hill on the northern side, at a short distance from the second group and is quite inaccessible. Caves 10 and 11 are unfinished cells and are totally dilapidated. Cave 12 is a monastery. The period of the third group is difficult to establish in the absence of any identifiable features.

Ellora Caves

Location: 26 km north of Aurangabad

Ellora Caves, more popularly known as 'Verul Leni' in the local dialect were more or less known to the world throughout their existence. Extending in a linear arrangement, the 34 caves contain Buddhist chaityas, or halls of worship and viharas or monasteries, as well as Hindu and Jain temples. Spanning a period of about 600 years between the fifth and eleventh centuries AD the earliest excavation here is in Dhumar Lena (Cave 29).

The first 12 caves in Ellora are the earliest and were excavated by Buddhists over a period of 200 years from 550-750 AD. These caves are located on an ancient route connecting the ancient ports of Sopara, Bharuch, etc., on the Arabian coast with inland ancient cities like Ujjain, Paithan, Ter which ultimately connect with south Indian cities.

The Buddhists were the first to have undertaken excavations in Ellora. The period corresponds to the first phase of work in Ajanta and is contemporary to the Aurangabad caves. Their period of occupation was between circa 450-650 AD. During this period, 12 caves were excavated by the followers of Buddhism. These caves can be divided into two groups based on the architectural developments of these caves. Caves 1-5 are the

▲ Sculptures at Ellora

earliest among the 12 and Caves 6-12 form a separate group, which belong to a later period.

These two groups consist of a single chaityagriha and monasteries. In the earlier group, there is a unique excavation, which is Cave 5, also known as Maharwada. This is the largest vihara and there is an image of a seated Buddha in the main shrine attended by Avalokitesvara on one side and Maitreya on the other side.

Among the second group, consisting of Caves 6-12, the Teen Tal is the biggest and most elaborate. Cave 6 is notable for its antechamber which has several interesting sculptures and figures from the Vajrayana pantheon. Cave 10, known as Visvakarma or the Carpenter's Cave, is the only proper chaitya hall in Ellora. Its facade, richly decorated, resembles masonry work. A porch surmounted by a gallery leads to another gallery inside the chapel. The chaitya hall is the third largest in India. Besides the large number of seated and standing Buddhas, there are a number of images of the Bodhisattvas. A staircase leads to a large pillared court and a gallery with a railed terrace.

Cave 11 and Cave 12 are large three-story high structures alike in design and represent the style that peaked in Ellora. Cave 12 is the bigger of the two and is more impressive, it is known as Teen Tal and is a vast excavation. The interiors make a striking contrast to the undecorated facade for the hall in each floor and has galleries of images of the Buddha, and almost all the deities of the Vajrayana pantheon. Among the huge Buddha figures, with Avalokiteavara, Padmapani, and Vajrapani in attendance, the one in the shrine, with arms folded and the face deeply meditative is the most impressive one.

Pitalkhora Caves

Location: 80 km north-west of Aurangabad

Pitalkhora most probably represents the ancient Pitangalaya where yaksha Sankar resided according to the Buddhist text *Mahamayuri*. Pitalkhora is deep in an utterly secluded scarp of the Satmala hill, overlooking a narrow glen. It is a remarkable series of caves with a picturesque wild setting and perfectly calm atmosphere. Pitalkhora lies on the ancient trade route used by the caravans from Sopara and Nasik crossing the Indrayani hill near Pitalkhora on their way to Paithan.

There are some 13 excavations in two groups. The first group comprises Caves 1-4 with 6, 6A, 7, 8, and 9 being the result of the westward extension of the rock excavation activity. The earliest belong to second century BC (Caves 1-4), while Caves 6–9 are ascribed to the first century BC and Caves 10–11 to the first century AD. The Pitalkhora group consists of some three shrines (chaityas and a stupa with a cell) the others being viharas accommodating probably 75 members.

The main groups, in the form of a rough crescent, start near the head of the ravine and face south, south-west, and west. The fronts of almost all the caves have disappeared, and in most instances the upper portions of the walls have crumbled too. The large number of fissures that admit rainwater into the caves existed even when the caves were in use.

The crowning glory of Pitalkhora are Caves 3 and 4, both conceived and executed on a magnificent scale; the exuberance and the rich texture of their façade decoration unparalleled in the pre-Christian caves. Sharing a common forecourt facing the narrow stream in the bosom of ravine, both are roughly contemporaneous. Apsidal on plan, Cave 3, the chaityagriha, consists of the usual nave and apse, demarcated from the aisles by an elongated U-shaped row of 37 tapering octagonal pillars inward rakes. This cave was inhabited till about seventh century AD, which is proved by the faded paintings, and a few painted records, on its pillars, walls, and ceiling.

▲ Cave 4, huge in scale, has some beautiful art on its pillars and walls

The second group, consisting of four caves is nestled on the other side of the ravine, the first cave in this group is almost opposite the last cave of the first group. As one proceeds towards this group from the head of the ravine, one gets a panoramic view of the first group of caves. Curiously enough, all the four caves of this group are associated with stupas – three apsidal chaityagrihas and one cell, with extensions at the back and left sides, containing three rock-cut stupas, evidently made in memory of some distinguished resident monks as at Bhaja.

Junnar, Nasik and Paithan Group
Junnar Caves
Location: 90 km from Pune

Junnar is a derivative of 'Jurna' (from 'jirna') nagar, meaning old town. Junnar was an important center of Hinayana Buddhism. It was the largest such center in Maharashtra. This town lay on an ancient trade-route which ran through the narrow pass of Naneghat (possibly named after the Satavahana queen Nayanika, who improved the pass) to Kalyana (the modern town of Kalyan), an important commercial center. Junnar, is a town of considerable antiquity and was once of greater importance than Pune.

Junnar has the largest number of caves to be found in any one place in India. There are in all 324 rock-cut excavations of which ten are chaityagriha, 174 are viharas and other chambers, 115 cisterns and the remaining are unfinished excavations.

There are rock-cut caves on four distinct hills in various directions, but within a radius of 5 km from Junnar. Among these, the earliest seems to be an inscribed cave at Naneghat with a cistern that had full-length bas relief portraits of the early rulers of the Satavahana dynasty.

In terms of occupational capacity, the Junnar community could have numbered several hundreds, probably between 200-300 monks and nuns. This may have been the strength at the peak period, about AD 100, for the settlement was created out of the hills around Junnar in several stages reflected in the changing architectural style.

These caves can be divided into four main groups:

The Sulaiman hill group situated to the north of Junnar contains a large number of caves and cells for the use of monks, but the most important are the Ganesh Lena cave and the chaitya cave marked 'No. 6'. Ganesh Lena is now converted into a place of worship by the locals. It is reached by a staircase. The front verandah, which is extremely narrow, is supported by eight pillars. There are two rows of pillars – five in each – surmounted by figures of lions, tigers, and elephants. The stupa is one of the usual pattern, but is remarkably well-proportioned and finely executed.

Manmodi Hill lies to the south-west of Junnar. Here are three groups of viharas and chaityas. Several of the caves in this group appear to be half-finished probably on account of the unsuitability of the rock. The most important in the group is the chaitya Cave No. 2. The front is well-made with four pillars and an Ashoka railing below.

To the south-west of Junnar lies the Shivneri hill group of caves, famous for the fort of the great Maratha Shivaji, where he was born. In this group, the most important cave in the chaitya is marked No. 48 which is different from the others on account of its flat roof. In the rear there is the usual stupa. On the summit of the hill is a large tank cut of the rock.

The Tulja Lena group is about 4 km to the west of the town. Here are a series of caves excavated out of the face of a rock. The main object of interest is the circular chaitya cave. This is the only one of its kind we have come across. The rock was first bored into and then excavated in the form of a circle. In the middle is carved out the stupa and all around it are twelve octagonal pillars which support the dome. Pradakshina can be made all around the stupa from outside as well as from inside by walking around the pillars.

Nasik

Location: 8 km south-east of Nasik town

One of the largest Buddhist monastic settlements was in the Junnar-Nasik area. The Buddhist caves, locally known as the Pandu Lena, are in one of the isolated hills, close to the Mumbai road and about 8 km south-west from Nasik town. They are situated about 300 feet above the level of the plain and are easily approached by a pathway leading from the road, a distance of about 2 km.

▲ Buddha's Mahaparinirvana is depicted on the walls of the caves in Nasik

Nasika or Nasikya of yore was situated on an important caravan-route. The chief interesting feature of this group is not only the number of inscriptions on the wall referring to events of great historical significance, belonging to the reign of the Satavahanas and Kshetraharas, a Saka family temporary eclipsing the fortunes of the Satavahanas, but also in its representing a brilliant phase in the rock-cut architecture of the second century AD to which period are ascribed the majority of caves. They almost entirely belong to an early date and were excavated by the Hinayana sect, the first great division of Buddhists. It was originally devoid of images or any representation of Buddha as an object of worship, or in fact any of those characteristics which marked the introduction of the Mahayana philosophy. There are altogether 23 excavations, though many of these are small and unimportant.

Cave 3 is the biggest vihara here and contains 18 rooms in all and is well suited as a residence for the monks. On three sides of the hall, benches or tables are well-arranged. Above the door, are engraved symbols of the Bodhi tree, chaitya and dharmachakra. The sculptures here include dvarpalas and the scene of the abduction of a woman. An interesting feature of the vihara is the stupa in relief on the back wall of the hall with worshippers on two sides.

Cave 10 is almost a copy of this cave but the pillars are very elegant. The hall can be entered by three doors.

Cave 17 has a back room separated by two pillars with elephant designs. On the wall is a Buddha image.

Cave 23 is enlarged a second time by Marma, a lay follower. The ante-chamber is somewhat elevated and has two carved pillars in the front. The dvarpalas here are large, inside the shrine is an image of Buddha, he is shown preaching the first sermon.

Paithan

Location: 48 km from Aurangabad

Of the most major cities and towns, the most ancient was Patithana or modern Paithan. It lay on an ancient trade route near Aurangabad. In the *Sutta Nipata* (collection of Buddha's sermons mostly in verse) it is called the capital of the Alaka country. By the time of Buddha, Paithan had already become a thriving town with trade links with the south and north.

Karle – Bhaja – Bedsa – Kondana group

Karle Caves

Location: Halfway between Mumbai–Pune (200 km) easily accessible from both cities

In the hills known as Bhorghat between Mumbai and Pune, some of the most important groups of early period caves are found. This was an important trade route connecting the Pune–Junnar area with Sopara on the west coast. These caves are at Bhaja, Kondane, Bedsa, Karle, and Shelarwadi, which belong to the beginning of the Christian era.

Sculptures at the entrance of Chaitya hall in Karle ▶

The Great Chaitya of Karle would rank among the most important monuments of the world. It is described in one of its own inscriptions as the 'most excellent rock mansion in Jambudvipa (India)'. On stylistic and paleographic grounds, this monument is attributed to the beginning of the second century AD.

The Karle establishment received munificent gifts from a variety of sources. Probably the beginnings were made under the patronage of local communities of lay devotees led by the Maharathis (Somadeva of Okhalaiyas) but soon itinerant merchants added their contributions.

There were originally two free-standing pillars, surmounted by four lions, one on each side of the facade and near the beginning of the entrance. These lion pillars were at least 45 feet in height, equal to that of the Ashoka columns at Sarnath. The pillar on the right was destroyed when a flaw or fault in the rock damaged the right side of the frontage. The temple of goddess Ekvira now occupies the place where this pillar stood.

The outer porch is wider than the main hall. It consists of two thick octagonal pillars without bases and capitals. It forms a triple entrance and supports a mass of rock in which four pillars stand between pilasters which provide the effect of a dwarf colonnade above. Below the ledge of the rock is a rail band. The front screen covers most of the façade.

Several modifications were made later by the Mahayana Buddhists. The friezes above the elephants were cut away to insert figures of the Buddha and his attendants. There is a miniature temple, the front of which is crowned with chaitya arches and in between them are carved figures which are among the finest sculptures in India. Above this, the rail and chaitya arch patterns are again depicted at the top. On the front wall, both friezes of rail at the bottom and at the top were replaced by images of Buddha and his attendants. On the other side of the door, couples are depicted, which is part of the original decoration. In the space between the central and the right door there is an image of Buddha attended by Padmapani and Manjushri. Buddha is seated on a lion throne with the feet dangling on the lotus over a wheel supported by two deer. Beneath the wheel are naga (serpent) figures and above the Buddha are shown two Vindhya-Dharas holding a crown.

The entrance to the hall of the chaitya has three doorways. The inner hall has magnetic properties. Fifteen pillars on each side separate the nave from the aisles. The pillars depict the same design and the theme of the lion pillars. Its area is about 1700 sq. feet, a veritable cathedral among chaityas, and is therefore called the Great Chaitya of Karle.

Theravada architecture reached its climax with the construction of the Great Chaitya at Karle.

The inner hall is majestic. Nearly 2,000 years have passed since the sound of pilgrim's feet or the chanting of saffron-robed monks broke the silence of this pillared hall. On the inner side, that is, within the aisles, horses take the place of the elephants. The eight pillars on the right are sixteen-sided and have a dagoba carved on it, flanked by a chakra symbol and a sinha-stambha; the latter was probably the design of the lion pillars outside the porch.

There are seven pillars behind the dagoba. The dagoba is very unique and is made up of a two-storeyed drum with a rail design on the upper edge, probably for circumbulation. The top of the dome has a capital decorated with rail patterns and a wooden umbrella, and on the underside a lotus is carved. Around the edge of the capital are eight holes for fitting a metal rail for hanging drapes, which serves for enclosing the relics when they are exhibited.

The unique feature of the chaitya is the chaitya-arch and window, on which the whole system of lighting depends. There are several inscriptions that help in deciding the dates of construction.

In addition to the chaitya cave, the remaining excavations are viharas and monasteries.

The village Vehargaon near Karla, so called because of the monasteries nearby and the modern township of Lonavala or Lonauli, which means an abundance of 'lenas' or caves, are strong indications that this area, which includes Bhaja and Bedsa, was a stronghold of Buddhism with Karla as the center of pilgrimage.

Bhaja Caves

Location: At a distance of 7-8 km from Karla

This group consists of 22 excavations on a hill, near the village Bhaja. The view from the cave facing the valley of Indrayani river, with two towering Maratha forts, Lohagarh, and Visapur, along the adjoining hilltops is arresting.

▲ The Bhaja caves were created before the image of the Buddha was introduced

The caves here are the product of the early phase of excavation, dating back to the period when the image of Buddha was not introduced here. The latest excavation here is a cistern, dated to the end of the second century AD, based on the evidence of the paleography of an inscription. The caves, however, remained in use at least till the fifth–sixth centuries AD which saw the embellishment of the chaityagriha with the painted figures of Buddha.

There are a total of 18 excavations, stupas and viharas (among the former a very interesting chaityagriha, regarded as the earliest in its class). The rows of pin-holes on the front of the arch suggest some embellishments, most probably in woodwork. The façade is effectively carved mainly with the simple motifs of railings.

Among the monasteries, Cave 18, which consists of a pillared verandah with a cell on the right and a recess on the left and an astylar hall with a bench along the left side and two cells each on the back and right sides, is of unique interest on account of the florid treatment of the wall-surface, unusual in an early monastery. The columns of this monastery are square below and above and octagonal in the middle.

The other monasteries are ordinary with a verandah and an astylar hall with cells, on two or three sides.

Bedsa Caves

Location: 18 km from Karla caves

In the same spur as the caves of Bhaja, but on the southern side and facing the Pauna River some 300 feet above the plains, is a small group of caves known as Bedsa, or Karunj Bedsa.

The caves consist of a chaityagriha, a monastery, two single independent cells, an unfinished cave, a few cisterns within recesses, a tiny apsidal roofless excavation with a stupa and an unfinished circular cell with stupa.

▲ The Bedsa caves are a small group but the viharas here are quite unique

Though the smallest, this group of caves has to its credit several novel features. The group consists of an old chaitya and viharas of unique shapes and a few cells and cisterns. The chief focus of attraction has been the evolution of the rock-cut chaityagrihas. The chaityagriha has four pillars, horses, bulls and elephants with male and female riders have been carved on them. Its ribbed roof is supported by 26 octagonal pillars.

The verandah has cells at either end; one of them on the right side is a gift from a banker from Nasik, his name being inscribed on its façade. Its walls are decorated with the conventional but effective array of chaitya-arches, semblances of roofs and railings. In contrast to the ornamental exteriors, the interior of the hall is severely plain.

Kondane Caves

Location: 16 km north-west of Karla caves

The small but interesting group of caves at Kondane or Kondhana is excavated in the western face of a high hill. The Kondane group is in the same range of hills as the forts of Rajmachi and Srivardhan. Due to its utter isolation amidst the mountain-ranges, the group seldom receives the attention it merits.

The first excavation to the south-west is a chaityagriha, it is strikingly similar to the Bhaja façade. The dagoba is 9 feet in diameter surmounted by a double-storied capital with provisions for a wooden umbrella and shaft, to the north of the chaitya at a higher level is a large vihara. It consists of a rectangular pillared hall with attached cells and a pillared porch in front.

Much of the floor and façade of the porch is damaged. On the right wall is carved a dagoba in half-relief under a chaitya arch. The ceiling shows traces of paintings (floral and geometrical designs). The façade is carved with a railed balcony, the upper part is crowned by a row of chaitya arches or windows.

There are two short inscriptions on the façade, which form the paleography, and appear to belong to the early part of the first century BC. The third excavation is a plain ruined vihara with nine adjoining cells. Beyond this, to the north, is a row of nine cells cut into the far end of what may have been a natural hollow in the cliff.

The rest of the group consists of a pondhi half-filled with mud, two small cells, and two small cisterns.

Ambivale

Location: Approximately 90 km from Mumbai

The Ambivale cave is about half a mile from the village of Ambivale, north of Karjat, under the hill fort of Kotalgadh and to the east of it, and thus not far from Kondane. The cave overlooks the river, being 20 feet above it – the sloping rock leading up to it from the water. It consists of a large square hall, about 42 feet by 30 feet, and is 10 feet high, having four cells each on the three sides making it twelve cells in all.

Kanheri – Kondivate – Sopara Group

Kanheri Caves

Location: North of Mumbai and east of the township of Borivali

The hill in which the extensive group of caves is located is known as 'Krishnagiri', or 'Kanhagiri', 'Krishna's hill'. Its summit is formed by a large mass of compact rock under which a softer stratum has in many places been washed away. The entire group consisting of 109 caves is one of the biggest monastic settlements in India. They lie scattered on different tiers of the hill in small groups of three to five or more.

▲ The Kanheri Caves are in Mumbai and date back to the first century BC

Beginning with the first century BC the genesis and growth of this group of Buddhist caves excavated in the mass of volcanic turf in the hills of Kanheri or Krishnagiri covered a period of more than a thousand years.

The Buddhist monks of Hinayana faith were the first to commence with the excavations of these caves and the famous chaityagriha (Cave 3), bearing an inscription of the time of King Yajna-Sri Satakarni Goutamiputra (second century AD) is a product of Hinayana.

Caves 41, 67, 89, and 90, have on their walls a dazzling profusion of reliefs, mostly of Buddha, displaying admirable poise and subtlety, with a dignified expression of transcendental bliss. Buddha is generally shown as either standing with his right hand in vara-mudra, or seated in dharma-chakra-pravartana-mudra. In the latter kind of image, he is often shown with all his paraphernalia. Seated in pralambapada-asana with his feet resting on a lotus, he is flanked by two Bodhisattvas, the latter themselves, in larger composition, in the company of female

▲ The art in the Kanheri Caves are intricate and of immense value

deities. The stem of the lotus is held by a pair of nagas, sometimes accompanied by nagis. This type of composition is very popular in the western Indian caves of sixth century AD.

In Caves 2 and 41 Avalokitesvara is represented in the company of two female deities, one of them most probably Tara. Cave 41 consists of a court, a small portico in front of a pillared verandah, an astylar hall with a cell on either side and a shrine with figures of Buddha on a wall, also one sees a representation of the four-armed eleven-headed Avalokitesvara, the only known relief of this form in India.

One of the reliefs in Cave 67 depicts the Dipankara Jataka, where Buddha, in one of his existence as a bodhisattva, was born as a learned Brahmin, named Sumedha, Sumati, and Megha. Excavated in the reign of Yajna Satakarni, Cave 3 has a court with a rock-cut fence in the front, access to which is provided by a flight of steps. The façade of its fence is exuberant with an ornamental railing pattern with a row of animals at the base, lotuses on the shafts and cross-bars and half lotuses alternating with human busts on the coping.

There were large structural stupas in front of the chaityagrihas. One of them, of stone, yielded two small copper urns, containing ashes, a small gold box with a piece of cloth, a silver box, a ruby, pieces of gold and two copper-plates, one of them dated to 324 AD. Near the chaityagriha and guarding the way to the hill is the opening of Cave 1. It was designed to have a double-storied verandah and a porch, besides the pillared hall, the last in the initial stage of excavations. Cave 11, called the Darbar cave, consists of a verandah with eight octagonal pillars, a small pillared chapel at the left end, a flat-roofed hall with pillared aisles along the three sides, and has a shrine of Buddha in pralambapada-asana.

Nearby, cut steps leading from one group of caves to another and the fine rock-cut benches beside the caves, and the provision of cisterns for water supply, are some of the noteworthy features of this site. These caves contain numerous inscribed records of considerable interest to the Buddhist pilgrim.

A majority of these rock-cut cells follow more or less a standardised form of a single or double room (Bhikshugriha) that invariably has a rock-cut bench, and in front is a narrow veranda.

Kanheri is the only place in India where monastic caves were continuously occupied by Buddhist monks from the second century BC to tenth century AD and even beyond that time. This is evident from a Japanese inscription made by a Buddhist pilgrim of the Nichiren Sect which is engraved on the walls of Cave 66.

By the tenth century, Buddhism was declining and with the Mughal invasion it can be said that it disappeared from India for all practical purposes. Small bands of monks continued to reside in these damaged and deserted monasteries till the advent of the Portuguese. Kanheri did not escape the religious zeal of these new conquerors and in 1535, Fr. Antonio da Porto, a Franciscan priest, not only converted the remaining Buddhist ascetics to Christianity, but renamed the chaitya the church of St. Michael.

Kondivate Caves

Location: 20 km south of Kanheri

The total number of excavations here is 18, of which one is a chaitya, two are chaityagrihas and the rest are viharas, probably accommodating no more than 25 members. The chaitya is assigned to the same age as the one at Bhaja (about first century BC) the Mahayanists, probably in the sixth century AD.

Though small and few in number, the caves at Kondivate are of interest because a chaitya there is one of the earliest in Western India. The plan of the chaityagriha consists of a long astylar hall with a circular sanctuary at the back, and bears a striking similarity to that of the Sudama cave in Barabar hills. The entrance to the hall is in the front, directly opposite the door of the sanctuary. The ceiling of the hall is flat, and the hall is approached by a central flight of steps (now badly decayed). On the right wall of the hall were added, in the fifth and sixth centuries AD, several reliefs of Buddha. The largest composition depicts the Master in the preaching attitude, seated in bhadrasana on a lotus, the stem of which is held by two nagas. In this panel, Buddha is attended by Padmapani and another Bodhisattva.

Cave 13 has a verandah with carved pillars and pilasters, two each, a hall with four pillars arranged in a square, eight cells, and a shrine in the center of the back. The door frame of the shrine in this monastery is decorated with the motif of a pillared pavilion.

Cave 4 has a pillared verandah with a bench and a spacious astylar hall with benches too, and a pillared corridor excavated along the side and back walls. Approached by a flight of steps from a moulded platform in the front, Cave 2 has a verandah and an astylar spacious oblong hall. Besides these caves, there are scanty remains of a structural stupa and several monolithic votive stupas.

Sopara

Location: 70 km from Mumbai, easily accessible by local trains

Sopara was the capital of the Konkan from about 500 BC to AD 1300. Sopara is approachable from Nala Sopara railway station of the Western Railways.

Under the names of Shurparaka, Sopara appears in the *Mahabharata* as a very holy place, where the Pandavas rested on their way from Gokarn in North Kanara to Prabhas or Veraval in South Kathiawar.

It is mentioned in the *Harivansha* as a city of 500 bows a thousand yards broad, and 500 arrows about five hundred yards high, and is said to have been built on the land recovered by the arrow that was shot by Parshuram when he won the Konkan from the sea.

According to a Buddhist writer, in one of his former births, Gautama Buddha was Bodhisatta Supparat, i.e. Bodhisattva of

Sopara. In 540 BC or thereabouts, it is said to have been visited by Vijaya, the mythical conqueror of Ceylon.

Sopara was also known as 'Ophir' or 'Sophir'. 'Ophir' is written as 'Sophir' by Josephus, a Greek writer, and according to several authorities, 'Sophir' is the Coptic or Egyptian word for 'India'.

The Sanskrit dictionary *Yadavas Kosh* appears to point to 'Sopara' as the chief place in Aparanta where it says, 'Aparanta is the western country, Shurparaka and others'.

For a place whose importance as a religious and trade center lasted for over 2,500 years (1400 BC–AD 1300) Sopara yields few remains of this exalted past. Some excavated remains are now preserved at the Asiatic Society in Mumbai.

Very recently, a local governing body has launched a programme to preserve the stupa here and initiate a tourism development project.

Konkan Area

The Konkan is a narrow strip of lowland along the west coast of India. There were several Buddhist settlements here, both along the coast and interiors. These were at Kuda, and Dabhol, along the coast, and at Mahad, Chiplun, Kol, and Nadsur. In the interiors, they total some 150 excavations, the largest groups of which are at Kuda, Mahad, and Nadsur.

Kuda Caves

Location: 200 km from Mumbai, or 100 km from Pune in Konkan area

The caves at Kuda have perhaps the most picturesque location. On the eastern shore of the northern arm of the Murud-Janjira creek, there are 24 Buddhist caves near the village of Kuda, of which four are chaityagrihas and 21 viharas, which could have accommodated a fraternity of some 60 monks and nuns. They are assigned to a period of first and second centuries AD and a few of them were reoccupied by the Mahayanists in the seventh century AD.

▲ Kuda Caves

All the caves are exceedingly plain and very much alike in size. The lowest and farthest to the north, is one of four caves which contains dagobas. It consists of a verandah with a cell on the left, a benched recess on the right and a large square hall with two plain octagonal pillars rising from a dwarf wall at the far end. These pillars serve as an antechamber to the shrine, which has a plain dagoba reaching to the ceiling.

Cave 5 is a square vihara devoid of cells. There are three shallow recesses in the rear wall and a low plinth runs along the other three sides. An inscription in the verandah records that this cave and a cistern were the gifts of a female ascetic, Paduminika and her followers, Bodhi and Asalpamita.

The principal excavation of the group is a chaitya, numbered 6. The roof front of the verandah is supported at the other end on the head and shoulders of carved elephants. One broad door flanked by a window gives access to the inner hall, which has a plinth on three sides. Two plain shafts rising from low benches separate the antechamber from the hall. The back or outer side of these benches is decorated with animals and dwarfs between bands of floral patterns above and below.

To the left of the antechamber is a cell with a bench, behind which is a small chamber, probably used for the storage of temple property. The large oblong shrine has a plain dagoba. There are two interesting reliefs at the corners of the far end of the hall. These panels have life-size male and female figures with a dwarf attendant.

The verandah has several reliefs of the Buddha, one of which depicts the Buddha seated on a lotus throne, below which is a wheel supported on a pillar held by nagas and naginis. On either side of the pillar are three deer. These sculptures are later additions from the fifth or sixth century AD. To the south of the Caves 8 and 15, are chaityas that are similar to Caves 1 and 6. The remaining excavations in the upper terraces are plain viharas, verandas, cells with benches and attached pondhis.

Kuda must have been important probably due to its location on the creek and may have served as a port in the Satavahana period.

Mahad Caves

Location: 205 km from the south of Mumbai, on the Konkan or west coast road

Only about 1 km from the town is the village of Pala, and these caves are sometimes referred to as the Pala Caves. The Mahad group of caves faces west and affords a view of the Savitri or Bankot River. There are 31 excavations, 20 in the upper scarp and the rest about 18-27 feet lower down. Of these, except for Cave 1, with inscriptions that can't be easily deciphered, all the caves belong to the Hinayana faith and have been dated to the early centuries of the Christian era. They continued to be occupied later in the fifth-sixth centuries AD when the Mahayanists carved images here. The place appears to be of considerable importance in the Satavahana period as it was on the ancient highway joining Konkan with central Maharashtra.

The majority of the excavations consist of a hall with a pillared verandah in front and a shrine or cells in the far end. Several caves are in ruins and many are unfinished. The only decorative motifs, and this appears rather infrequen-

▲ Situated on the ancient highway connecting Konkan with the rest of the state, the Mahad Caves initially belonged to the Hinayana sect

tly, is the rail pattern on the parapet or wall between and pilasters. Several cells have benches, which indicate that they were excavated in early Hinayana times. The inscriptions that are donative and the sculptured images of the Buddha with attendants, however point to later Mahayana occupation.

Cave 1, at the south end of the upper scarp, though unfinished, is a large chaitya-vihara built along the same plan as the later Mahayana chaitya halls at Ajanta, Ellora, and elsewhere. It consists of a pillared verandah (only one of the six pillars that were finished) and a large hall, wider at the rear than in front. There are four incomplete cells on the left wall. A plinth runs around all four sides of the hall. In the center of the rear wall is the shrine containing a square mass of rock rising to the roof. In the front is an image of the Buddha seated on a wheel, in the teaching attitude, with deer beneath, attended by chauri-bearers and vidhadharas above. Other standing figures are carved on either side of the square mass of rock, and on the back wall a second seated figure of the Buddha has been outlined.

The largest excavation in this group is Cave 8, another chaitya. It bears some resemblance to that at Kuda. All the pillars of the verandah are broken, and the dagoba in the shrine at the far end has been worked upon by time and weather, but the carved umbrella and shaft on the roof are still visible.

Cave 15 is a small excavation consisting of a verandah, a small hall, and a recess containing a dagoba carved in high relief with a broad band of the rail pattern around the upper edge of the drum.

In the lower scarp at the south end of the group is Cave 21, probably the oldest excavation in Mahad. It is a small chamber containing a dagoba five feet in diameter, reaching the roof, with a seated Buddha carved, attended by chauri-bearers and vidhyadharas, the latter holding a crown over the Buddha's head.

Kol Caves

The establishment at Kol, south-east of Mahad, has two small groups of caves, and two to the north-east have a few small cells and cisterns.

Sudhagarh Caves

Location: 120 km from Mumbai and near Pali town, famous for a Ganesha temple

There are two groups of Buddhist caves in this area, one at Thanale and the other at Nanavali, which are located in the Sudhagarh taluk, or in the sub-division of the Kolaba district of Maharashtra.

The Thanale group of 23 excavations is about 18 km from Pali, a small town at the foot of the Sarasdagh Fort. The principal cave here is a vihara, consisting of a hall, a plinth on three sides with cells in the walls, which are level with the plinth, and from which steps lead down to the hall.

The entrances to the cells are decorated with the chaitya arch motif. The recesses between the doors are also ornamented with the same motif, the spaces between these arches are filled with the rail pattern and lattice windows.

Each cell has a stone bench. Stone plaques have been set into the northern and eastern walls, six feet above the plinth, two of which have inscriptions in the Brahmi script of the second century BC testifying to donations made towards the construction of these caves. Above the recess on the northern wall is a bas-relief of a five-headed serpent, which is repeated in miniature on the southern wall. Adjacent to this is another relief of a couple standing on a fish. A much later addition is a lotus painted on the ceiling of the vihara.

The chaitya cave is devoid of interest, the facade having fallen away. It is a plain cell with a dagoba 12 feet high at the far end. The upper portion of the drum is carved with the rail pattern. Steps leading from the chaitya cave to the adjacent excavations have long since crumbled, and the only path now available is along the face of the rock.

An interesting excavation is the stupa gallery. It consists of a large low-roofed chamber with eight stupas carved out of rock. They bear a close resemblance to the stupas in the gallery at Bhaja. The remaining caves to the north are single cells excavated at different levels.

Nanavali is about 35 km from Pali, or a further 17 km from Thanale, via the villages of Bhairampada and Pachapur. The 37 caves at Nanavali are also referred to as the 'Khadasambla'. They are in an advanced state of ruin and in several cases the overhanging rock has collapsed, thereby blocking entry to the caves.

The principal excavation here is Cave 13, a large chamber consisting of 15 cells and one chaitya cell carved in the three walls. It is made up of a large assembly area nearly 16 m. sq. with a plinth similar to that at Thanale, running around the three sides. The southern wall has five cells, the northern has four and the western has seven, the second from the right being the chaitya cell. All the residential cells have benches. Steps lead down from the plinth to the hall whose floor is level with that of the chaitya cell.

The chaitya is apsidal with a vaulted roof and contains a dagoba 7 feet high. There are signs of water seeping through the roof and being led around the dagoba across the floor to the edge of the cliff. This tunnel is flanged so that it could be covered with stone slabs.

Remnants of a short flight of steps at the northern and southern ends of the hall lead to the caves beyond. The existence of square and round sockets in the ceiling and in the floor indicates that a structural screen was once in place to screen off, or segregate the chaitya.

The remaining excavations consist of single, double, and even triple caves, similar in plan to those at Mahakali, the entrance to the inner cells being through in front. All these cells have stone benches and recesses. The inner cells were furnished with wooden doors, as sockets for such arrangements are noticeable.

Panhale Kaji – Ancient Pranalaka

Location: 19 km by road to the village Wakavali, on the Khed-Dapodi road

Panhale Kaji is a small village consisting of 12 separate localities (wadis) in a small area, measuring about 3 sq. km.

There are 29 caves here, and of these 28 are situated on the right bank of Kotjai, on a hill-slope, on the top of which lies a commanding hill fort. Caves 1-16 are about 150-300 feet away from the riverbed. Caves 18-28 lie close to the river bank. Cave 29 which lies near Bagwadi, about 2 km away from the main group, to its south, overlooking the stream called Dhakti.

The caves which had disappeared into oblivion some time after the 14th century remained unknown to the outside world. The 29 caves here were brought to light by the Department of Archives and Archaeology in 1973 and 1974.

The local people knew of only one cave called Ganesha Lena (Cave 21) as it was partially accessible and the image of Ganesh in the verandah of that cave was worshipped by villagers.

Panhale Kaji of Dapoli taluk of Ratnagiri district must have been a place of importance during the Silahara times. It finds mention as 'Pranalaka' in two Silahara inscriptions of AD 1100. The word 'Kaji' which goes with it, appears to have been added after the area came under the possession of the Adil Shahi Sultanate of Bijapur, early in the 17th century, when the Sultans captured the port of Dabhol and appointed a Qazi to look after legal and other related functions.

Palaeographic evidence pushes back the antiquity of these caves to the third century AD.

Khed – Chiplun group

Khed

Location: 218 km from Mumbai

In the Buddhist cave group of Khed, there is a large vihara, with an oblong cell in the back wall containing a stupa, and three cells for monks, excavated in the side walls of the main hall. The group also has four other smaller caves provided with rock-cut water cisterns.

Chiplun

Location: 250 km from Mumbai

At Chiplun, about a half km south of the town, there is a group of four Buddhist caves, known as Pancha Pandava caves. Of these Cave 3 is a chaityagriha. It appears that with Khed as the principal center, Hinayana Buddhist monks took up excavations of monastic centers at Chiplun and Panhale. The mercantile community of Dabhol perhaps contributed to the excavation of the caves and maintenance of the religious community.

Shirwal – Wai – Yerpal – Karhad – Pohale

Shirwal

Location: 48 km south of Pune

There are 15 caves at Shirwal, the majority of the excavations are either ruined or filled with debris. They are all similar, and very plain, as are all the early caves.

Wai

Location: Lohari as a small hamlet situated 4 km north of Wai

The hill on the outskirts of the village has a group of eight caves cut into the soft trap rock from south-west to north-east and facing the south-west. The group consists of two damaged viharas, one of which was decorated with figure sculptures, now much mutilated, a few cells and one chaitya.

Yerphal Caves

Location: 1 km from the village Yerpal on the Karad – Patan road.

The group of caves consists of a small chaitya cave, two cells and an unfinished excavation. It was discovered by Dr. MK Dhavalikar and Dr. Suresh Jadhav on December 9, 1979. Although the caves were unknown to the world, the people of the village know about their existence. The caves were full of silt and debris but have been recently cleared by one Ramachandra Lugade, a saintly character who lives in the village, and has recently also laid a path that one can take to the caves.

The chaitya hall, the main cave, is apsidal on plan. It has a vaulted roof, about 4.20 m high. The hall is astylar with a stupa in the apse, which has been considerably destroyed. Adjoining the stupa, on the south, are two cells. Of these, the one that is close to the chaitya, has a bench and there is a cistern at the eastern end.

Karhad Caves

Location: 500 km from Mumbai and 200 km from Pune

Karhad is a flourishing town in Karhad district. It was a very important trading and religious center in the Christian era, in the Satavahana period. The fact is evident from the donative records of the merchant of Karhataka (ancient name of Karhad) in places as far away as Bharhut in Madhya Pradesh. The present township is situated on the ancient remains on the confluence of the Krishna and Koyna.

Karhad was a town of great antiquity. There are three groups of caves located about 5-7 km southwest of the town, viz. Jakninwadi and Agashiva groups, and the third group is situated in the hill near Chachegaon.

This group comprises of about 65 caves, of these, five are chaityas, the rest are viharas.

The absence of pillars, and considering the small size of many of the excavations, the frequency of stone benches, the simple forms of the dagobas indicates their early age. The inscriptions are weather-worn but appear to belong to the Karle period. The Karhad group was excavated about the same time as the groups at Kuda, Mahad, and Shelarwadi and are not far from those at Nasik and Junnar.

There are several chaityas in this group. The first chaitya in this group, Cave 5, is badly ruined, the front having fallen away.

The second chaitya, Cave 11, was not only unfinished, but has also suffered damage.

The third, Cave 16, is smaller than Cave 5, its verandah is supported by two square pillars without base or capital, and a square recess at the far

▲ The Viharas

end of the hall contains a dagoba in better condition than those in the two chaityas already described.

A vihara of interest is Cave 24. At either end of the verandah is a row of chaitya arches between bands of the rail pattern. Below, the wall has been divided into compartments, but no trace of the carving now exists.

The only other excavation with lattice windows at Karhad is Cave 29.

The only sculptured figure in the Karhad group, occurs in Cave 48. It consists of a broad pillared verandah with five cells in the rear. The central chamber which is much larger than those flanking it, contains a traditional dagoba in good condition.

Cave 60 is apsidal and bears some resemblance to the Bedsa Vihara. Above the entrance is a row of chaitya arches, and though there is no trace of a dagoba in the apse, this cave may have been a primitive form of chaitya, with a structural dagoba.

The Government of Maharashtra with the help of the Ministry of Tourism and Ministry of Environment and Forests has undertaken an extensive plan for the development of the Karhad Caves as a tourism promotion project. The work has been undertaken on a war footing. The roads from the main highway to the spot are almost complete. There will be all the facilities like guides, restaurants, local transport, special arrangements for helicopters, etc. The Kolhapur, Pohale caves are also an hour-and-a-half drive from the Karhad caves. In the near future, Karhad, Kolhapur will also get their place on the international map like Ajanta, Ellora, and Aurangabad.

Pohale Caves

Location: 18 km north-west of Kolhapur

A group of six, mostly ruined, caves are situated 3 km north-west of the village Pohale, at the foot of a low hillock, locally known as Jyotiba Hill. Of these, the chaitya and vihara are interesting. The most remarkable feature of the chaitya is that it is apsidal on plan, and is astylar, but has a flat roof.

The stupa in the apse is considerably destroyed, but the chhatra carved in the flat roof can still be seen; the shaft (danda) of the chhatra and the harmika however, are broken. The cave is comparatively wider and there is sufficient room for circumambulation. The entrance door is similarly wide.

▲   Author at Pohale Cave

Pauni

Location: 82 km south-east of Nagpur

It was first noted as an ancient site by the archaeologist Cousens in 1897. Subsequently J Marshal and H Hargreaves noted the picturesque fort wall and moat at the site, indicating its medieval occupation. In 1936, GC Chandra in his unpublished official communication reported on the different mounds at three localities in Pauni – Hardolala Tekdi, Jagannath Tekdi, and Ghoda Ghat and indicated the possibility of there having been stupas here, following the discovery of large stone pieces, Brahmi inscriptions from the second century AD, small images, and a stone relic with bone pieces, now of unknown origins.

Later, two important antiquities came to light – a chaitya-stambha with the inscription of the kshatrapa Rupiyamma and a copperplate grant of Pravarasena Ii of the Vakataka dynasty.

The discovery of a railing pillar with Hinayana motifs carved on it in association with an inscribed coping stone near the ancient mound, was enough to prove the existence of the Buddhist faith in the Vidharbha region in the early times.

The excavations in Pauni have strengthened the possibility of the existence of Buddhism during the Ashoka period in Maharashtra, during recent excavations. The newly discovered evidence indicates that the existence of Buddhism here goes back to the pre-Mauryan period to the Satavahana period (circa AD 250) as far as the Buddhist remains are concerned. The remains are scattered over a wide area locally known as the Jaganath Tekdi, the Chandakapur Tekdi, and the Hardobala Tekdi.

The general picture, as presented by the archeological remains, is that of a Theravada Buddhist community which began its existence probably a little before, or during, the Mauryan period.

The resurfacing of the stupa complexes and its re-enlargement indicates the changing fortune of this community and the monuments themselves fell into disuse probably by the third century AD.

Very recently, the Pannya Metta Sangh has inaugurated a newly constructed Vihara Maha Samadhi Stupa under the leadership of the Venerable Sangha Ratna Manke, on the charming banks of the Ganga Bhumi Pauni, Bhanadara district, in Maharashtra.

The Venerable Sangha Ratna Manke is a versatile and dynamic religious activist who has devoted his whole life for the propagation and protection of Buddhism in Maharashtra. He has opened several religious centers and helps people in need. This stupa was inaugurated on February 8, 2007 and today it has become a picnic-spot and an educational center for school and college students around Nagpur area.

For further details contact: Venerable Sangha Ratna Manke
Email: psmasangh@satyam.net.in; www.prmj3.com

Ter

Ter is situated on the western bank of the river Terna in the district and taluka Usmanabad. Ter is widely known to the Marathi-speaking people chiefly by virtue of its association with the celebrated saint poet Gora Kumbhar. The village however has long earned a reputation as a site of archaeological interest owing to the discoveries of surface finds and a large number of important antiquities in the private collection of Mr. Ramalingappa, a prominent resident of the village.

The excavations at Ter testify to the inhabitation of the site during the early historical and Indo-Roman period. The excavations reveal that the site was occupied thrice during a period ranging from the third century BC to the third century AD. Antiquities tend to shed light upon the religious affiliations. The triratna symbol on pottery finds, reveal the prevalence of Buddhism as followed by various sections of the society.

Ter seems to have had links with the Hellenic world. The earliest literary reference is to be found in the Periphus of the Erythraean Sea written by an anonymous author of Egyptian-Greek origin in the first century of the Christian era.

Maharashtra has 35 districts. All major cities are connected by well-maintained highways.

Maharashtra State Transport operates buses, from air-conditioned buses to standard buses, to the remotest parts of the villages. The private transport system in between cities operates day and night. Facilities for tickets booked online are also available for bus reservations.

Major towns have the Maharashtra Tourism Development Corporation offices.

Unfortunately, very few Buddhist sites are popular in Maharashtra. Suitable and comfortable Buddhist routes can be as follows: start from Mumbai or Pune from where public as well as private transport is easily available. Popular sites like Aurangabad circuit, Karle circuit has trained guides for support.

Buddhist Circuit of the State

Ajanta, Aurangabad, Ellora, Pitalkhora

Junnar and Nasik

Karle, Bhaja, Bedsa, Kondana, Shirwal

Near Mumbai – Kanheri, Kondivate, Sopara

Konkan Area – Kuda, Mahad, Kol, Sudhgarh, Nadsur, Panhale-Kaji

From Pune – Shirwal, Wai, Yerpal, Karhad, Pohale (Kolhapur)

General Information

Area: 3,07,731 sq. km

Capital: Mumbai

Boundaries: Gujarat, Madhya Pradesh, Andhra Pradesh, Karnataka, Goa, Dadra and Nagar Haveli, Chhattisgarh, and the Arabian Sea.

Chief Languages: Marathi, Hindi, Gujarati, English

Main Towns: Mumbai, Pune, Nagpur, Nasik, Aurangabad, Kolhapur, Sholapur, Shirdi, Pandharpur, Satara, Sangli, Wardha

Air: Mumbai, Pune, Nagpur, Nasik, Kolhapur, Aurangabad

Rail: Mumbai (Mumbai Central, Chhatrapati Shivaji Terminus, Bandra Terminus, Kurla Terminus for outgoing trains), Pune, Sholapur, Satara, Kolhapur, Nagpur, Jalgaon, Bhusawal, Nasik

Road: Length – 2.66 lakh km; NH – 4,367 km; SH – 33,406 km; District roads – 47,922 km; Village roads – 97,913 km

13

NORTH-EASTERN STATES

Connected by an infinite chain of pearly threads, intricate as a spider's web, the north-eastern states of Arunachal Pradesh, Assam, Manipur, Meghalaya, Mizoram, Nagaland, Sikkim, and Tripura offer visitors a rare feast – a kaleidoscopic fiesta that lures visitors with its magical richness and stunning variety.

Arunachal Pradesh

Buddhism was introduced in Arunachal Pradesh by Guru Padmasambhava himself, who spent some time in the Tawang area in meditation, and while preaching the Dhamma. He came to Tibet in AD 747. He had been invited by the King of Tibet, Khri-sron-Ide-btsan to help propagate and spread Buddhism. Guru Padmasambhava is said to have established two shrines – one at Takstang and the other at Baggajanga.

Mahayana and Theravada, both forms of Buddhism, are prevalent in Arunachal Pradesh – Mahayana in the north-western zone and Theravada in the south-eastern zone. The Mahayana Buddhists are Monpas and Sherdukpens (descendants of the Mongoloid race are now tribes of Arunachal Pradesh), of Tawang and West Kameng districts.

The Mongoloid race originally immigrated from Tibet and Bhutan; the Monpas are Buddhist by faith and follow the Gelukpa Sect of Mahayana Buddhism. Before embracing Buddhism, they were believers of the Bon faith, characterised by the spirit of worship and animal sacrifice.

The Theravada Buddhists are the Khamptis and Singhpos of Lohit and Tirap districts, they migrated from Burma.

◀ Monks prepare for the Kalchakra ceremony at Tawang Monastery

▲ The Tawang Monastery is the largest in India and the second largest in Asia

◀ This statue of Buddha towers over disciples

Tawang Monastery

The crown of Buddhism in Arunachal Pradesh, the Tawang monastery, forms the core of the Lamastic faith of the Mahayana school of Buddhism in the region, making it the largest monastery in India and the second largest in Asia. The current Dalai Lama had passed through Tawang while escaping from Tibet. The Tawang monastery was established by Merak Lama Lorde Gyamtso in 1860-61.

As the legend goes, Lama Gyamtso went out in search of the perfect site for the monastery. One day he left his horse outside a cave, and went in to pray for divine guidance. When he came out, he saw that his horse, who had never wandered away, was nowhere to be seen. After looking for him frantically, he finally found the horse standing calmly on the top of a hill. Lama Gyamtso realised that a divine hand had guided him via the horse, to the hallowed spot where he decided to construct the monastery. He called it Tawang ('ta' – horse; 'wang' – chosen). The monastery was constructed with the help of volunteers from surrounding villages. Even today, these villages are responsible for the maintenance of different sections of the monastery.

The Tawang monastery, was built 10,000 feet above sea level, amidst the picturesque Himalayan ranges that slope towards the east. The monastery offers an imposing and picturesque view of the Tawang Chu valley. The monastery appears like a fort from a distance, as if guarding the wide valley below. The Tawang monastery can house 700 monks, and is the main source of the spiritual feelings of the people of this region.

The drive to this place is spectacular; one goes past oak, pine, rhododendron and bamboo forests, with breathtaking views of mountains and valleys. You will have to cross the Sela Pass, the second highest motorable pass in the world, at 13,700 feet. You also pass the ruins of Dzong, a Tibetan fort at the Dirang valley.

The majestic monastery can be entered from the northern side, along the ridge, by the Kakaling gate, which is a hut-like structure, the walls of which are made of stone. The ceiling or the interior roof of the Kakaling is painted with mandalas that depict the saints and divinities. After Kakaling, comes the main gate of the monastery in the northern side. Its eastern wall is about 925 feet long while its height is 10-20 feet.

The Tawang monastery houses several structures within its premises, the most prominent being the dukhang. The dukhang or the assembly hall, which is the main building of the monastery, stands on the northern side of the main court. This three-storeyed complex houses a temple and a labrang, which is the establishment of an Abbot. The interiors of the dukhang are equally well marked with magnificent works of art. Its inner walls have been painted with the sketches of several saints and Bodhisattvas, whereas the northern walls of the hall are covered with an altar, used for religious ceremonies; and again, towards the altar's left is a silver silk casket holding the Thangkas. The Thangkas have been dedicated to the chief deity of the monastery, Goddess Sri Devi, also known as Palden Lhamo.

There is a Thangka here, which was painted (the painting is known as Ja–Droi Ma) with blood drawn from the fifth Dalai Lama's nose, and was given to Merak Lama by His Holiness the fifth Dalai Lama himself. On the northern side of the monastery, is a huge statue (26 feet high) of the Lord Buddha, standing in the middle of the hall.

Another prominent structure in the monastery is the Court, situated at the back of the Gonpa (monastery). The stone slab court hosts religious dances and other ceremonies, held according to the lunar calendar of Monpa. On the western side of the court is a three-storied building, known as Par–Khang, or the Liberty. The Par–Khang houses numerous sacred scriptures and Buddhist texts.

A two-storied structure is located in the southern side of the court, with one part used to store the monk's provisions, while the other one is occupied by monks. Lastly, on the eastern side of the court is the rhumkhang, a two-storied structure. The rhumkhang is used for cooking sacred food required for rituals and as refreshment for the monks on festive days.

The Sha or hut (60 in all) is another important structure in the monastery, used as residential quarters by the monks. The Center for Buddhist Cultural Studies is an integral part of the monastery. Young monks are taught traditional monastic education here along with several other subjects like English, Hindi, and Arithmetic.

As per tradition, every Buddhist family with more than three sons has to send one son to the monastery to become a monk. Every family also contributes a share of its foodgrains and other items for the Lamas who live in the monastery. At a distance, on another hill, is another monastery which houses women monks – a rare phenomena in India.

The Tawang monastery is associated with the famous Torgya festival, which is held in the eleventh Monpa month called the Dawa Chukchhipah (December-January). Varied dances are performed during the three-day celebration. This festival is celebrated to drive away evil spirits so that people may enjoy a happy prosperous life in the coming year. Each dance is associated with some myth or legend.

After spending a couple of hours in the monastery, lighting the small prayer lamps and incense sticks, turning the grant prayer wheels, and feeling the vibrations of the prayer chants, the all-pervading solitude creates an ambience which kindles the spiritualism lying dormant in all of us.

Bomdila Monastery

Close to the Tibetan border and perched at a height of 8,000 feet is the town of Bomdila, famous for its Buddhist monasteries.

The landscape of Bomdila is breathtaking with the surrounding snowcaps and apple orchards. One can stop at Sela Pass on the way to the Tawang monastery from here, as well as visit the orchid centers at Tippi and Sessa. The craft center at Bomdila has a beautiful range of local woollen rugs and carpets with colourful Tibetan designs.

Home to Buddhist Lamas and monks at Bomdila in the west Kameng district, Bomdila monastery is one of the most prominent centers of the Lamastic faith of Mahayana Buddhism. A replica of

▲ A centre of the Lamastic faith of Mahayana Buddhism, the Bomdila Monastery is a replica of the one in Tibet

the Tsona Gontse monastery at Tsona in the southern Tibet, the Bomdila monastery (also known as Gentse Gaden Rangyel Lling monastery) was set up by the 12th incarnation of the Tsona Gontse Rinpoch. The reincarnate who was born in Morshing west Kameng had established this monastery in 1965, before his death in 1966. However, the Rinpoche, the 13th incarnation, Tsona Gontse Rinpoche renovated and enlarged the monastery. He also included a huge prayer hall, which was blessed by His Highness the 14th Holiness Dalai Lama in 1997.

The Gonpa comprises a prayer hall, used by the Lamas and the monks for penance and as residential quarters. The prayers and tantrayana practice of monastic life are followed by the senior Lamas or the monks of the monastery.

Rigyalling Monastery

Located amidst the panoramic lush green trees and serene atmosphere in the Tawang district, the Rigyalling monastery is a major center of Buddhist learning in Arunachal Pradesh.

The efforts of the Lama Changsey to amend for the urbanisation gradually creeping in, has resulted in rows and rows of trees of all types such as the pines, fir, oak, and the rare *crytomeria loponica*. His green thumb has turned the place into a picturesque abode where the silence is broken only by the chirruping of birds and the rustle of the wind in the tree.

Taktsang Monastery

Also known as the 'Tiger's Den', the Taktsang monastery lies 45 km away from Tawang. The monastery is surrounded by a dense coniferous forest and snowy mountains, thereby presenting a calm picture, making it a prefect center for meditation. The Taktsang monastery is also said to have been visited by Guru Padmasambhava in the eighth century AD.

Urgelling Monastery

About 5 km from the heart of town is the Urgelling monastery established by the Lama Urgen Sangpo who came here from Bhumithang in Bhutan. Dating more than 460 years ago, the monastery is the birthplace of His Holiness the Sixth Dalai Lama. Apart from being a treasure trove of many ancient relics, the monastery has the footprints and fingerprints of the Dalai Lama preserved for darshan.

The Nunneries

The Anis or the nuns are called to join the monk life voluntarily. No rules or compulsion forces them to embrace the rigorous and hermit life of a monk.

Brama Dung Chung Ani Gompa

The oldest of the Ani gompas, it was commissioned by Lama Karchen Yeshi Gelek in 1595. It houses 45 nuns and is 12 km from the town.

Gyangong Ani Gompa

Situated on a hillock, surrounded by pristine beauty, is the Ani gompa at a distance of 5 km. It has about 50 inmates.

Singsur Ani Gompa

About 28 km from Tawang, built by the Rev. Gonpaste

General Information

Arunachal Pradesh

Area: 83,743 sq. km

Capital: Itanagar

Boundaries: Assam, Nagaland.

Countries – Bhutan, Myanmar, China

Chief Languages: Monpa, Aka, Sherdukpen, Nyishi, Apatani, Tagin, Hill Miri, Adi Dinaru Mismi, Miju Mishmi, Nocte, Tangsa, Wancho

Main Towns: Itanagar, Seppa, Daporijo, Along, Pasighat, Tezu, Khonsa, Yingkiong, Anini, Walong, Tawang, Bomdila, Ziro

Air: Itanagar, Daparjio, Ziro, Along, Tezu, Pasighat

Rail: Bhalukpong

Rimpoche, this nunnery is the home of about 45 nuns.

Gorsam Chorten

Situated 92 km from Tawang at Zemithang is this stupa looming high into the sky. It was constructed in the 12th century and is the largest stupa in the area.

Major cities offer suitable accommodation to suit every tourist's budget. Buses and private sumos are available from Tezpur in Assam to reach Tawang. For further information, contact tourist offices or travel agents.

Assam

Assam is the home of the Brahmaputra (son of Brahma). Assam is a land of rich archaeological heritage. Ancient relics have been discovered along the entire Brahmaputra valley.

Sri Suryapahar

One finds vestiges of Buddhist relics in the form of rock-cut votive stupas, although it is commonly believed that Buddhism was not prevalent in the cultural history of ancient Kamarupa. The stupas are in various sizes, and lie on the hill at Sri Suryapahar. These stupas are highly significant, and appear to be archaic in shapes, designed in the form of a hemispherical drum, except one stupa which is hewn in the form of a cylindrical drum. The archaic nature of these carvings shows that the stupas at Sri Suryapahar were hewn during

General Information

Assam

Area: 78,438 sq. km

Capital: Dispur

Boundaries: Meghalaya, Arunachal Pradesh, Nagaland, Manipur, Tripura, Mizoram, West Bengal

Chief Languages: Assamese, Bengali, Bodo, Mishing, Karbi

Main Towns: Guwahati, Dispur, Tezpur, Silchar, Jorhat, Dibrugarh, Sibsagar, Diphu, Barpeta, Dhuburi, Bongagaon, Nalbari.

Air: Guwahati, Dibrugarh, Jorhat, Silchar, Lakhimpur, Tezpur

Rail: Length – 2,391.76 km. Main Railway Stations – New Bangaigaon, Maligaon, Dispur, Rangia, Lumding, Jorhat

Road: Length – 34,000 km. National Highway – 22,038 km.

▲ Author at Suryapahad

the Hinayana phase of Buddhism and is therefore assigned to the early Christian era. Any more relics that depict the development of the faith in later phases could not be seen at the site, although the neighbouring territories of Bihar and Bengal witnessed the later phases of Mahayana and Vajrayana esotericism.

Major cities offer suitable accommodation to suit every tourist's budget. Buses, and private taxis are available from major cities. For further information, contact tourist offices or travel agents.

Tripura

A promising site of the Pala period has been located at Pillack, in the south Jotabari area in the Belonia sub-division of Tripura. The remains found here consist of mounds of bricks and brick-bats. Some of the mounds yielded images of Buddha and deities of the Mahayana-Vajrayana pantheon. A small standing figure of Padmapani in bronze was discovered in south Jolaibari.

Pilak

About 10 km away from Agartala is Pilak, famous for its eighth-ninth century AD archaeological remains. The site represents an old civilisation, yielding evidence of both Hindu and Buddhist linkages. The main attractions here are the massive stone sculptures of Avalokitesvara and Narasimha and numerous carvings in stone as well as terracotta plaques. The site is still being excavated.

Mahamuni

Location: 150 km from Agartala

Mahamuni is famous for its ancient Buddhist temple. The temple draws Buddhist pilgrims from as far off Thailand, Mayanmar, and Sri Lanka apart from those nearer home from Bangladesh.

Major cities offer suitable accommodation to suit every tourist's budget. Buses and private taxis are available from major cities. For further information, contact tourist offices or travel agents.

General Information

Tripura

Area: 10,491.69 sq. km

Capital: Agartala

Boundaries: Assam, Mizoram.

Country – Bangladesh.

Chief Languages: Bengali, Kokkorak, and Manipuri.

Main Towns: Agartala, Belonia, Kumar-ghat, Kailashahar, Udaipur, Khowal, Kamlapur

Air: Agartala

Rail: Manughat, Dharamnagar

Road: Length – 14,395 km.

14

ORISSA

The existence of Buddhism in Orissa is as old as the religion itself. While Lumbini, Kapilvastu, Bodh Gaya, and Sarnath are places associated with Lord Buddha's life, Orissa was associated with his teachings.

The entire length and breadth of Orissa is dotted with 4,000 monuments and archaeological sites, which include Buddhist monasteries, chaityas, and stupas established centuries ago. Most of these monuments are dated between third century BC and 12th century AD, which speaks of the great tradition of architecture and sculptural excellence.

'Utakal', 'Kalinga', 'Odera', 'Kangoda' are some of the ancient names of the state of Orissa. Though its boundaries have always varied from time to time, Orissa has been occupying an important position in the cultural history of India right from the time of Buddha, till today.

It is well-known the world over how the Mauryan Emperor Ashoka turned into an important patron of Buddhism after his expedition in Kalinga and earned the name 'Dharma Ashoka' which has immortalised him.

The earliest reference to 'Odra' is found in the Buddhist text *Lalitavistra* in connection with Buddha's relic, popularly known as *Kesaasthi* carried by two Orissan merchants, Tapassu and Bhallika, during the Buddha's lifetime. In subsequent periods, we find references to two more relics in Orissa, viz. the nail and tooth.

Even though the Buddha did not visit Orissa, according to early *Vinaya* texts, the two merchants Tapassu and Bhallika became the first lay disciples of the Buddha. These two merchants, while on their way to Madhyadesa with 500 trading carts, met the Buddha under the *rajayatana* tree on the last day of the seventh week after

◀ A statue of the Buddha still waiting to be excavated in Ratnagiri

His Enlightenment. A spirit of their departed relative directed them to pay their respects to the Buddha, so they readily offered the Buddha rice-cakes and honey. As related in the commentary of the *Anguttara-Nikaya*, the Buddha gave them eight handfuls of his hair, which the merchants took home to their native city (Asitanjana) where they placed it in a magnificent chaitya erected for this purpose. According to the *Theragatha*, these two merchants also visited the Buddha at Rajagriha. In time, Tapassu became a sotapanna and, as a devachikaopasaka, was included in the list of eminent upasakas while Bhallika entered the sangha and became an arhat. The *Pujavaliya* in Sri Lanka records that Tapassu and Bhallika, sometime after their conversion, visited the east coast of Sri Lanka where they erected a chaitya to commemorate their visit.

Unfortunately, we do not have a continuous or chronological history of the development of Buddhism in Orissa. After a gap of over 300 years after the Mahaparinirvana or demise of Buddha, we come across the Kalinga war, the conquest of Kalinga by Emperor Ashoka, and his devotion to Buddhism.

In 261 BC, the over-ambitious Emperor Ashoka invaded Kalinga and unleashed a bloody battle around Dhauli. One-and-a-half lakh people were taken captive, one lakh were slain and as many as that number succumbed to the after-effects of the war. Emperor Ashoka smiled and then laughed heartily, for he had won the war. But what came next was beyond his imagination. He saw heaps of the dead, heard the wailing of the wounded and saw the tears rolling down the cheeks of those who suffered. The terrible massacre made him remorseful. His victory echoed defeat.

At this juncture, appeared Upagupta, the Buddhist monk and showed him the path of peace and non-violence. Ashoka was rejuvenated with Upagupta's *vani* and realised the essence of conquest by Dharma/Dhamma in preference to a conquest by force. Then Ashoka surrendered the sword and embraced Buddhism. History took a U-turn as he renounced violence for good.

After the great war of Kalinga, a new chapter in the spread of

Buddhism began, not only in Kalinga, but through the world. Emperor Ashoka, who had led the troops to conquer Kalinga was greatly moved by the bravery of the Kalingan people. This war has gone down in the annals of history as one of the greatest wars in ancient times.

The history of the war has been described in detail on the XIIIth Rock Edict of Ashoka, which bears living and perceptible evidence about the great war. Ashoka, the tyrant monarch embraced Buddhism and followed the path of peace and prosperity thereafter.

This happened only in the holy land of Orissa, where people of many religions lived peacefully and harmoniously over the centuries. Ashoka had issued two special edicts only for the people of Orissa stating how the vanquished people of Orissa should be treated. One such rock edict is located at Dhauli, only 10 km away from Bhubaneshwar and the other edict is at Jaugarh (Ganjam district) 35 km away from Brahmapur.

Emperor Ashoka sent his son Mahindra and daughter Sanghamitra to Sri Lanka entrusting them with the mission of preaching the principles of Buddhism. Tissa, Ashoka's brother chose Kalinga as the place of his retirement and for him Ashoka built a monastery known as Bhojakagiri-vihara, which functioned as the Theravada school of Buddhism.

Learned scholars of Buddhism namely Dharmaraksita and Dhjtika had visited Orissa and influenced a large number of devotees by their impressive teachings. Two other great acharyas – Nala and Posadha – also visited Kalinga and made remarkable contributions to the spread of Buddhist faith in Kalinga.

The message of peace and non-violence spread across the world. Thus began a new era of art and education, peace and pilgrimage. Dhammarakhita, Tissa's preceptor, came to Kalinga to spend his last days with Tissa and other monks in this monastery.

The Kalinga war showed the people the way from war to peace and became the torch bearer to the world. Despite the physical devastation wreaked by the war, there was intense spiritual regeneration. The brutalised people took refuge at the feet of

Mahakarunika Buddha. Orissa sought medicine for its wounds and was blessed.

After the Mauryan kings, Orissa was ruled by the Kings of the Chedi dynasty who were Jainas. The Jain caves on the Udayagiri and Khandagiri hills date to the first century BC and were carved during the reign of Kharavela.

That Buddhism was spreading throughout Orissa in the early centuries of the Christian era is evident in various inscriptions. It is known that a Mahayana center existed at Jayarampur, in the northern Balasore district, near the mouth of the Subarnarekha river as early as the sixth century AD, since it is recorded in a copperplate inscription from the time of Maharajadhiraja Gopachandra (circa fifth to sixth century AD).

The Chinese pilgrim Hiuen–Tsang visited Kalinga in the seventh century AD. He mentioned in his notes that at least ten Buddhist monasteries and many stupas were found in Kalinga where large numbers of scholars and disciples of Buddhism were practising and preaching the philosophy of Buddhism.

Although very little is known about the history of Orissa during the seventh-eighth centuries AD, the construction activities at Lalitagiri, Udayagiri, and Ratnagiri appeared to have gained momentum in the seventh century, at which time numerous monasteries were constructed, and this was further accelerated during the eighth century. The active patronage of the rulers of the Bhaumakara dynasty played a major role in the phenomenal growth in the construction activities (Ratnagiri-Udayagiri).

The Bhaumakara dynasty lasted for more than 200 years with royal patronage being especially heavy during the first hundred years. Orissa was at the forefront of new developments taking place during the eighth century including Vajrayana.

In the loosely-constructed administrative policy followed by the Bhaumakaras, a certain amount of autonomy was generally allowed to the minor ruling families in Orissa.

Somavamsi rulers ruled over Orissa between AD 1040–1065. Although they were primarily followers of Brahmanism, they apparently were tolerant towards other religious faiths.

The later part of the Ganga period was one of continuous warfare against the Muslims, Orissa lost her independence to the Mughals, while the southern dominions were in control of the sultans of Bahamani.

Modern Orissa is proud to have carefully preserved centuries of Buddhist heritage, nurtured by ancient Kalinga, the land as sacred as Lumbini or Sarnath. The land was believed to have been declared by the Buddha as one of the 12 places where one could attain perfection.

Buddhist Sites

Balasore District

Ayodhya

Location: 25 km west of Balasore

This was at one time the capital of the Vairata-rajas and throughout its long history was considered a sacred site both for Hindus and Buddhists. A chain of irregular caves in the hills nearby suggest there was a large Buddhist establishment dating to a period much earlier than the surviving sculptures.

This place in particular is very important since it has the temple of the Buddhist Goddess Marichi. The original temple of Marichi was located about a half mile west of the present temple and the old place was found to have huge remains of carved stones, Amalaka sila, and large granite pillars. Some of the granite columns are as big as 16 feet long and three feet cubits. In the sanctuary of the present Marichi temple, beautiful images of Manjushri, Lokeshvara, and Varahamukhi were found.

The three-faced and eight-armed Marichi image stands in the conventional alidha-pose on a chariot drawn by seven pigs. The face to the left is that of a sow. The popular Buddhist chant '*Ye-dhama-Hetuprava*' is inscribed on the top of the slab fashioned with the image of Dhyanibuddha Vairochana.

Apart from the major sites, remains of the monasteries and stupas, temple foundations, Buddhist images and antiquities have been found scattered through the villages of Avana, Badgaon, Badia,

Balasore, Bardhanapur (Tikarapara), Basta, Bhuinpara (Shergarh), Dhupsila (Nilgiri), Gandhibedha, Gohiratikra, Jayarampur, Kasba, Kaupur, Khadipada, Khaira, Khangara, Kupari, Mangalapur, Orasahi/Dakinesvari-pitha, Shergarh/Patana, Soro, and Sujnagarh.

Bhadrak District

Khadipada

Khadipada in Bhadrak district, must have been a flourishing site for followers of Mahayana Buddhism. Several life-sized images of Buddha are found in the village. In 718 AD, images of Vajrapani and an inscribed Padmapani have been found here and are now housed in the State Museum at Bhubhaneshwar.

The two images of Buddha were constructed from several stone slabs. The first image depicts Buddha seated in Vajraparyanka with his right hand in the bhumi-sparsha-mudra and the second image, badly broken, depicts the Buddha in dharmchakra-mudra and may have served as the Tathagata Vairochana on a large stupa. Numerous smaller images of the Vajrayana pantheon have been retrieved from the vast mound at Khadipada and are presently kept in a village shrine. Many images are still found here.

Solampur

The village of Solampur, mentioned in the Neulpur plate of Subhakar Dev I (AD 790), lies on the bank of the river Vaitarani. The village has grown on the mounds and ruins of Buddhist edifices. A number of broken idols of Mahayana and Tantric deities can be seen in and around the village. Some of the images are fixed to the walls of the Raghunath temple. Among such images is a slab representing the eight great events associated with the life of Buddha called 'The Eight Miracles' (coined by Mr. M Foucher). The main image shows Buddha in the bhumi-sparsha-mudra, indicating his Enlightenment at Uruvela. Immediately above his head, and below the Mahaparinirvana scene, at the apex of the pointed back-slab, is a row of six seated Bodhisattvas which, along with one on either side of the nirvana scene, form a set of eight corresponding to the mandala cult of Bodhisattvas in Orissa.

To the left, at the bottom, is depicted Buddha's birth – Mayadevi stands with a female attendant holding the branch of an Ashoka tree in Lumbini garden. There is a standing two-armed image of Padmapani, and Avalokitesvara flanked by two Tara figurines.

Placed beneath a tree in front of the Santesvari Thakurani temple are numerous fragmented images, including Avalokitesvara, Jambhala, and Vajrapani. Several small broken images of Buddha are placed on the porch of the shrine along with a large image of a four-armed, seated, Amoghapasa Lokesvara.

A two-armed image of Tara standing is found in the area. Images of Buddha and mutilated figures of other Buddhist icons are kept in another temple. The majority of the images can be dated from the 9-11 century.

Cuttack District

Banesvarnasi

Banesvarnasi is a picturesque hillock, on the bed of the river Mahanadi near Narasimhapur. The place is easily accessible by road from Cuttack and was originally a leading Buddhist establishment like that in Lalitgiri and Ratnagiri during the later part of the sixth century AD.

An image of Prajnya-Parimita was found below the roof of a shed. The goddess sits in the Vajraprayanka pose on a lotus pedestal, with a lotus. The images of Buddha, Padmapani and Avalokitesvara were taken from here and housed in the State Museum at Bhubaneshwar. Two images of Tara were also found here, one of which has been taken to Patna.

The Mahanadi riverside and a number of temples close by create a picturesque sight and offer enduring satisfaction to the visitors.

Jajpur

The city of Jajpur, situated on the Vaitarani river at the edge of the Assia hills, is an old and prominent pitha of Sakta (Shakti)/ Tantrism whose history goes back at least as early as the

▲ A votive stupa and an image of Buddha that can be seen at Vajragiri Mahavidyalaya in Jajpur

Mahabharata. It is more famously known as Viraja Kshetra. This place was once integral to scores of ancient cultures and was also a place of pilgrimage, unfortunately at present, everything is in ruins.

This place is also very closely associated with Buddhism. The Bhaumakaras made their capital at Viraja and called it Guha-deva-pataka or Guhesvaro-pataka.

The kings of the Bhaumakara dynasty were all ardent Buddhists and during their rule in the eighth and ninth centuries AD, they erected Buddhist monuments not only in and around the area, but also in different parts of their kingdom. Images of Buddha, Avalokitesvara, Manjushri, Maitreya, and Tara are found in different areas, testifying to the glory and greatness of Jajpur.

Stupas and monasteries built under the patronage of the Bhaumakaras at places like Ratangiri, Udayagiri, Lalitgiri, Vajragiri, Langudi, etc. can be easily reached from Jajpur.

The famous temple of Mother Goddess Biraja is located here, which is worshipped by thousands of devotees. This is also called the Nabhi Gaya, sharing equal status with the famous Gaya in Bihar where respects are offered to departed souls of ancestors according to Hindu customs.

Teacher opens a window to the past

Dr. Nursingha Sahu presently works as the Principal of the Dharamsala Mahavidyala in Jajpur District. He also devotes some of his time to his noble passion – researching ancient Orissa's historical and archaeological findings. He has brought to light a lot of hidden information since 1979. His research-

oriented articles on the lost and dilapidated Buddhist monuments in Dharmashala areas have solved many mysteries surrounding the State's socio-economic and cultural life. His research has proved ancient Orissa's marine trade relations with Rome and south-east Asian countries.

During my visit to Orissa in February 2009, I heard about him from one of his college colleagues, Dr. Manorama Sahu, a lecturer in English, while we were on a journey from Bhubaneshwar to Cuttack and Ratnagiri.

I will always be indebted to Dr. Sahu for all the help he gave me. He was kind enough to accompany me to Langudi, and Radhanagar Fort area in spite of his busy work schedule.

According to Dr. Sahu there are many unseen Buddhist sites around Jajpur district. Due to his sincere endeavour and excavation work, carried out through the Department of Culture, Government of Orissa, the places discovered so far are Kayama, Langudi, Tarapur, Neulpur, Bajragiri, Kantigadia, Deulipal, Panturi, the hills and Radhanagar port and fort, Singhapur, Chandapur, Uttarpratap, Chainihuda, Mirzapur, Sulia, Andeigoda, Kusunpur, Kshemeswar and Beruda.

Dr. Sahu has conducted comprehensive studies in an area of about 516 km around Jajpur area. Search towers, Ashokan stupas such as those at Anuradhapur, stone inscriptions and stone carvings in the Brahmi script, rock-cut Buddha images from the initial stages, objects of cultural heritage like dancing figures, mrudungam, votive stupas, inscribed Buddha images on lotus panels, meditation places and caves (the Pushpagiri monastery as mentioned by Hiuen–Tsang), and Panchdhyani Buddha etc. are the many significant places and objects that he has discovered.

Called Gajaraja Museum (at his native village Kaima), the three rooms of his house contain a virtual treasure trove of rare antiquities collected during his research through a period of 31 years. After a day's hard work in the college, Dr. Sahu spends some of his time in his personal museum. Every Sunday and on holidays, he goes to remote and distant places to collect antiquities for his studies. There are rare coins, centuries-old palm leaf manuscripts, Chinese vases, ancient and architectural images, and effigies displayed in his personal museum. Dr. Sahu has single-handedly built up a considerable wealth of information for research scholars from Tirupati, Pune, Raipur, Utkal University of Culture, Aligarh Muslim and Jawaharlal Nehru University, and enabled them to dig deep into Orissa's ancient cultural heritage.

Also, several researchers from Japan, Germany, America, Sri Lanka, China, Myanmar, and Thailand have visited the museum to collect information. Some rare significant materials under this roof include stone-age axe, tools, earthen pot, usable domestic instruments, copper ornaments, and raw clay toys that are contemporaries of the Mohenjadaro civilisation.

Roman emblems commemorating trade relations with Rome, clay pots with the mark of Roman coins, figures of Roman security guards, clay masks of royal personalities, various coloured wares, stones, ornaments, rice fossils, coins of Nanda, Gupta, Ganga, Kushan, Mather, Mughal, Maratha, British and some foreign countries all have place of honour in his museum. The museum has been registered by the Government of Orissa.

Dr. Sahu has received several laurels, including the prestigious Rajiv Gandhi Sadbhavana Award by the Rajiv Gandhi Youth Forum, Orissa Vyasadev Samman, Saraswata Saransa award of Jajpur and he was felicitated in Dharamsala Mahotsav, Korei Mahotsav, Sukarnika Museum, Banki for his unique love and passion for collecting historical artefacts and publishing research articles on the discovery of forgotten sites in Jajpur.

Dr. Sahu's ultimate objective is not only to help visitors and

> scholars, but also to create awareness among the people about the importance of the preservation of dilapidated monuments and archaeological remains.
>
> For further details and any information about Buddhist sites in Orissa, contact:
>
> Dr. N. C. Sahu – Principal
> Dharamsala Mahavidyalaya via Jajpur
> District – Jajpur, Orissa
> Pincode 755 050
>
> Residence:
>
> Village Kaima, District Jajpur via Dharamsala
> Pincode 755 008,
> Phone: 06725 273370, Mobile: 09437808824

The most important places among the above sites are the nine small hills on which Emperor Ashoka built nine Hinayani Buddhist stupas where Buddha delivered his powerful religious speech in ancient Kalinga. This fact has also been noted in the travel report of Hiuen–Tsang. Interestingly, the nine Hinayani stupas are situated within a 10 km radius in the area under Dharamsala Police Station.

Tarapur Hill

These hills are probably named after the Buddhist goddess Tara. On the top of the hill is a stupa now damaged, broken railing pillars, cross-bars and burnt brick-bats. One rock-cut cave was hewn for the Buddhist bhikkus. Four railing pillars are inscribed. The inscription contains the names of Tapusa, Kalingaraja, Kesa-stupa, and Bheku Tapasu Danam. The researchers link the discovery with the two merchants of Orissa, Tapassu and Bhallika and the stupa they built.

Kayama Hill

The full shape rock-cut elephant is a unique piece of Kalingan art and probably erected during the Mauryan rule. Inscriptions like

▲ This elephant cut from rock represents Kalingan art

'Gajaraj', 'Tisa Sri Sri Buddha', 'Gogul raba', 'Purugaditya', seven prehistoric caves, a damaged Hinayana stupa, have been discovered from the hilly area. The hill is identified by Dr. Nursingh Charan Sahu as ancient Surabha Giri described in the Buddhist text *Ganda buhya*, and recently identified as Radhanagar.

Langudi Hill

Hinayani, Mahayani, and Tantric Buddhist remains have been discovered from the Langudi Hill. The most important objects among them are two inscribed stone images of Emperor Ashoka, with the inscription 'Puspa Giri vihar', handmade stupas of Ashoka, Panchadhyani Buddha, votive stupas, Buddha images, etc.

Deuli Hill

Rock-cut caves and damaged Hinayani stupas have been discovered from the hill area. Inscriptions containing the words *'Bhalluka lane'* is considered an important find, since like the inscription *'Bhikhu Tapassu daman'* discovered on Tarapur hill, the word *'Bhulluka'* proves that the area is the birth place of two of the first disciples of Buddha – Tapassu and Bhalluka.

Deulipal Hill

Adjacent to Deulipal hill on the bank of river Brahmani are caves and ancient damaged stupas.

Panturi Hill

Situated in the western direction of Deulipal hill, Panturi hill contains a stupa on the top with several objects from the pre-Christian era.

Neulpur Hill
Near Tarapur hill, Neulpur hill contains ten rock-cut caves and a damaged Hinayani stupa.

Kantigadia Hill
This hill is close to Neulpur, Langudi, and Vajragiri hills. There is a damaged stupa, a rock-cut idol of Vairava, and some rock-cut caves.

Vajragiri Hill
Along with Hinayani Buddhism in the initial period, even Tantric Buddhism spread here. Many tantric images have been shifted to the state museum from the hills. Some images have been preserved in the campus of Vajragiri College and in the locality.

Radhanagar Fort and Port
The ancient Radhanagar fort is akin to the fort of Shishupalagada near Cuttack.

Dr. N C Sahu's deep research brings to the limelight new information which needs further research and study. He has proved that ancient Orissa had marine trade relations with Rome and south-east Asian countries from Radhanagar fort. Dr. Sahu has collected Kushana coins, punch marked silver coins of the Nanda dynasty, copper coins of the Mather dynasty from 4th century A.D., etc. Historians and researchers have also identified Radhanagar fort area as the place of the Kalinga war, because excavated items had inscriptions in the Brahmi script mentioning Kalingaraj, Toshali, and Sadabhu Tissa. Ashoka had divided his kingdom into north Toshali and south Toshali. The word 'Toshali' does not exist at or near Dhauli in any other archaeological find. Hence, a few people believe that Radhanagar is the capital of Ashoka's empire and not Dhauli.

Lalitgiri, Ratnagiri, Udayagiri

Location: All three places are located about 100 km from Bhubhaneshwar, within a radius of 30-40 km

Lalitgiri

Lalitgiri, Ratnagiri, and Udayagiri are isolated hills in the Assia range, Cuttack district. Lalitgiri is one of the points on the Buddhist Triangle, popularly known as the Diamond Triangle of Orissa, which sings the glory of a past heritage, spanning from 3 BC-AD 15. Udayagiri is the eastern-most hill and is separated from Ratnagiri.

Lalitgiri and Udayagiri were seats of a university, known as Puspagiri, whose fame spread far and wide. To this university trudged a Chinese pilgrim, 1,400 years ago, in the quest of knowledge. Hiuen-Tsang in his itinerary states he visited Wu-cha (Odra) and found that most of the people in that country professed Mahayana Buddhism. There were about 100 monasteries in the country then.

The extensiveness of the remains and the topographical features that are easily visible, support the hypothesis that the two stupas on the two hill monasteries mentioned by Hiuen-Tsang, were situated on the Lalitgiri hill, which is distinctly visible from the top of the Udayagiri hill.

The entire area is practically littered with images of the Mahayana and Vajrayana pantheons. Among many noteworthy discoveries at this site is an ancient stupa containing relics preserved in a stone casket. Its antiquity and silver and gold contents have led to specula-tions that these are relics of Lord Buddha. Further findings of black polished pieces of

▲ Part of the Diamond Triangle of Orissa, Lalitgiri has a treasure trove of Buddhist relics

pottery inscribed in Ashokan Brahmi and a number of inscriptional evidences such as Kushan inscriptions, ornamental Brahmi, etc., have corroborated in establishing Lalitgiri as a flourishing center of Buddhism in the second century BC.

Lalitgiri is composed of three separate hills – the Olasuni, the Parabhadi and the Landa. The Olasuni is famous in Orissa as the seat of the prophet Araksita Das who resided there during the latter half of the 18th century. On the northern slope of the Parabhadi hill is a long gallery cut out of rock in which a series of large Bodhisattavas were originally placed, though today it is mostly a heap of ruins and is known as the Hathikhali (elephant pit). Landa hill, covered with the extensive ruins of ancient brick buildings and scattered sculptures, had become in the past an ideal site for a brick quarry run by the locals. So, despoliation and plundering have robbed the hill of many of its treasures. The Landa hill peak slopes towards the base of Parabadi peak. In the passage in between the two hills, was a Buddhist shrine that has collapsed and the rubble from this shrine was used to construct the temple of the Tantric goddess Basuli. The image, still worshipped by the locals, is believed to be the image of Vajra Tara.

There were six large images of Padmapani Avalokitesvara within the temple premises of Basuli, but these are now housed in the sculpture shed at Lalitgiri. On the back of one of the images of Padmapani Avalokitesvar are the words – *'Ye Dhamma Hetu Prabhava, Hetus Teshan Tathagata'*. This tells us that Tathagata (Buddha) preached about the causes of human sufferings and offered ways to overcome them.

Four monasteries have been excavated, with the smallest, Monastery No.2, on the north-east corner of the hill where it faces east. It consists of a sanctum and five cells. The monastery was ravaged at an early date and sometime later was converted into a Hindu temple.

Monastery No.1, midway up the hill and near the Basuli Thakurani temple, also faces east. The sanctum is fronted by a large courtyard, which is framed by four cells at the front, two on either side of the entrance, and five cells aligned on both north and south sides.

Monastery No.3 is just like Monastery No.1, but faces south towards the area of the apsidal shrine. Its 18 cells are aligned in the same manner as of Monastery No.1. Numerous pillars unearthed here are stylistically similar to the niches and doorjambs in the late sixth – early seventh century brahmanical temples at Bhubaneshwar.

When excavated in early 1992, Monastery No.4 of the apsidal shrine and facing north-west, still retained its colossal Buddha in the sanctum, though its head was missing and its right shoulder and part of the left arm was damaged. He is seated on a simhasana with his right hand displaying the bhumi-sparsha-mudra.

A large number of antiquities in the form of terracotta objects, stamped or inscribed pieces of pottery, sculptures of Buddhist divinities, scenes from Buddha's life, images of Buddha in standing and seated poses, in different sizes and shapes, have also been found. Terracotta seals, sealings, miniature figures of Avalokitesvara, votive stupas, silver slages over 200 gm, gold rings are also noteworthy finds. Among the glorious treasures found in Lalitgiri, are three standing images of Buddha dressed in a loose outer garment, of which two have been shifted to Bhubhaneshwar and preserved in the Department of Archaeology museum.

The drapery is an illustration of Gandhara art. The third one is a large-sized image of Buddha kept behind the gateway. One can also see in the sculpture shed a huge statue of Buddha sitting, the hand touching the floor, in the bhumi-sparsha-mudra.

Two small heads of Buddha (two feet in height), an image of Nagaraja, a seven-hooded canopy, an image of Maitreya, an image of Manjushri are also kept in the sculptural shed. Many more are believed to be buried.

These excavations push back the nucleus of the site to at least the second-third century AD to indicate that Lalitgiri is the earliest of these three major Buddhist sites in the Assia hills. The site must have been in existence by the third century AD and apparently was the most developed site during the visit of Hiuen–Tsang, it had been postulated that it might have been Puphagiri/Puspagiri-vihara.

Ratnagiri (Sri Ratnagiri – Mahavihra)

Another point of the Diamond Triangle, 100 km away from Bhubaneshwar, Ratnagiri has a rich concentration of Buddhist antiquities. Extensive excavations have unearthed large monasteries, a big stupa, numerous Buddhist shrines, sculptures, and a large number of votive stupas.

The village named Ratnagiri is presently located around the hillock containing Buddhist remains, which is an isolated hill of the Assia range bounded on all sides by the three rivers, the Brahamani, the Kimira and the Birupa. The top of the hill still offers a panoramic view of the surroundings, which was chosen for the Buddhist establishment.

It is said that Ratnagiri and Udayagiri were the nucleus of Tantric Buddhism and it was from here that Buddhism spread to other parts of India and the world. The antiquity of tantric tradition in Orissa is corroborated by a discovery of a fragmentary stone inscription, most likely containing a Buddha tantra, which on paleographic grounds, can be dated to at least the sixth century AD.

Stratigraphically, the earliest strata of Ratnagiri has been dated to the fifth century AD. Since then the continuous growth of art and architecture was seen up to the end of 13th century AD. The name of the site – 'Ratnagiri Nahavihara Aaryavikhu Samghasya' – comes from the terracotta seals here. Recent excavations (1998-99) near the Mahakala temple revealed unique images of Avalokitesvara and still some artefacts remain buried. The excavation revealed the establishment of the Buddhist center at least from the time of the Gupta King Narasimha Gupta Baladitya (first half of the sixth century AD).

Buddhism had developed here unhindered up to the 12th century AD. Initially, this was an important center of the Mahayana form of Buddhism. During the eighth-ninth century AD, this became a great center of Tantric Buddhism or Vajrayana art and philosophy.

Pag Sam Jon Zang, a Tibetan arhat, a guru, indicated that the institution at Ratnagiri played a significant role in the emergence of Kalachakra Tantra during the 10th century AD. This is evident from numerous votive stupas with reliefs of divinities from the

Vajrayana pantheon, separate images of these divinities and inscribed stone slabs and moulded terracotta plaques with dharanis.

There is also a smaller monastery, a stone temple, and brick shrines here. In the midst of these magnificent monuments, is the beautifully carved stone door-jamb at the entrance of the brick monastery.

The overwhelming majority of the sculptures at Ratnagiri can be grouped into two phases, an early phase dating to the eighth-ninth centuries, dominated primarily by images of the Mahayana pantheon, and a later phase dating from the $10^{th} - 11^{th}$ centuries in which Vajrayana imagery is more dominant, though both the forms of Buddhism co-existed, with the latter evincing early and late aspects.

Aside from the images of Buddha, included among the large stone sculptures on the site are various forms of Avalokitesvara, Manjushri, and Tara along with examples of Arya-Sarasvati, Cunda, Hariti, Heruka, Jambhala, Maitreya, Marichi, Sambara, Vajradhama, Vajrapani, Vajrasattva, Vasundhara, and Yamantaka.

Of the numerous Avalokitesvara forms, particularly popular in the early phase are images of Amoghapasa and Jata-mukuta/Mahakaruna, suggesting the extreme importance of the cult of Bodhisatta-as-saviour during this period in Orissa, while this form of Khasarpa is more popular in the later phase. The Asatmahabhaya form of Tara depicting her as a saviour, in contrast, appears in both phases. One of the most unique juxtaposition of images in the late phase occurs in the sanctum of Temple No. 4 located in the area in the front of Monastery No. 2.

The largest number of monolithic stupas (dated between the 9-13 centuries), as many as 535, were found on the south-western side of the main stupa area, immediately outside the compound wall of Stupa No. 1. Of particular iconographic interest are the numerous sculptural-mandalas at the site which include groups of eight and 16 Bodhisattavas, the latter seemingly based on the Vajradhatu-mahamandala of the *Sarvatathagata-tattvasamgraha*.

Over the years, numerous sculptures have been removed from the site with examples now housed in various museums, including the Indian Museum at Kolkata, the Patna Museum, the National Museum at New Delhi, the Orissa State Museum at Bhubaneshwar. Other examples are scattered in neighbouring villages.

An excavation site in Ratnagiri also yielded 27 metal images, the most interesting from an iconographical viewpoint being the image of Krsna-Yamari.

In the overwhelming number of monolithic stupas, Ratnagiri can safely compete with Bodh Gaya. Ratnagiri was a great learning center and hundreds of scholars both from within and outside the country used to throng here for Buddhist studies.

Udayagiri (Sri Madhavapura-Mahavihara)

One of the largest Buddhist complexes in Orissa, Udayagiri is about 90 km away from Bhubaneshwar. The ancient name of this complex was Madhavapura-Mahavihara. Udayagiri forms the easternmost peak of the Assia range. The two arms of the hill, one extending to the northwest and the other to the southeast, form a

▲ Udayagiri home to a colossal image of Padmapani, has yielded many precious idols, some dating back to the seventh century AD

bay opening to the east. Exploration reports of the several scholars published by the Archaeological Survey of India indicate that on the slope of the valley-like site there were at least 3-4 monastic complexes and many Mahayana-Vajrayana images scattered all round a rock-cut well. The excavations proved that this was a Madhavapura-Mahavihara site that flourished from the 7-13 centuries AD. The name of this site also revealed from terracotta sealings to have been 'Madhvapura-Mahavihara Arya Vikshu Sangha'.

The hill contains two spurs, extensively covered with Buddhist remains. At the foot of the hill there stood an elaborately carved colossal image of Bodhisattva Padmapani holding a large lotus in the hand. The figure bears an inscription recording the name of the donor Kesava Gupta, a monk. It was carved out of a single slab of chlorite and was more than seven feet high. The upper portion of the image, now broken into two parts lies on the ground.

There is a rock-cut well, at the base of the terrace of the hill, the inscription records that the well was dedicated by Ranaka Vajranaga. About 50 feet higher up, is a platform upon which once stood a shrine of Buddha. There are remains of a shrine consisting of a cell and a porch. The cell contains the colossal image of Buddha. The image of Buddha is in bhumi-sparsha-mudra, made of three pieces of bluish chlorite stone and is 5 feet, 6 inches high.

In the southern part of the terrace, at some height from the base, is a temple of Mahakali. From a ruined brick mound near this temple, an image of Vaisravana was dug out and subsequently removed to the Indian Museum. A little higher up the terrace, stands a four-armed image of Avalokiteswara, the legs of the image are broken.

The northern part of the terrace was covered with extensive remains of stupas. The niches on four sides of this stupa contain four images of Buddha. Being an object of worship, the stupa was encircled by a compound wall. The stupa is about 16 feet high and the dome is on a square platform. This stupa has a significant place in the development of Buddhism in Orissa. There are four images fixed on the four sides of this stupa (one of the images has fallen down from the original place). This signifies that these images were Dhyanibuddhas.

> It is in the tradition of Vajrayana Buddhism that Vajrasattva is the Adi Buddha (the primal enlightened one) who possesses five kinds of knowledge, conceived as His five attributes, from which five kinds of meditation (Dhyanas) emanate. From these five deities known as five Dhyani Buddhas, Tathagata emanates.
>
> They are:
> 1. Vairochana
> 2. Ratnasambhava
> 3. Amitabha
> 4. Amoghasiddhi
> 5. Akshobhya

These Dhyanibuddhas are generally represented on the four sides of the stupa, which is the symbol of the Buddhist universe. Vairochana is the deity of the inner shrine, so it is generally not represented. Amitabha faces the West and is seated on a full bloomed lotus on the western side of the stupa. Akshobhaya faces the East and is carved on the eastern side of the stupa. Likewise, Amoghosiddhi and Ratnasambhava are carved on the North and South side of the stupa facing north and south respectively. The theory of Dhyanibuddhas and various tantric practices are described in *Guhyasamaj Tantra* (third century AD).

The Dhyanibuddhas together with their different shaktis, the various yogic, and other means of worshipping, constitute the kernel of Tantrisum or Vajrayana. Thus, the stupa shows that this site was a very prominent Vajrayana center during the medieval period of Orissan culture.

During the course of excavations here, there were about 50 unique sculptures of Buddhist divinities like Buddha, Bodhisattva, Avalokitesvara, Tara, Jambhala, Aparajita, Heruka, etc. Also many sculptures were found scattered and half-buried at the site, and such findings are still being made.

This settlement occupies an important place in the development of Buddhist culture in Orissa. Lalitgiri, Ratangiri, Udayagiri with its excavated treasures are the finest Buddhist complexes discovered so far in India. Still many more monasteries and mounds remain buried beneath the debris.

Langudi

Close to the Lalitgiri–Ratnagiri–Udayagiri complex is Langudi Hill, another important site of Buddhism. This hillock is a congregation of cluster of low-lying hills and is surrounded by other Buddhist sites like Vajragiri in the east, Radhanagar and Kaima hills on the north.

▲ Dr. NC Sahu and the author examining temple panels at Langudi hill

Excavations revealed abundant evidence that a large stupa with many Buddhist images was constructed here and was known as Pushpagiri Vihara. On the middle portion of the hill, evidence of a monastery made with bricks was discovered. The southern spur of this picturesque hillock, yields Buddhist monuments exquisitely carved in an extensive panel, with four sculptures and two clear-cut compartments.

The main discoveries here were the Tara image, a four-armed image of Parjanaparamita, rock-cut images and a stupa at the center, images of Avalokitesvara and Dhyani Buddha. This marks the religious merit of the place, which was the center of religious activities during the fourth-fifth centuries AD. Besides rock-cut monuments, the excavations also brought to light a number of terracotta Buddha images. Few early Brahmi inscriptions were also reported from this Langudi hillock.

The most remarkable and prized discovery here was in 2001 when two inscribed images of Emperor Ashoka, one with his two queens and another with just one was found. Ancient Kalinga, which includes the Langudi hill area, was very much a part of his empire.

Tarapur

Tarapur village is situated on the Cuttack–Paradeep road. Sculptures were discovered by locals while they were renovating a portion of the Taladanda canal. They found figures and edifices of Buddha, Avalokitesvara, Prajnyaparamita, Mairichi, and Tara. The Buddha and Avalokitesvara sculptures represent characteristics of eighth century AD techniques and the Mairichi and Parjnyaparamita can be placed in the 11th century.

At present, the images have been assembled under a Kendu tree where they are worshipped as Hindu deities. Ruins of a brick structure are still visible on the embankment of the canal.

Apart from the captioned major sites, the following towns and villages have yielded remains of monasteries and stupas, temple foundations, Buddhist images and antiquities, etc.

Adasapur, Amaravati-kataka, Ali (Aul), Bagalpur, Bhattarika, Chudar, Cuttack, Dharamsala, Dondua-matha (Kalyanapur), Duburi hill, Durgapur, Fakirpatna, Kaduapara-Dihasahi, Kalanapur (Brahmavana), Kapila, Kaupada (Kaduapara), Kendrapara, Kendupatna, Khaira, Kulangiri, Kundesvara, Mahanga, Maricipur, Mudupur, Nagaspur, Narasinghapur, Nasikakotian, Natara, Nathuvara, Odisoandeigoda, Oratapurgarh, Paradipgarh, Sakuntalapur, Salipur, Singhapur, Taranga, Tiadi-sahi (Kaduapara), Tirthamatha (Turanga) Vajragir, and Varahapur.

Ganjam District

Following towns and villages have yielded remains of monasteries and stupas, images and antiquities: Buddhakot, Ganjam, Jaugada (famous for Ashoka Rock edicts), and Kayima.

Keonjhar District

In Keonjhar distrct, remains of monasteries and stupas, images and antiquities have been discovered in Banchua, Deogaon, Sadha and Talagarh.

Khudra District
Aragarh Hill

Aragarh is situated in the Haripur Panchayat area near Khudra, on the banks of the river Daya. The site is remarkably picturesque. The undulating hill site is about 3 km long. It can be inferred from some evidence that a Buddhist settlement had existed there for more than 400 years.

There is a stupa complex buried beneath the mound at Aragarh, which is evident by the discovery of Buddhist images, railing fragments and votive stupas. Included among the images are examples of Avalokitesvara, a multi-armed Tara, and the lower half of a four-armed Avalokitesvara with images of Mahavairocana, Vajrasattva, and Hayagriva on the pedestal. On the top of the hill is a flat-roofed pillared chamber with openings on four sides, the back opening is now walled-up, while the other openings are secured with stone window grilles. The openings are framed on each side by a naga-stambha.

A lower chamber has a door opening on the front of the structure while the huge size of the mound indicates the existence of a large Buddhist complex, which is still buried. The exposed structure and surface images can be dated to the 10th or 11th early century.

Mayurbhanja District
Boud/Baudh

Boud, a district headquarter, is rich in Buddhist antiquities. Perhaps the name 'Boud' is reminiscent of the Buddhist heritage the place has inherited. Situated on the bank of river Mahanadi, Boud was on a trade route connecting south Kosala and the plain lands of Kalinga. Buddhist antiquities have been found in Boud town and at villages Paragalpur and Shyamsundarpur. A large image of Buddha is seen in Boud. This image is seated in the bhumi-sparsha-mudra and is 6' 9" high and 4' 6" wide. In the Ramesvara temple, a Tara image with an inscription that dates it to the 10th century AD is seen. Several bronze statues of deities from the Buddhist pantheon were found in this area. Two small bronze images dated to the 9th – 10th century were also discovered at Boud. One is a two-armed Maitreya seated in the lalitasana. The second image is four-armed and represents a form of Sankhanthan Lokesvara.

Khiching

Location: 25 km from Karanjia subdivision of Mayurbhanj district

Khiching has several Buddhist monuments. Excavations carried out since 1920 reveal magnificent features of Buddhist heritage. One mound revealed the remains of a stupa with a casket of ashes enshrined. A colossal image of Mahakarunika Buddha in bhumi-sparsha-mudra has been preserved in the local museum at Khiching. The figure is seated on a lotus throne in the Yogic pose, it has a graceful face, is adorned with dangling earrings and the branches of Ashvattha tree akin to the Bodhi tree under which Siddhartha attained Enlightenment are also depicted.

Some images of Vajrasana Buddha were also found in this site. The inscription *'Ye Dhamma Hetu'* on a slab suggests that Buddhism flourished here before the 10th century AD.

The brick structure known as Itamundia was partially excavated in 1908 by Dr. NK Bose. The brick building consists of three small rooms and a verandah. In the middle room, Dr. Bose found inscribed images of Avalokitesvara and Marichi. The Marichi image is now in Baripada Museum. Square plinths of several votive stupas together with a circular one, all made of bricks, existed in front of the structure.

About 20 years ago, several sculptures were retrieved from a tank on the outskirts of the village including an image of Tara and an image of Manjuvara Manjushri. The Buddhist images at Khiching are made of a hard chloritic (muguni) stone quarried in the neighbouring villages of Kesra and Adipur. In respect of facial features, body ornamentation and coiffure, this particular style of

Khiching has a blend of Orissan and Pala characteristics. The majority of the images can be dated to 10th century AD.

Apart from captioned major sites, remains of monasteries and stupas, images and antiquities have been found in Baripada, Koisarigarh, and Ranibandh

Puri District

Achyutrajpur

Achyutrajpur, one of the oldest Buddhist centers, achieved eminence under the Bhaumakara dynasty (eighth-ninth centuries AD), though it might have been established in the sixth century AD. The Bhaumakara dynasty is responsible for spreading Buddhism from Orissa throughout India and also in China. While in all other Buddhist centers, stone sculptures gained prominence, at Achyutrajpur bronze sculptures of Buddhist icons forms a bulk of the idols created.

Achyutrajpur came into prominence in AD 1963 with the discovery of a hoard of metal images and objects when the foundation for a local college was being laid. The area is picturesque with the Ghantasila hill about a kilometer north of the site and the Salia river flowing closeby. The entire area between this stream and the road to the south of the local college (Godavarish Mahavidyalaya) was formerly a mound containing the ancient ruins of religious structures (primarily Buddhist).

The antiquity of the area is proved by the discovery of two sets of copper-plates pertaining to the Sailodbhava dynasty of Kongoda.

Other copper-plates found in the area attest to its continued prosperity during the Bhaumakara and Somavamsi periods while in the Ganga period a temple dedicated to Daksaprajapati Shiva was built in Banpur. It has been proved that the area not only nourished Buddhism and Brahmanical cults, but also, to a limited extent, Jainism as well.

The largest hoard of bronze images of deities from the Buddhist pantheon including 19 votive Buddhist stupas were recovered in Achyutrajpur. Two big earthen pots containing the entire hoard of bronze images besides a set of copper-plates of Indranatha, a king of Somavamsi dynasty were also found here. Of the 95 metal images which were part of the hoard, at least 75 icons are Buddhist with 17 being of Tara. The other images include 16 of Buddha, 10 of Avalokitesvara, five of Cunda, five of Vajrasattva, four of Majushri, three of Maitreya, two of Bhrkuti, and one each of Asokakanti-Marichi, Heruka, Jambhala, Kurukulla, Pandara and Vajrahunkara. There are five unidentified Boddhisattvas and four female icons. Two of the latter are six-armed with one possibly representing Tara. Of the 16 Buddha images, 13 display the bhumi-sparsha-mudra, two exhibit the abhaya-mudra and one is depicted in the dhyana-mudra. Fifteen of the images are seated while one is standing. None are accompanied by Bodhisattva, attendants, or devotees. Of the 20 stupas contained within the hoard, four have images of deities, including one Buddha in the bhumi-sparha-mudra and other with a Bodhisattva, possibly Maitreya. The most interesting stupa is also the largest; in its niches are depicted Tara, Bhrkuti, Pandara and possibly Ashokakanta Marichi or Yasodhara. A similar group of four goddesses appears on stone sculptures of Lokesvara at Ratnagiri and Udayagiri.

Benupada
Location: 7-8 km from Delanga railway station of Puri district
There is a temple here where five clay stupas are presently worshipped. These five stupas perhaps represent the five primordial elements of five Dhyani-buddhas. The area surrounding Benupada was once the stronghold of Buddhism as Dinanaga, the great Buddhist exponent, resided in the Bhora Saila monastery. The monastery has not been identified. Buddhist relics have also been found in the nearby villages of Haripur, Jharpada, and Ghoradia. There are also several caves at Tapanga hill near Narangarh, Barunai hill near Khurda and Aragarh hill near Delang, specifically used by Buddhist monks for teaching yoga.

Dhauli
Location: 8 km south-west of Bhubaneshwar
Dhauli is identified as Toshali, the seat of Ashoka's vice-royalty in

Kalinga. From the available remains at Dhauli, it can be safely assumed that it was a great Buddhist center in the past. The major rock edict XIII and two special edicts found on the hill indicate the glory of this region during the third century BC. The Dhauli hilltop provides a panoramic view of Bhubaneshwar.

It was here that Ashoka's great transformation took place and Buddhism was revitalised. The transformation of Emperor Ashoka from a ruthless invader to a lover of peace, after the colossal carnage of the Kalinga war, was a significant event not only in Ashoka's life, but also in the history of India. The Emperor then made an appeal to all citizens to embrace Buddhism.

After conversion, Emperor Ashoka made several administrative reforms to alleviate the resentment among the people of Kalinga against Magadha's domination, restore peaceful co-existence, for which he issued elaborate instructions through rock edicts installed at various places in the empire.

The early habitation extended in a radius of more than one kilometer around Dhauli. On the northern side of the southern hill, Ashokan edicts are inscribed on a huge rock. Crowning the inscription, the famous elephant sculpture about 4' high, the forepart of an elephant, cut out of natural rock can be seen. This sculpture can be regarded as the earliest specimen of Orissan sculptural art. The elephant was originally designed to be the emblem of Gautam Buddha. Ashoka being a Buddhist, elected to have an elephant as his kingly insignia. Gautam Buddha's mother saw in her dream a white elephant entering her womb and the child born was Buddha. Since then the elephant has been very auspicious for Buddhists.

In Orissa, about 14 Rock Edicts of Ashoka, and two sets of Rock Edicts have been discovered – one at Dhauli and the other at Jaungarh. Ashoka instructed the Mahamantras or judicial officers not to punish his subjects without trial. In the second, he expresses to the Royal Prince or Governor of Tosali his concern for the forest folk, to whom he was like a father. The thirteenth edict of Ashoka describing the horrors of the Kalinga war has been prudently omitted here.

Kuruma

Location: 8 km north-east of Konark

Villagers collected a large number of antiquities from a mound, including terracotta ornaments, beds, small terracotta images, red-ware pottery, and a terracotta seal inscribed with an inscription in characters of the 9-10 century AD. In a temporary shed erected over the mound are images of Buddha, Yamantaka, Jata-mukuta Lokeshvara, and Mahakaruna. Of these Buddhist images housed in the shed, the largest is a crowned Buddha in the bhumi-sparsha-mudra. An image of Heruka mounting a buffalo and a crowned Buddha seated in the bhumi-sparsha-mudra are worshipped by the locals as Yama and Dharma respectively. Hence the village is also popularly known as Yama-Dharma.

Apart from the captioned major sites, the following towns/villages have yielded remains of monasteries and stupas, temple foundations, and Buddhist images and antiquities: Amaraprasadgarh, Amrsevara, Arkavata, Astaranga, Bada-Tara, Banpur, Batesvara (Tulasipur), Bhillideuli, Bhubaneshwar, Denua, Durdurabasta, Gada Beguniapada, Ghorodia, Gopalpur, Jiunti, Kapilaprasad, Kapilesvara, Kenduli, Kukimundia, Lataharana, Avalokitesvara, Manitri, Phiriphira, Ramacandi, Renugala, Sundaragram, and Virabalabhadrapur.

Bargarh District – Old Sambalpur District

Ganiapalli

The Ganiapalli ruins were partially excavated by the Post Graduate Department of History of Bargarh district, in 1978. The village is situated on the banks of the river Ang. The ruins consist of a monastery complex constructed of bricks. The excavations reveal that the monastery had structural buildings. Burnt bricks were used for the construction of the monastery and have been seen used in the walls and in the foundation. Two life-size Buddha images, worshipped as Siddharthamuni and Nagamani depicting the Mucilinda form of the Buddha were found in this area. The images and the brick complex may tentatively be dated to AD 617.

Other objects found here include one iron safe and a lot of shards of bowls and sprinklers.

The remains of another Buddhist vihara dating to the same approximate period has been discovered at Nagaraj on the left bank of the Ang river, about 18 km from Ganiapalli. Bricks and brick-fragments are spread out almost continuously from the monastery of Ganiapalli to this mound.

There are many places all over Orissa where Buddhist monuments and remains can be found that bear testimony to the observations of a galaxy of historians that Buddhism had been embraced, taught, learnt, preached, propagated, and flourished for about 1400 years in Oddra desa, Utkala, subsequently named as Kalinga, and then Orissa with geographical variations in the dimensions of the area, over this long period of time.

Important Buddhist sites are connected to the cities by fairly good roads, taxis and auto-rickshaws.

Package tours are offered during tourist season from Bhubaneshwar, Puri, and Cuttack. Ranging from budget to star hotels, there are a number of reasonably priced places, some of which are located near Buddhist sites.

General Information

Area: 1,55,707 sq. km

Capital: Bhubaneshwar

Boundaries: Andhra Pradesh, Chhattisgarh, Jharkhand, West Bengal; *Sea* – Bay of Bengal

Chief Language: Oriya

Main Towns: Bhubaneshwar, Cuttak, Puri, Sambalpur, Balangir, Baragarh, Raurkela, Bhadrak, Rayagonda, Behrampur

Air: Bhubaneshwar. There are 13 airstrips and 16 helipads in the state.

Rail: Bhubaneshwar, Puri, Cuttack, Brahmanpur, Balangir, Raurkela, Sambalpur

Road: Length: NH – 3,194 km; SH – 5,014 km

Buddhist Circuits
Bhubaneshwar – Dhauli, Kuruma
Cuttack – Lalitgiri, Ratnagiri, Udayagiri, Langudi

15

PUNJAB

Long considered to be the state of heroes, Punjab is called the sword-arm of India. Punjab, the land of five rivers and integrated cultural history, is a treasure trove for an avid tourist. Ancient Punjab is the land of the Vedas and the Indus valley civilisation,

The word 'Punjab' is made up of two Persian words 'Panj' and 'Aab'. 'Panj' means 'five' and 'Aab' means 'water'. This name was probably given to the land of five rivers by the Persians.

The creation of many viharas, stupas, and other monuments during the reign of Ashoka gave a great fillip to the spread of Buddhism in Punjab. In fact, the unprecedented activities in the cause of the Dhamma created a stir in the land of five rivers, which resulted in the advent of renowned Buddhist scholars and philosophers in the following centuries.

During the reign of Ashoka and immediately thereafter, there also flourished a local kingdom in Punjab with Srughna, modern Sugh, near Jagadhari in the district of Ambala, as its capital city. It covered an area of about 1000 miles. Raja Dhanabhuti, the pre-eminent king of this royal family ruled from 240-210 BC. This pious Buddhist king did not only build magnificent stupas in his capital city, but he also made donations to the world famous stupa at Bharhut in Central India, which was constructed between 250-200 BC.

Inspired by Ashoka, Raja Dhanabhuti also raised a number of stupas in and around his capital, Sugh. Hiuen–Tsang, who visited Sugh in AD 635 saw there, besides an Ashoka stupa, a number of stupas containing relics of Buddha, Sariputta, and Moggallana (His two disciples) and other great Arhats (an enlightened person who has extinguished cravings and achieved nirvana).

◀ Dating back to the third century BC, the stupa in Sanghol was built by Emperor Ashoka

In the *Janavasabha-Sutta* of the *Digha-Nikaya* (collection of long discourses), Kuru is mentioned along with the other Janpadas where Tathagata delivered a number of religious discourses. According to the *Jatakas*, the size of Kuru was 300 leagues and Indapatta (Indra-prastha, near modern Delhi) was its capital. The ancient Kuru country, according to Dr. BC Law, may be said to have comprised the Kurukshetra or Thaneswar. The district included Sonepat, Amin, Panipat, Karnal, and was situated between the Sravasti on the north and Drishadvati on the south.

During His visits to the Kuru country, Lord Buddha generally stayed at Kammasadhamma, a market town of the Kuru people. Kammasadhamma, is believed to be present day Kaithal, a market town, 56 km west of Karnal.

Thullakotthita was another important town in the Kuru Desa. The city is mentioned as the capital of King Koravya of the Kuru kingdom with whom Ratthapala (Rashtrapal) held a religious discussion. Here, after hearing a discourse by the Buddha, Ratthapala, a Kuru noble, joined the Buddhist Sangha.

As Hiuen-Tsang's account makes Thanesar the westernmost country of the Buddhist Majjhimadesa, SN Mazumdar has identified Thuna with Sthaneswar or Thaneswar. Thaneswar is now a tehsil headquarter in the Karnal district. It is situated on the banks of Saravasti and is a sacred place for the Hindus.

That the Buddha had visited some other places in Punjab as well seems a possibility. Lord Buddha, while on a missionary tour of Punjab, had stayed at Srughna (modern Sugh near Jagdhari), at Kuluta (modern Kulu) and at Taki (modern Asrur in Gujranwala district, Pakistan). Further, in the last 'bhanavara' or 'the portion of tales' of the section on remedies in the text *Vinaya Pitaka* (contains Buddha's teaching regarding the rules of conduct of the monks and many episodes and events associated with the development of sangha) it is said that the Buddha once went from Vaishali to Bhaddiyanagara and then returned to Saravasti via Anguttarapa, Apana, Kushinagara, and Atuma. The same journey is related in the Tibetan version of *Vinaya* of the Mula Sarvastivadins. In his treatise *Ancient People of the Punjab*

Przyluski has identified Bhaddiyanagara or Bhaddiya with Sakala (Sialkot) and Angutarapa with Agroha, an ancient city, 20 km north-west of Hissar. In the ancient days, there was a great route of commerce which passed through Sialkot, Agroha, and Rohtak (Rohitaka) connected Taxila with the Gangetic Valley. The Buddha is said to have travelled by this route. The Buddha may have visited Taxila also, which is not in India now.

On the basis of whatever little evidence is available after so many centuries, it is clear that Buddha had sanctified the land of the five rivers.

Hiuen–Tsang, the Chinese pilgrim, who was in India from AD 634-644 saw the Ashokan stupas at the following five places in Punjab, Haryana, and Himachal Pradesh.

Place	*Identification*
Satadru	Modern Sanghol (Punjab)
Sathanesvara	Modern Thanesar (Haryana)
Srughna	Modern Sung near Jagadhari (Haryana)
Kuluta	Modern Kulu (Himachal Pradesh)
Tamsavana	Modern Sultanpur or Raghunathpur (Himachal Pradesh)

Of the numerous pillar edicts issued by Ashoka, one major pillar edict was in the plains of Punjab. This pillar was at Topra, a village near Ambala from where it was removed by Feroz Shah Tughlaq in AD 1356 and taken to Delhi. Now it stands on the ruins of Feroz Shah Kotla, and is known as Delhi Topra pillar.

Sanghol

The recent excavations at Sanghol in Tehsil Samrala, district Ludhiana, has brought to light the rich heritage of Buddhism in Punjab. The name Sanghol has originated from Sanghpur, a town that has a Buddhist monastic nature. The most important monument unearthed by the Department of Archaeology in 1985 is the stupa, which appears to have been first built by Ashoka in the third century BC, inspired by the pattern of the Dharma

Chakra (Wheel of Law). The cylindrical stupa is of 52 feet diameter on a 55 feet square platform. There is also a murram pathway (a type of stone) about 18 feet in width all around the stupa. In the east, is a paved pathway along which a number of votive stupas of solid mud were erected by the devotees.

From the central portion of the stupa, were recovered a tooth, ashes, and some bones as also the bottom portion of a relic casket, most probably the body relics of the Buddha. The excavations also yielded a lid with a Kharosthi legend of the first and second century BC. Upasaka Ayabhadra mentioned in the legend may have been responsible for enshrining the relics in the stupa.

General Information

Area: 50,362 sq. km

Capital: Chandigarh

Boundaries: Jammu & Kashmir, Himachal Pradesh, Haryana, Rajasthan, Pakistan

Chief Language: Punjabi

Main Towns: Ludhiana, Amritsar, Bathinda, Jalandhar, Patiala, Gurudaspurk

Air: Amritsar, Chandigarh, Bathinda, Ludhiana

Rail: Length – 3726 km; Main railway stations – Patiala, Jalandhar, Amritsar, Bathinda

Road: Road length – 48,543 km

The priceless discovery of 117 sculptures from the Kushana period in the railing around the stupa on the square platform is quite stunning. These railing pillars were found in a pit between the monastery and the stupa. The valuable parts of the railing include four corner pillars, 58 upright pillars, seven double-sided pillars, 35 cross-bars and 13 coping stones.

Tihara

Tihara is a place in the north-west corner of Jagraon tehsil. Tihara has been identified with the city of Varat mentioned in the *Mahabharata*. On the mounds here, a large number of small square copper coins were found, which had on one side the Buddhist wheel and on the other side the names of the Rajas in old Sanskrit. Besides coins, impressions of seals in burnt clay, large bricks, dice glazed pottery and many other antiquities, including the impressions of coins of the Yaudheyas in clay have also been found.

16

RAJASTHAN

There are very few artefacts of any value to Buddhists and pilgrims in Rajasthan. Two of Ashoka's edicts were found at Bairat (Jaipur district) 85 km from Jaipur. One of them, on a rock still in situ, is a version of the Minor Rock Edict, found in several other places also. The other, on a detached block of granite is unique in its importance, and is now in the collection of the Asiatic Society, Kolkata. Fragments of a pillar and an umbrella on the two terraces of the Bijak-ki-pahadi overlooking the township, the circular chaityagriha, the ruined monastery (which is a restoration of a later period) etc., were found by Alexander Cunnigham, all possibly dating back to the first century AD.

The names of the monuments, which were erected during the reign of the Mauryas at Lal Sote, 95 km from the town of Jaipur, are intact. In about the sixth and seventh centuries AD, Buddhist settlements came up in Kolvi, Binnayaga, and Hathiagor, all in the extreme south of Jhalwar district, which borders Mandasor district in Madhya Pradesh. The rock-cut caves here are off-shoots of the same Buddhist movement, which resulted in the caves at Dhamar.

Buddhism did linger in a few places for a few centuries more. The inscription by the side of the Barkhari gate of the town of Shergarh (in Kota district) records the construction of a Buddhist temple and a monastery to the east of the mountain Kosavardhana, built by the feudal chief Devadatta, in the Vikrama Somavat period (Hindu calendar period corresponding with first century AD).

Another center was in the vicinity of Chittorgarh. On the top of the hill and by the side of the Fath Jamal tank approximately ten portable monolithic votive stupas were found. The words on them were written in characters used in the ninth century AD, one of the stupas is now housed in the National Museum, New Delhi.

The caves, near the village Kolvi (Jhalwar district) have been excavated, out of the precipitous face of a laterite hill with a flat top. Many of them have suffered much on account of natural denudation. The exposed caves are excluding the free-standing stupas, but there is a reason to believe that there are still more caves buried in the area. The majority of the residential caves are generally flat, and house plain cells, oblong or square, with a single door.

General Information

Area: 3,42,239 sq. km

Capital: Jaipur

Neighbouring states or Boundaries: Gujarat, Madhya Pradesh, Uttar Pradesh, Delhi, Haryana, Punjab, Pakistan

Main Towns: Jaipur, Kota, Tonk, Jodhpur, Bikaner, Udaipur, Bhilwara, Sikar, Alwar, Sawai Madhopur, Ajmer, Chittorgarh

Air: Jaipur, Jodhpur, Udaipur

Rail: Main Railway Stations – Jaipur, Jodhpur, Kota, Alwar, Sawai Madhopur

Road: Length – 1,53,734 sq. km

At Binnayaga, nearly 22 caves have been exposed so far. Most of them are monastic abodes of small units, similar to the ones at Kolvi and are of little interest to tourists.

17

SIKKIM

The cultural development and political history of Sikkim has been associated with the historical development of Tibet from the very start. In Tibet, Sikkim was known as 'Den Zong' meaning the 'Valley of Rice'. According to some sources, the name of the state was 'Su' meaning 'new' and 'Him' meaning 'house'. According to some sources again, the word 'Sikkim' is derived from the Sanskrit word 'Sikhim' which means 'crested or mountainous country'.

Whatever the name may mean, it is possible to trace the recorded history of Sikkim from the reign of Srongtsane Gampo in Tibet in the seventh century AD.

Sikkim is blessed by the great Guru Padmasambhava himself who passed through this land in AD 747 while on his way to Tibet, since he had been invited by the King to help propagate Buddhism. However, Buddhism struck roots in Sikkim only in the 17th century, when Gyalwa Lhatsun Chhenpo, a missionary Lama in Tibet, vigorously preached and propagated Dhamma in this region. Born in 1595, in the Kongbhu district of eastern Tibet, Lhatsun Chhenpo focussed on preaching the Dhamma amongst the simple and gentle Lephca people of Sikkim. Having won their confidence, the patron saint of Sikkim, Lahtsun Chhenpo, decided to establish Buddhist temples in order to meet the spiritual needs of the people.

As Tantric Buddhism made its way to Sikkim from Tibet, the culture in this mountainous region developed quickly. The schism in Buddhist sects in Tibet played a vital role in the establishment of the new kingdom headed by Phuntshog Namgyal as the first Chogyal in AD 1641, which ushered Sikkim into a new era of vigorous political, religious, social, and cultural activities under a

◀   This ancient mural painting is a mesmerising combination of Buddhist art ideologies, colour, and devotion

settled government. It was because of this religious fervour and zeal of the Chogyals (Dharam Raja) and the Lamas of different Buddhist sects that a number of religious structures in the form of Tak-phu or rock caves, Gumphas or monasteries, Chortens/mane (stupas), and Mendongs came into being in the state which was much bigger in size, going beyond its present boundaries. Many other secular structures were also constructed, keeping pace with the shift of the capital from one place to another. Some other important Tak-phu or rock caves in Sikkim are Lha-ri-nying-phu, Kah-do-song-phu, Pe-phu, De-chhen-phu, etc. Some of the ancient monasteries in Sikkim which are still today famous centers of Buddhism are Sangachhelling, Dubdi, Pemayangtse, Tashiding, Ralong, Rumtek, Enchey, Labrong, Fodong, Namchi, Singtam, and many others.

There are many old chortens (stupas) throughout the state, but special mention should be made of the Thangwa Rangdol of Tashiding monastery, which is considered to be the holiest of all and the other is in front of the Coronation Throne of Norbugang at Yuksom. The Mendong at Geyzing is believed to be the oldest and longest Mendong that enhances the glory of Sikkim.

Apart from different types of religious structures, the secular and old architectural remains in this state are also noteworthy, including the remains of the first capital at Yuksom known as Tashithenka, Rabdentse the site of the ancient capital of Sikkim, ruins of the capital at Tunlomg, etc.

The monasteries of Sikkim are places of religious discourses, worship, meditation and are the storehouse of many handwritten religious books and manuscripts. The monasteries constitute an important element of Sikkimese cultural heritage.

The monasteries are known as gompa/gonpa, which means a solitary place. Isolation was seen as an aide to meditation, so monasteries were built in remote locations. Tradition maintains that a monastery should look out towards the east to catch the first ray of the rising sun. The building should lie along the long axis of a hill and it is desirable to have a lake in front of the monastery. Following these prescriptions, the sites occupied by monasteries in Sikkim are usually commanding and picturesque. The monastic buildings cluster round the temple used as an assembly hall. The outer detached buildings provide dormitories for the monks. Lining the approach to the monastery are tall prayer flags and chortens (stupa). The temple is referred to as Lhakhang. It is also called Dukhang, which means a meeting place, and Tsuglakhang, which means an academy. A monastery in Sikkim combines all the functions of chapel and school.

Monasteries Around Gangtok City
Enchey Monastery

Situated on a beautiful hilltop near the Gangtok TV tower is the magnificent Nyingmapa monastery of Enchey.

A beautiful story encapsulates the importance of this monastery. Many years ago, a saint called Drubthob Karpo, a resident of Lingding Gangtok, once went to Ralang Monastery, in south Sikkim for learning and practising monastic education. He spent many years learning rituals under the learned Lamas and held the post of Chinyer or General Manager in the monastic administration. One day, a jindag (devotee) from Barfung came to Ralang Monastery to offer prayers through the whole day in the name of his departed family members. However, that day the weather was not good, and the fire in the kitchen was not burning well. Therefore, Chinyer Lama failed in making the morning rice soup (solthuk) and tea in time for the assembly of monks. This displeased the jindag who immediately complained and an argument started. The jindag angrily told the Lama to choose between him and Chinyer Lama. Eventually, the Lamas favoured the jindag and expelled Chinyer from the monastery.

However, that incident was a blessing in disguise for Chinyer. On the way back to Gangtok, the Chinyer Lama made up his mind to meditate in a cave at Mainam Hill above Ralang. It took him a few years to attain the stage of Dubthob or Shidha/Siddha but he also acquired the power to fly. As a sign of his achievement, he laid his footprint on a rock there.

One day, a hunter from Yangang village came across this cave and saw him. He was quite amazed to see him and called him 'Dhubthob Karpo' which means 'White Saint'. The hunter invited the saint to his dwelling house at Yangang to receive his blessings. Thereafter, the saint flew from Mainam Hill and landed at the present monastery site, near Gangtok TV tower.

Afterwards, he built a small shrine at this spot where he spent a few years and later he meditated at the Taktse hilltop. Thereafter, he flew to Dromo in Tibet and then flew to Bhutan.

A hermit called Karma Sherab came to the shrine of Enchey for a retreat. And amazingly after a few years, he also acquired the power to fly and flew back and forth between Gangtok and Pakyong. So, the place became very significant. The saint spent the rest of his life in this shrine. After he passed away, the lineage holders of Dhubthob Karpo, with their profound faith, developed the old shrine into a full-fledged monastery in AD 1840. Fifteen monks lived there and gave the monastery the religious name 'Sang-naga-Rabtnling' which means 'Sacred Stable Place'. In 1908, during the reign of the tenth Chogyal Sidkyong Tulku (1879-1914), the monastery was rebuilt and given its present shape, which is an artistic adaptation of the Chinese Temple of Gyanak Riwo Tsenga.

The monastery performs its annual mask dance on the eve of the Sikkimese Losoong corresponding with the months of December-January. Today, it is a major monastery in Sikkim.

Sang-Ngor Chotshog Monastery

Sang-Ngor Chotshog Monastery, in Rongneck, is the only monastery in the state which belongs to the Sakyapa Sect of Mahayana Tibetan Buddhism. Established in 1961 by His Eminence Luding Khen Rinpoche, Head of the Ngorpa sub-sect of the Sakyapa Sect. It was blessed by HH Sakya Trizin Rinpoche who is the supreme head of the Sakyapa Sect, and subsequently by His Holiness the Dalai Lama. The Lamas in this monastery observe a Summer Retreat called Yarney in the summer. Above this monastery, amidst a lush green forest, is a retreat center maintained by this monastery where there are Lamas who have been meditating for three years and three months.

Dophenling Monastery

Dophenling Monastery situated in Chandmari, Gangtok, is the only Gelugpa/Gelukpa monastery in the state. It is a newly built monastery, which was inaugurated by His Holiness the Dalai Lama in April 2005. The place is called Bod Lha Solsa, which means 'the place where the Tibetan Guardian Deities' are worshipped. The Tibetan community of Gangtok gathers here during their festivals like Losar or the Tibetan New Year, or Trungkar Dhuech, which is the Dalai Lama's birthday, to worship their gods and goddesses by unfurling prayer flags and burning incense. The Tibetan community in Gangtok, under the instruction of His Holiness the Dalai Lama, built a stupa near this monastery for world peace.

Tsuglakhang, the Royal Chapel

Tsuglakhang is situated in the premises of the Palace where all the official ceremonies of the government were held during the reign of the Chogyals of Sikkim, until the merger of Sikkim as a State of the Indian Union, in 1975. It was here that royal ceremonies like the coronation of a new king or the wedding ceremony of a royal family used to take place. Previously, the famous Kagyad Chham (Annual Mask Dance) in winter and a warrior dance called Pangtoed Chham in summer was performed for the guardian deity of Mount Khang-chen-dzonga known as Pang Lhabsol.

However, after the abolition of monarchy, the performance of Pangtoed Chham here was discontinued.

The Buddhist Organisation of Sikkim still observes the Buddhist festivals like Saga Dawa, Drukpa Tshezhi, Guru Trugkar, Lhabab Dhuechhen, and other Mantra recitation ceremonies from time to time.

Sichey Dechen Choling Tamang Monastery

This is a Buddhist monastery belonging to the Tamang Buddhist in the state capital. The full name of this monastery is Tamang Dechen Choling Gonpa, and it was established in April 2005. The monastery performs all Buddhist ceremonies and organises religious programmes from time to time.

Burtuk Uugen Pema Choling' Tamu Monastery

The All Sikkim Gurung Tamu Buddhist Association established this monastery in AD 2000 and His Eminent Gurung Rinpoche Ven. Karma Wangchuk laid down the foundation stone on September 13, 2000. The monastery belongs to the Nyingmapa Sect of northern Buddhism. The structure was started with contributions and donations made by devotees and well-wishers.

The monastery observes all Buddhist festivals. In the future, the monastery will be a center of learning for Gurung Buddhist followers.

Tingkey Gonjang Monastery

Situated in Fatak Bojhogari, near the Tashi View Point, is the Tingkey Gonjang monastery, which was established by HE Tenth Tingkey Ganjang Tulku. The monastery site was blessed by HH Dalai Lama in 1981. This is a Nyingmapa monastery and inside the monastery one can see the idols of Khen-lop Cho-sum and the engraved statues of the 25 disciples of Guru Padmasambhava called Je-bang Nyer-Nga. The full name of this monastery is Ugyen Dongak Chokhorling Gonpa.

Namgyal Institute of Tibetology

The Namgyal Institute of Tibetology on the way to Deorali Chhoedten has a rich collection of rare volumes of Buddhist books and Tibetan texts on diverse subjects like astrology, philosophy, and the like. It's a vast treasure of Lepcha, Tibetan, and Sanskrit manuscripts as well as Buddhist arts and icons, and attracts scholars from all corners of the world.

The foundation stone of this world-renowned institute was laid down by His Holiness the Dalai Lama on February 19, 1957 and was inaugurated by Pandit Jawaharlal Nehru, the then Prime Minister of India on October 1, 1958. The XIth King Sir Tashi Namgyal (1893-1963) and his son Palden Thondhub Namyal offered immense contributions for the establishment of this institute. Without their noble vision and thought, the institute would not have come into existence.

▲ The Namgyal Institute of Tibetology contains rare Buddhist books, arts and Tibetan texts on varied subjects

Dud-Dul Chhoedten

Dud-Dul Chhoedten at Dotabu, Deorali, is one of the most famous attractions both for Buddhist devotees as well as for the tourists in Gangtok. This stupa was built under the supervision of the late most Venerable Tibetan Lama Kyabje Trulshig Rinpoche in 1945-46, in accordance with the prophecy made in 1944 by His Holiness Dudjom Rinpoche, Head of the Nyingmapa sect.

Placed inside the Chhoedten is the complete Mandala of Vijra Kilaya (Dorje Phurpa), one complete set of Kangyur holy books, various rare relics, important Zungs (books containing the Buddha's teachings), and other precious religious articles. This Chhoedten is one of the most

▲ The Dud-Dul Chhoedten subdues the evil spirits on its hillock and houses several important artefacts

sacred stupas in Sikkim. The purpose of erecting this sacred stupa is for subduing evil spirits on this hillock. It is particularly famous as the seat of Kyabje Dodrupchen Rinpoche who is one of the most accomplished Nyingmapa Lamas in the world today. This Chhoedten is surrounded by the monk quarters of Chhoedten Gonpa and Guru Lhakhanng, which houses two huge statues of Guru Padmasambhava.

Guru Kubum Monastery

Guru Kubum Gonpa is located near Deorali Petrol Pump. HE Dzonang Rinpoche (one of the celebrated Nyingmapa Lamas) built this monastery in 1962, under the instruction of His Holiness the Dalai Lama, for world peace. The Government of Sikkim provided the site for this Lakhang. Later, the Lakhang was extended and developed into a small Gonpa under the guidance of Ku-ngo Nyima Zangpo, the highly respected and learned Lama of Nyingmapas. Housed in this monastery are a 100,000 miniature images of Guru Padmasambhava, the Patron Saint of Sikkim.

The Tshechu Puja is performed on the tenth day of every Tibetan month, which is the birthday of Guru Rinpoche. This monastery also houses the magnificent statues of eight different manifestations of Guru Padmasambhava. The monastery is presently called Guru Kubum Gonpa.

Lingdum Zurmang Monastery

HE Zurmang Gharwang Rinpoche, who is the twelfth successive incarnation of Zurmang Gharwang of Kagyudpa sect, founded the Lingdum monastery. The incarnation of Zurmang can be traced as far back as the 14th century, to the time of the Fifth Karmapa Lama Deshin Shegpa (AD 1384-1415). The ground-breaking ceremony was held on the 22nd day of the ninth month in 1992, according to the Tibetan calendar.

This day is considered auspicious as it was on this day that Lord Buddha descended from Tushita (according to a *Jataka* tale, Buddha went to heaven (Tushita) to preach the Dhamma to his mother). The construction was completed and inaugurated in 1999.

The monastery performs attractive Lama dances during religious festivals like Gutor/Gustor in winter.

Rumtek Dharma Chakra Center

Rumtek Dharma Chakra Center located about 24 km from Gangtok, is a center of learning for the Kagyupa Sect of Tibetan Buddhism. The XVI Gyalwa Karmapa Rangjung Rigpe Dorjee founded this monastery in 1962.

In 1959, His Holiness the Sixteenth Gyalwa Karmapa (1923-1981) and his retinue of followers had to leave Tibet after the Chinese invasion. His Majesty, the Eleventh King Sir Tashi Namgyal invited Karmapa Lama to Sikkim. The Karmapa made his seat at old Rumtek Gonpa for a few years. The King offered 74 acres for the establishment of this center to preserve the wealth of his lineage and spiritual treasures.

▲ Author at Rumtek Monastery

The architecture of this four-story building is said to have been based on the original style of the Tshurphu monastery that is in Tibet. Perched high at 5,800 feet, the monastery comprises the main shrine temple, a retreat center, a stupa, a protector's shrine and other establishments of the community, along with a number of other religious institutions.

The Rumtek Monastery possesses some of the world's most unique art pieces, ancient manuscripts and icons, and religious art objects. Behind the main monastery is a small hall where a beautiful jewel studded chorten, which contains the ashes and bones of the Sixteenth Gyalwa Kramapa is displayed. Half a kilometer uphill from the monastery is a hermitage, monks go to for complete seclusion and can meditate for a period up to three years.

Lama dances are performed here during religious festivals like Saga Dawa (birth anniversary of Lord Buddha), Guru Trungkar Tshechu (birth anniversary of Guru Padmasambhava) and Gutor Chham on the eve of the Losar (Tibetan New Year). Being the seat of the Gyalwa Karmapas, the Rumtek Dharma Chakra Center is now the international headquarters of the Kagyupa Sect.

Old Rumtek Monastery

Just half a kilometer away from the Dharma Chakra Center is the original Rumtek monastery, which was found by the fourth Chogyal Gyurmed Namgyal and completed by Lamas in AD 1740 and is regarded as one of the oldest Kagyupa monasteries in Sikkim. Before completion of the construction of the Rumtek Dharma Chakra Center, the Sixteenth Gyalwa Karmapa stayed in this monastery. Karma Chokhor Thubten Ling is the original name of old Rumtek Gonpa.

Buddhist Monasteries – East District

Kathog Monastery (Dorjeden)

Kathog Monastery is located above Pakyong Bazar, East Sikkim. The lineage of saint Kathog Kuntu Zangpo founded it in 1840 A.D. Kathog Lama was one of the three pioneering Lamas who played a part in the coronation of the Phuntshog Namgyal as the first King of Sikkim in AD 1642 at Yuksam, West Sikkim. Kathog Lama founded a small shrine as Kathog Lhakhang at Yuksam in AD 1643. Later, due to damages during the Gorkha war and frequent war tension, his lineage holders moved their religious center to the present place. It follows the Nyingmapa Sect of Buddhism. Now it has become one of the major monasteries in east Sikkim and observes all the major ceremonies with a mask dance.

Pathing Matsang Monastery (Chokhor Yyangtse)

A saint called Trungwang Pema Tsondu built this monastery in 1860 and named it Linkoed Chokhor Yangtse gonpa, since at that time most of the followers lived in the Linkoed village. The present monastery was rebuilt in 1982 after an earthquake. The government offered aid in 2005 to remodel it slightly. It is now renamed Pathing Matsang gonpa since the monastery is properly located on a small hillock of Matsng village within Pathing area. It belongs to the Nyingmapa sect of Buddhism.

Today, it has become one of the major monasteries in East Sikkim and observes all the major ceremonies.

Rinak Monastery (Paljor Phuntsog)

Saint Konchhog Gyaltsen originally founded the Rinak monastery in East Sikkim with a small shrine. Later his lineage holders reestablished it in AD 1841 after the earthquake damaged it. The monastery follows the Drukpa Kagyu lineage and the late Kagyu Tulku was its spiritual head.

It also observes all the major ceremonies.

Buddhist Monasteries – North District

Kabi Monastery (Sanga Dhargyeling)

Kabi monastery is located 25 km from Gangtok on the way to North Sikkim. This monastery earlier was Manilhakhang or Nun monastery built by the public for the purpose of the pujas that were performed regularly. The place was upgraded into a full-fledged monastery in 2003. The monastery belongs to the Nyingma sect of Sikkimese Buddhism and observes all major ceremonies. A famous place of worship called Kabi Longtsok, where the blood brotherhood oath takes place by Bhutia-Lepcha is situated just above it.

Phensong Monastery (Sanga Chhoding)

Phensong Monastery was built on the gentle slope from Kabi to Phodong, and has perhaps one of the best landscapes in the region. This is one of the six biggest monasteries and has the largest number of monks in Sikkim. Lhatsun Jigmed Pawo founded this monastery in AD 1721. When it was destroyed by a fire in 1947, the Lamas had it rebuilt in 1948. The Lamas, with government aid, once again rebuilt it in 1985, when torrential rains destroyed it in 1983.

The monastery belongs to the Nyingmapa sect and observes all the major ceremonies with the annual mask dance.

Phodong Monastery

Phodong Monastery is a major Kangyupa sect monastery in northern Sikkim. The monastery was actually founded by the fourth King Gyurmed Namgyal but unfortunately, he passed away in 1734. However, the Lamas with a support of the people completed the monastery in AD 1740. When an earthquake struck and destroyed the monastery, the Lamas rebuilt the monastery in AD 1977, made it bigger with financial assistance from the government along with their own contributions.

The main festival is the annual mask dance fair in the winter, i.e. December and January.

Labrang Monastery (Palden Phuntshog Phodrang)

Labrang Monastery located a few kilometres away from Phodang Gonpa is one of the important monasteries of the Nyingmapa lineage in northern Sikkim. It was founded by Prince Rigzin Chhenpo, the son of the eighth ruler Sikyong Namgyal (1819-1874) in 1844. Records reveal that he installed a precious bronze statue of Karma Guru (presently seen in the shrine on the top floor). Its walls are adorned with life-like frescoes depicting Buddhist legends. A major renovation project was undertaken in 1978 with government aid. Its architecture is unique, with the Rinchen Surgye or eight-pointed diamond symbolising the indestructible, and is therefore the only monastery of its kind in Sikkim.

The monastery observes all the major Buddhist festivals with a mask dance.

Ringyim Rigzin Choling Monastery

This monastery is located above Mangan Bazaar, the North District headquarters and is a Lepcha monastery and follows Nyingmapa Sect of Buddhism. It was built in 1852 during the reign of seventh Chhogyal Trsgphud Namgyal (1785-1864). The monastery was damaged by an earthquake in 1981 and renovated in 1985 with government aid.

It also observes all the major ceremonies throughout the year.

Tingbung Rigzin Tharling Monastery

Tingbung Rigzin Tharling Gonpa is located in Tingbung village in upper Dzongu and follows the Nyingmapa sect of Sikkimese Buddhism. It was built in 1912 by a monk called Lama Tambi.

It celebrates all the major ceremonies with an annual mask dance called the Drankmar Chham in winter.

Tholung Monastery (Rigzin Chhodubling)

This monastery is located in the remotest part of upper Dzongu, and is one of the most sacred monasteries in Sikkim.

The Fifth Lhatsun Pema Dechen Gyatso built it in AD 1789. It follows the Nyingmapa sect of Buddhism.

The monastery possesses ancient holy texts, invaluable art and artefacts, which had been brought here in AD 1788. It is said that the Gorkha invasion from Nepal had caused havoc and fear among the Buddhist monks in the west, during the reign of Chogyal Tenzing Namgyal (1769-1793). Therefore, Lama Gyatso transferred all the precious collections, valuable texts, religious objects and many other things that belonged to former Lamas from Dubde and Sangag Choling monasteries in the west, to Tholung via Yangang Gonpa, in the south.

The religious treasures kept in the monastery are taken out for sunning and cleaning once every three years during the Kamisil Ceremony, under the supervision of the Ecclesiastical Affairs Department, Government of Sikkim. The present monastery was reconstructed in 1980, since the earlier monastery was dilapidated. The route to this monastery diverts from Mangan.

Sheep Gyer Monastery (Kunzang Choling)

This monastery is located in one of the most difficult and hilly areas of North Sikkim and came into existence in AD 1900. It follows the Nyingmapa sect of Buddhism. The present building was rebuilt in 1985 with government aid. Now it has become one of the major monasteries in north Sikkim and observes all major ceremonies throughout the year.

Tsunthang Monastery (Rigzin Choling)

The location of the Tsunthang Monastery is associated with historical importance and religious significance. During the eighth century AD the Great Guru Padamsambhava, the founder of Tibetan Buddhism, visited Tsunthang to subjugate a mischievous demon called Duetsen who had been reluctant to come under the Guru's spiritual domain. The people believe that the Guru Rinpoche personally consecrated the present site where later Lepcha Buddhist followers built a monastery in AD 1788. The present monastery was built in 1968 during the reign of the last King Chhogyal Palden Thondub Namgyal. The monastery follows the Nyingmapa sect and performs all major Buddhist ceremonies. As per the *Dejong Ney-yig* text, the present day Tsunthang is known as Tsemo Rinchen thang (top precious plain) which is marked by a sacred rock called Lhe-do or Ney-do by Buddhists and bears the footprint of Guru Padmasambhava.

Lachung Monastery (Samten Chholing)

The Lachung Monastery in north Sikkim was built in the Iron Dog year corresponding to AD 1850 and remodelled in 1983. The Nyingmapa sect of Buddhism is followed here. The monastery observes all major ceremonies with an annual mask dance in winter. Today, the Lachung monastery is one of the major monasteries of north Sikkim.

Lachen Monastery (Ngodub Chholing)

The Lachen Monastery is located 28 km above Tsunthang Sub-Division office. It was built in AD 1858 and follows the Nyingmapa sect of Buddhism. It was fully reconstructed in 1977 and the number of monks increased with time. Now it is recognised as one of the major monasteries in north Sikkim. Today, the monastery functions under the guidance of His

Eminence Lachen Gomchen Rinpoche.

The monastery observes all major ceremonies with the annual mask dance.

Thangu Monastery

The Thangu Monastery is a branch of the Lachen Monastery and is located 29 km from its parent monastery on the way to Guru Dongmar Lake. It was earlier a small Lhakhang (temple) built in the twentieth century. However, in 2003, the locals rebuilt the temple and made it bigger with government assistance. The history of this monastery is unique. In the summer, the people of Lachen shift to Thangu, which is at a higher altitude than Lachen. They carry out cultivation and observe ceremonies in Thangu Monastery. When winter approaches, they return to Lachen. This practice exists till this day.

Guru Dongmar Holy Lake

The Guru Dongmar Lake is situated in the lap of Mount Khang-Chhen Gyao, which was named Guru-Dongma (Guru's first visiting place in Dejong), after Guru Padmasambhava's visit to this place in AD 700. Guru Padmasambhava was the founder of Tibetan Buddhism and is regarded as a celebrated Buddhist saint of that era. As per religious history, Guru Padmasambhava visited this Lake before entering the hidden land of Domojong (Sikkim). He recognised this Lake as a place of worship where the famous Dorje Nyima or Chhoedten Nyima performed his meditation. This lake is one of the 109 sacred lakes in Sikkim and is a landmark for the northern door, for entering the hidden land of Domojong. HE Lachen Rinpoche wrote that this lake used to be clear like the sky about 40 years ago and one could see straight down to the bottom of the lake. Some devotees had been fortunate to see their future forecast in the lake. It holds the power to give a pregnant woman the boon of a son. Unfortunately, the colour of the lake has gradually become white as people began defiling it. It is an indisputably powerful Buddhist place of worship. It is protected under the Place of Worship (Special provision) Act 1991, Government of India.

Tsho Lhamu Lake

Tsho Lhamu Lake is located a few kilometers away from Guru Dongmar Lake. It is worshipped by the yak herders as the Goddess Lake. 'Lhamu' means 'Goddess'; this beautiful lake in northern Sikkim is a source of the River Tista. People can enjoy the beauty of watching the water change its colour, which it does frequently.

Buddhist Monasteries – South District

Sharchhog Beyphug

The holy cave in Sharchhog Beyphug lies in Sangmo village in south Sikkim. The name literally means Hidden Cave of Eastern Direction. It is a vast cavern, reputed to extend by bifurcation to both Mount Tendong and Mainam. Its height varies from 5-100 feet. As described in the text *Deyjong Neyig*, the clues of the sacred treasures in this holy land are hidden in this cave. The mystic patterns on the cave walls and roof bear religious significance ascribed to various deities and ritual objects. The devotees often commence their pilgrimage from this cave, as it is the starting point for a pilgrimage tour in Beyul Demojong. It is said that one can cleanse one's external negativity here.

Doling Monastery

Doling Monastery is located on a small hillock in the middle of a jungle, about 6 km south from Rabongla baazar. Lama Rigzin Loyang founded this monastery in the Earth-Dog year of the 12th Rabjung cycle year corresponding to AD 1718. The monastery follows the Nyingmapa sect of Shargter or Eastern Treasure. The Mongolian ruler Juggar's invasion of Tibet in AD 1718 led to the persecution of the Nyingamapa sect and as a result, most of the Nyingmapa saints left Tibet and took asylum in the southern hidden lands.

In the same year, Lama Ugen Dorjelingpa and his son Rigzin Loyang also left Tibet and entered Sikkim as per Lungten or the spiritual guidance imparted by Chogyal Terdag Lingpa (1646-1714) of Tibet.

As per the written record of the Lama Jigme Pawo (1682-1729), Dorje Lingpa and his son first came to Sangag Choling monastery in the west and met with Lama Jigme Pawo, who at the time became regent to the minor Gyurmed Namgyal (1707-1734) the Fourth consecrated ruler. Later, they moved eastward, and found the area which is at present the site of the Doling Gonpa, and as per a prediction they made it their seat permanently. Shortly thereafter, Dorje Lingpa went back to Tibet and his son Lama Rigzin Loyang started building a small monastery. On its completion, his father arrived from Tibet, consecrated the monastery, and composed a prayer manual to worship the local Guardian Spirits and instructed his son to foster his lineage. Dorje Lingpa stayed in Sikkim for a short period and proceeded to Bumthang (Bhutan) where, he had sent one of his younger sons for a spiritual mission.

The monastery had been rebuilt in three different periods – in 1840, 1940-50 and finally in 1984. The reasons were either dilapidation or earthquake damages. There are many sacred objects of worship in the monastery. Dorje Lingpa laid his footprint on the rock which is preserved by the Lamas till this day. Today, the descendants of Lama Rigzing Loyang are the custodians of the monastery.

The monastery observes all the major festivals.

Ralang Karma Rabtenling Monastery

Ralang monastery is the first monastery of the Kangyupa lineage built by Sikkim's fourth ruler Chogyal Gyurmed Namgyal in the Iron Dog year of 12th Rabjung cycle year, which corresponds to AD 1730. Out of distress caused by internal conflicts, the fourth ruler of Sikkim, Chogyal Gyurmed Namgyal (1707-1734), disguised himself as a religious mendicant and went on a pilgrimage to Tibet. No one in that country suspected his royal origin, until he came before HH Changchhub Dorje, the 12th Karmapa (1703-1732), who recognised him instantly and gave him a warm welcome. The King was surprised and felt uneasy, as he was totally unprepared and had nothing to offer to such a dignified Lama. Therefore, he promised to the Karmapa Lama that he would build a monastery of his sect in Sikkim and would provide Jindags (donor and devotees) to the monastery.

After his return from Tibet, he built a monastery at Ralang in AD 1730 and offered Bhutia and Lepcha village that lie in the regions between River Tista and Rangit namely Barfung, Lingdam, Burmiok, Temi, Sangmoo, Yangang, and Lingmoo as Jindag for the newly built monastery. On its completion, the Rabney (consecration) ceremony was said to have been performed by the Karmapa himself from Tibet. Amazingly, some Rabney grains fell on the roof of the monastery at Ralang, which was witnessed by all present there. The devotion and faith had taken root in the people's mind and soon such monasteries spread in other parts of Sikkim.

In the beginning of the 19th century, an incarnation of one Omje Lama of Shamarpa lineage was born in the family of Chhoedten Kal-on in the village Barfung, he was later enthroned as the Head of Lamas of Ralang Gonpa by 14th Karmapa Thegchog Dorje.

During this Lama's tenure, the monastery was reconstructed and made bigger. The number of monks increased with the development of a new monastery and once again, the Rabney ceremony was performed from Tshorphu, Tibet, but this time it was performed by the 14th Karmapa Thegchog Dorje (1798-1863). On this occasion, many auspicious signs were observed, such as rainbows and the appearance of a vulture that circumambulated the monastery three times and thereafter flew northeast towards Mainam Hill.

In the course of time, an earthquake damaged the monastery resulting in several cracks on the wall and therefore the present Lamas, reconstructed the monastery with Government aid, in 1981, and later in 2003.

The monastery observes all the major ceremonies with the annual mask dance in winter.

Ralang Plchen Choling Monastery (New Monastery)

This is another Dharma Chakra Center of the Kangyupa Lineage after the Rumtek Dharma Chakra Center which was established by his Eminence Goser Gyaltsab Rinpoche in 1995 at Ralang, in south Sikkim. It is located just above the old Ralang Gonpa.

The sacred Mahakala Dance is held every year in November. The Ralang Monastery plays host to an annual festival, known as Pang Lhabsol or the worship of Mount Khan-chen-dzonga. Chham masked dances are also organised every year on the fifteenth day of the seventh month and on the twenty-ninth day of the tenth month of the Tibetan calendar.

Serdub Choling Monastery

Serdub Choling Monastery is located above Alley Bhaichung Stadium, Namtse. The former Serdub Dungzing Jigma Wangchuk Rinpoche, who contributed to the building of a famous Sangdog Palri structure at Pemayangtse Monastery, established this monastery in 1967. The monastery observes all the Buddhist holy ceremonies throughout the year. Presently his son Ven. Serdub Dungzing Lodoe Chophel is the custodian of this monastery.

Samdruptse Guru Statue

Samdrubtse is situated above Namchi Bazaar, the district headquarters of south Sikkim.

Guru Padmasambhava was the founder of Tibetan Mahayana Buddhism and blessed this Holy Hidden Land in the eighth century AD. During his travels in Sikkim, he had concealed a great deal of major and minor treasures in its sacred places so that Dharma flourished and the Hidden Land remained prosperous.

To repay their gratitude, Dr. Pawan Kumar Chamling, the Chief Minister of Sikkim has built the world's tallest statue of Guru Padmasambhava at Samdruptse. It is said that Lama Nga-dag Sempa Chhenpo (one of the three Pioneer Lamas) while opening the southern door of this Hidden Land in the 17th century, entered via Darjeeling and Namtse. During his short stay at Namtse, he climbed Samdruptse Hill where he wished that Dharma would flourish in this Hidden Land. Later, his wishes were indeed fulfilled and the Hill was therefore called 'Samdub-Tse'. 'Samdruptse' literally means 'Wish fulfilling Summit'.

Located on a majestic hilltop, this wonderful statue can be seen from such far-off places like Kalimpong, Darjeeling, and Gyalshing. The funds for the construction of this statue were provided by the Department by Tourism, Government of Sikkim.

Khado Sangphug Holy Cave

Sikkim is blessed with four holy caves that are situated in four different directions of Tashidhing Hill. Khadosangphug is located to the south of Tashidhing on the other side of the river Rangit between Jorethang and Legship. Guru Padmasambhava blessed this cave in the eighth century AD when he visited Sikkim. On the roof of this cave is a clear impression of Guru Rinpoche's hat, into which one can place one's head. Outside the cave, there is a famous hot spring called Phur Tshachu which is renowned for curing various illnesses. Between November to March, people from all over the Himalayas come here to bathe.

Buddhist Monasteries – West District

Dubde Monastery

At a distance of about 3 km to the north-east of Yoksam valley is situated the Dubde (the Hermit's Cell) Monastery. The First ruler Chogyal Phuntshog Namgyal (1604-1670) founded this monastery in AD 1647 for the patron saint Gyalwa Lhatsun Chhenpo (1595-1652). Later it was fully reconstructed by the third Lhatsun Jigme Pawo in the Water Rabbit year (1723) during the reign of Chogyal Gyurmed Namgyal (1707-1733). The precious Debri painting of Maha Shidhas of Sikkim, the lineages of high Lamas, Guru Tshog-Shing, and various protecting deities which embellished the inner wall were painted by Sikkim's famous painter Lhari Rinzin, or Temi Lharipa, in 1945.

The monastery belongs to the Nyingmapa Sect of Tibetan Buddhism. However, Dubde Monastery today stands as the first monastery of Sikkim and is famed for its old mural paintings.

'Dubde' means 'the retreat'. The trail to Dubde winds through lush green forests high above the village, offering scenic backdrops and impressive views of the mountain. For bird watchers, an early morning or late afternoon visit is particularly rewarding.

Built in stone, this two-storied, south-facing structure is tapering upwards and topped by a roof of iron sheet with projecting eaves and surmounted by a small bell-shaped dome called 'Gyaltshon'. The interior surface is lavishly painted with the figures of various deities, Cheresi, Chakdor and Dolma occupy a very conspicuous position along with the pictorial wheel of life and four guardian kings of the vestibule's entrance doorway. The nave ends with an altar that contains the images of Buddha, Padmasambhava, and other ritual texts that are preserved at the end of two aisles.

Today the monastery is protected by the Archaeological Survey of India as a cultural heritage of Sikkim.

Sang-Ngag Choling Monastery

'Sang Choling' means the 'island of esoteric teaching'. Sang-Ngag Choling monastery is said to be founded by Lama Lhatsun Chhenpo during the reign of the first King Phuntsog Namgyal (1604-1670) but the date and year of its founding has not been specifically recorded.

However, as per other records found in the Gazetteer of Sikkim, it was commenced under the direction of Lhatsun Chhempo during the reign of the first King and brought to completion at the time of the second King Tensung Namgyal, by Lama Kunzang Jigme or Mikyoed Dorje who came from Tibet and is said to have succeeded Lhatsun Chhemop as his incarnation. As per records in the Gazetteer of Sikkim, Lama Lhatsun Chhenpo went back to Tibet, probably in 1648.

After Lama Lhatsun and Chogyal Phuntsog returned from Tibet, they proceeded to demarcate the Rabdentse site for building a palace in the future and then they built many places of worship such as the Golden Stupa, Bodhi Stupa, and built a small shrine called Tsangkhang at the west side of the present Pemayangtse. At the same time, Lama Lhatsun consecrated many sites in the surrounding areas and thereafter proceeded to Tibet. Later, he passed away at Sheldrak Monastery in the Water Dragon year which corresponds to AD 1652. Therefore, the Sang-Ngag

Chholing was probably founded by Lhatsun in AD 1649-50. However, Lama Jigmed Pawo reestablished this monastery in the Wood House year, i.e. AD 1714 during the reign of the third King Chhogyal Chhagdo Namgyal.

The monastery observes all the major ceremonies through the year.

Pemayangtse Monastery

Pemayangtse Monastery is situated in Pelling, on a hilltop, at an altitude of 6,500 feet. It commands a panoramic view of the Himalayan range, the surrounding hills, and countryside and an impressive view of Khan-chen-dzonga.

It was originally a small shrine called Tsangkhang built by Lhatsun Chenpo on the spot west of the present monastery almost at the same time of the founding of Sang-Ngag Chholing monastery. Later, Chhogyal Chhagdor Namgyaland Lama Khenchhen Rolpai Dorje (first head Lama of Pemayangtse Gonpa) shifted this Lhakhang to the present site and reestablished it in AD 1705. They established the new monastery with the enrollment of 108 monks from families of pure descent after having enrolled the King himself as the first member. The Pemayangtse was specially built for the pure celibate monks called 'dra-tsang' and to its Lama was reserved the honour of anointing and crowning the Chhogyal during the time of the Monarchy's rule. The monastery was remodelled with government aid in 1969.

The main attraction of this monastery is Sangdokpalri, the Guru Rinpoche's Heavenly abode, which is a beautiful wooden masterpiece, complete with rainbows, angels and a whole panoply of Buddhas and Bodhisattavas, designed and made by the late Dngzin Rinpoche in 1971.

The main festival observed here is Guru Drakmar Chham in the winter, some time between February and March. During those two days, religious dances are performed and pilgrims come from all over Sikkim to attend the ceremonies. The dance ends on the third day with the unfurling of the Ghyo-ku, a gigantic embroidered Buddhist scroll, and the devotees bend down in homage.

Khachoedpalri Lake

Khachoedpalri Holy Lake lies in the lap of a beautiful hill above Rimbi River in the west of the Peiling bazaar. 'Khadchoedpalri' means 'Mountain of Blissful Heaven'. Legend has it that this place was once a grazing ground, abound with stinging nettle. Native Lepchas had many uses for the bark of the nettle. One day, a Lepcha couple was peeling off the bark of the nettle, and saw a pair of conch shells appear in the sky and enter the ground. The ground shook violently and a spring of water engulfed the entire ground and turned into a huge lake. As per the *Nesol* text, this was recognised as the abode of Tshomen Gyalmo or the Chief Protective Nymph of the Dharma as blessed by Goddess Tara. Native Buddhists believe that the shape of the lake is a footprint, the blessing of Goddess Tara. Khachoedpalri has become an important pilgrim as well as tourist destination in Sikkim.

Khachoedpalri Lake is considered to be one of the sacred lakes in the state, both by the Buddhists and the Hindus. The lake remains hidden under rich forest cover, and the birds do not permit even a single leaf to float on the Khachoedpalri's surface. There is a motorable road from Pemayangtse right up to the Lake.

Tashiding Monastery

Tashiding Hill, from a religious point of view, is the navel of all the holy places in Sikkim. Tashiding Monastery is built on top of a heart-shaped hill with the sacred Khang-chen-dzonga in the backdrop. It is nestled on the top of the hill that looms up between the Rathong river and the Rangit river and is surrounded by a profusion of prayer flags that flutter in the air.

There are also many chortens dedicated to some Chogyals and some religious personalities of Sikkim. The saint Padmasambhava made his miraculous visit to this hill in the eighth century AD along with his retinue of followers and recognised it to be the heart of the holy places in Sikkim.

Later in the 17th century, three great Lamas from Tibet met at Yoksam, and visited Tashiding hill to unveil this most sacred place. When they got there, a brilliant light radiated from Mount

Khang-chen-dzonga and hit Tashiding hill and divine music was heard. This miraculous phenomena was witnessed by many people. Later, the second Lama Ngadag Sempa Chhenpo moved his seat from Yoksam to Tashiding and built a small Lhakhang on this hill known as Jhampa Lhakhang in 1651 A D.

The monastery was reconstructed by Panding Ongmu, the stepsister of Chhogyal Chhagdor Namgyal, under the spiritual guidance of Lama Ngadag Rinchhen Gon, in AD 1716 who gave it a new name – Chhogyal Lhakhang. When an earthquake struck, the Lamas rebuilt it in 1995 with government aid. At present, the monastery has 60-70 monks and it follows the Jhang-Ten lineage of the Nyingmapa sect.

The most important festival in this Gonpa is Bhumchhu, a sacred holy water ceremony which is held annually and attracts a lot of pilgrims and devotees from Bhutan and other adjoining areas. Lama Ngadag Sempa Chhepo introduced Bhumchhu ceremony in the 17th century with a gift of a precious vase that was brought from Tibet. The most holy chorten in Sikkim is at Tashiding. So sacred is it, that the mere act of beholding it would cleanse all sins; its full name is Thong-Warang-Drol (saviour by mere sight).

A vase here is said to contain the precious relic of the Mythical Buddha 'Wod-Srung', the precursor of Buddha Shakya Muni. Because of this, this vase is a sacred object for pilgrims. The Lamas built many other sacred stupas around the chorten Thong-Warang-Drol for the protection and prosperity of this holy land.

Later, the Lamas, according to the order and at the expense of donations, built Mendang around Tashiding Chhodtens. The Mendang bears mystic charms of the protective divinities of Lamaism and the picture of the protective divinities are carved into stone blocks.

Today, the Chhodtens and Mendang monuments have become part of the most important religious heritage structures of Sikkim, as well as of the Himalayas.

Yoksam Norbugang Coronation Throne

As per a prophecy in the religious text, three Great Lamas of Tibet entered the Hidden Land of Beyul Demojong through three different directions – North, South and West. The three Lamas met at this auspicious site called Norbugang and subsequently consecrated the Chogyal Phuntshog Namgyal from Gangtok as the first enthroned ruler of Sikkim in AD 1642. Thereafter, by collecting virgin soil and stones from different parts of Sikkim, they constructed the sacred stupa of Yoksam Tashi Wodbar Chhodten.

As proof of this historic event, one can still see the seats of the four spiritual brothers known as Trulpe Naljor Chedzhi Zhugtri. The three Great Lamas who came to Yuksam were Lhatsun Namkha Jigme or Gyalwa Lhatsun Chhenpo, Ngadag Sempa Chhenpo, and Kathog Kuntu Zangpo. 'Yuksam' in Lepcha language means 'three lamas'. Yuksam Norbugang is also blessed with the footprint of Lhatsun Chhenpo on a small rock near the Chhodten. Chhogyal Phuntsog Namgyal built his palace at the Tashi Tenka hill rock and thereafter initiated the beginnings of modern administration in Sikkim.

Kathog Holy Lake

Kathog Tsho is a holy lake blessed by Lama Kathog Kuntu Zangpo. It is said to be a Soul Lake or La-Tsho of Lama Kathog Kuntu Zangpo. The lake is near Yuksam Nobugang Coronation Throne and legend has it that in the ancient days, the colour of the water in this lake would change according to the luck and fortune of the person who looked at it. The Lamas perform the Trusol or purification ceremony, every year so that the Lake retains its sanctity.

In recent years, Kyabje Yangthang Rinpoche, for the benefit of devotees living here, restored the Kathog Hosel ling Lakhang on the hill rock called Mandalgang, which was the site of the ruins of the Kathog Lhakhang built by Kathog Lama in AD 1643, but unfortunately the fortunes of this kingdom declined during the Gorkha war. The monastery is located near the Holy Lake. On the

General Information

Area: 7,096 sq. km

Capital: Gangtok

Boundaries: West Bengal;

Countries – Bhutan, China, and Nepal

Chief Languages: Lepcha, Bhutia, Hindi, Nepali, and Limbu

Main Towns: Gangtok, Namchi, Gyalshing, Mangan, Pemayangtse. Lichen, Yuthang

Airport: Gangtok

Rail: Nearest railway stations are Siliguri (114 km), Jalpaiguri (125 km)

opposite hill called Langchhen Tse, another similar Lhakhang is revived as Ngadag Changchhubling Lhakhang by Rinpoche on the site of the ruins of Lhakhang Marpo, which was built by Lama Nagdag Sempa Chhenpo in the same year.

Buddhism is the official state religion of Sikkim. This small state is quite close to Tibet, and is dotted with gonpas/monasteries. The best way to visit the monasteries which are in remote places, is to hire private transport.

18

TAMIL NADU

The Tamil country had come under the influence of Buddhism via Andhra Pradesh, during Emperor Ashoka's reign. The earliest inscriptions in Tamil Nadu belong to the third century BC and are written in the Brahmi script of the time, on the walls of the natural caves in the districts of Madurai and Tirunelveli. It is learnt from these inscriptions that it was Ashoka and his son Mahendra, who may have introduced Buddhism in Tamil Nadu. In his Rock Edict 3, Ashoka says that his Dhammavijaya prevailed on the border kingdoms of the Cholas and Pandyas, but it was his son Mahendra who was responsible for the introduction of Buddhism in Tamil Nadu and Sri Lanka.

Buddhism in Tamil Nadu enjoyed a long spell, right from the early Christian era till the late medieval period. The reason for this appears to be the existence of several important port towns along the coast, which perhaps facilitated not only trade and transport, but also religious propagation. The glorious epoch of this religion was well recorded in the ancient Tamil literature, in *Manimekalai* and *Silappadikaram*. The *Mahavamsa* mentions that King Duttagamini (101-77 BC) invited monks and kings from this region to witness the construction of the Mahastupa in Sri Lanka.

According to historians, Buddhism began to make an impact on Tamil Nadu only in the third century AD. During the period from the third to the sixth centuries AD, Buddhism had spread widely in Tamil Nadu and won the patronage of the rulers. The remains of a Buddhist monastery excavated at Kaveripattinam, which could be assigned to the fourth century AD, is believed to be the earliest archaeological relic of Buddhism in Tamil Nadu. The major urban centers of Kanchi, Kaveripattinam, Uraiyur, and Madurai were not only centers of Buddhism, but were also important centers for learning Pali.

The Tamil Buddhist monks of South India used Pali in preference to Tamil in their writings. This is because the Buddha spoke in Magadi Prakrit (Pali) which was considered to be the sacred language of the Buddhists. It was at this time that Tamil Nadu gave some of its greatest scholars (Theravada and Mahayana) to the Buddhist world.

Tamil Nadu boasted of outstanding Buddhist monks, who had made remarkable contributions to Buddhist thought and learning. Three of the greatest Pali scholars of this period were Buddhaghosa, Buddhadatta, Dhammapala and all three of them were honoured in Tamil kingdoms. Buddhaghosa made a remarkable contribution to Buddhism in Sri Lanka. He studied Buddhist precepts at the Mahavihara in Anuradhapura.

The sixth century Tamil Buddhist work *Manimekalai* by Sattanar, is perhaps the most famous such text in Tamil Nadu. It is a work expounding the doctrines and propagating the values of Buddhism. The interaction between Tamil Nadu and Sri Lankan monks finds mention in *Manimekalai*, which is set in the Tamil towns of Kaveipumpattinam, Kanchi, and Vanchi.

There is mention of the presence of wandering monks from Sri Lanka in Vanchi, which was the capital of the Chera kings of Tamil Nadu. The Chinese traveller, Hiuen–Tsang, wrote that there were around 300 Sri Lankan monks in the monastery in the southern sector of Kanchipuram.

The situation in Tamil Nadu, however began to change towards the beginning of the seventh century AD when the rise of Vaishnavism and Shaivism posed a serious challenge to Buddhism. These religions wielded a significant influence over the people, and soon the worship of Shiva and Vishnu began to gain prominence. Buddhism came under attack when they began to lose the popular support and patronage of the rulers. Buddhism turned to Sri Lanka and assimilated with the Buddhist population there.

During the Chola period (AD 850-1250), Buddhism had been on the wane, except in a few centers populated by Buddhists and boasting of its culture. The Pandya King Rajasimha II (AD 900-920) is said to have granted gifts to Buddhists and Jains alike. The

Chola king Virarajendra (AD 1063-1070) was also a patron of Buddhism.

Today, the Palk Strait which lies between Tamil Nadu and Sri Lanka, is seen as a divider, separating two different distinct ethnicities, religions, cultures and political entities but Tamil Nadu and Sri Lanka once enjoyed very close ties. During the early period, the Palk Strait was not seen as a divider, but a unifier. At that time, Buddhism was the bridge between Sri Lanka and Tamil Nadu.

Several artefacts dating back centuries have been found in the districts of Arcot, Kanchipuram, Salem, and Thanjavur.

Chakrapalli

Chakrapalli is located 15 km north-east of Thanjavur. The name is apparently a derivative of the combination of two words 'chakra' and 'palli', which perhaps means that a temple glorifying the Wheel of Dharma had existed in this village. An icon of Buddha is found preserved in the Tamil University Museum, which was taken from Papanasam, near Chakrapalli. Its style and workmanship indicates that it was made during the Chola period.

There are villages like Budhalur, 16 km north-west of Thanjavur and Buddhagiri near Budhalur, whose names suggest a close connection with colonies of Buddhists. Budhalur, a combination of two words, 'Buddha' and 'ur', which means 'settlement', and Buddhagiri, made up of 'Buddha' and 'giri', meaning the mound or hill, although there is no hill as such as the name indicates. It might notionally indicate some kind of an elevation resembling the stupa or vihara in Budhalur and Budhagiri.

Nagapattinam

One of the important centers of Buddhism was Nagapattinam, an emporium on the east coast. All the Buddhist edifices, which for a long time adorned it, have been swept away. The uprooted remnants, in the form of hoards of bronzes, coupled with inscriptional references and short but significant notes made by foreign writers conjure the vision of a busy international port with its different quarters nurturing their own cosy places of worship, built in their native architectural styles.

The multi-storeyed Pagoda (90 feet high) reported by Walter Elliot in 1846 at Nagapattinam serves as a classical example of a non-Indian Buddhist monument constructed for the benefit of Chinese monks during the period of the ruler Xian Chun in AD 1267. However, the bronzes are found in different hoards, one near the Puduveli Gopuram itself. Numbering about 350, they range from the early Chola to Vijaynagara tradition and represent Buddha, Lokanatha, Shadaksharo, Loksvara, Maitreya, Tara, Jambhala, Vasudhara, arhats and votive stupas of diverse shapes, some in curious forms.

Tiruchirapalli District
Puducherry

The occurrence of many Buddha images from AD 900-1200 in and around Puducherry indicates that this area flourished as an important center of Buddhism at least in this period. The noteworthy facts are that almost all the places where the Buddha statues have been found were also found Chinese and South East Asian potteries datable to AD 900-1300. Arikametu, the famous trading station on the east coast of India, yielded many Chinese potteries in addition to the pottery and other materials brought from Italy and other western countries. The Chinese celadon wares found at Arikametu, characteristic of the Sung and Yuan Lung Chuan wares, may be

General Information

Area: 1,30,058 sq. km

Capital: Chennai

Boundaries: Kerala, Karnataka, Andhra Pradesh, Puducherry; Sea – Bay of Bengal and Indian Ocean;

Country – Sri Lanka.

Chief Language: Tamil

Main Towns: Chennai, Coimbatore, Madurai, Vellore, Salem, Thanjavur, Thoothukudi (Tuticorin), Tirunelveli, Uddagamandalam, Nagercoil

Air: Chennai, Madurai, Tiruchirapally, Coimbatore, Salem

Rail: Length – 4181 km; Main Railway Stations – Chennai, Madurai, Tiruchirapally, Coimbatore, Salem

Road: Length – 150,095 km

ascribed to circa AD 900-1100. The co-existence of the Chinese/ South East Asian materials and the Buddha images at Manappattu, Kirmampakkam, Arikametu (Ariyan Kuppam), Puducherry, etc. suggest a close relation between them.

It may not be erroneous to presume that the Buddhist vestiges found in this locality are either made for, or influenced by, the merchants who came to these trading stations for trade purposes from Chinese/South East Asian countries and settled there either permanently, or only for a while.

19

WEST BENGAL

It is not definitely known when Bengal first received the message of Sakyamuni. Literary evidence, mostly Chinese and Tibetan inscriptions, illustrations in Buddhist manuscripts, mostly from the Pala period, and several sculptures attest to the existence of numerous flourishing establishments – stupas, monasteries, and temples – from the 5-12 century AD. But coming to the actual structural remains, one is confronted with the extreme scarcity of archaeological evidence. Most such remains, especially those which were situated on the plains, were gradually denuded and levelled under by periodical floods and the farmer's plough. Only a few, situated on high lands and above the level of the floods, mostly in the northern and eastern Bengal (now included in Bangladesh), survive.

By the fifth century AD, Buddhism was firmly established throughout Bengal. We get a glimpse of a number of centers that flourished during this period, apart from Chandraketugarh during which a scaling was produced with the Buddhist creed written in Gupta characters. This particular site yielded, among other things, a stupa, and a bronze figure of Maitreya. This particular site is a brick structure in mud with a central sanctuary, four cells in the corner, and four chambers, open in the front between the cells, all built on a moulded plinth, the latter, having inconspicuous offsets at intervals.

The fragmentary image of Vajrasattva, which is now in the Khiching museum, is said to have been part of this structure. The structure, known as Kukudagarh, is a plain square temple of granite. Inside it was found a small image of Buddha in the bhumi-sparsha-mudra, now shifted to the Khiching museum. Among the architectural pieces lying in the compound of the museum are a few carved lintels with figures of Buddha and Lokesvara, besides the stone masonry stupa which was originally located within the village to the south-west of the Thakurani compound. Besides the images, there are several Buddhist images lying both inside and outside the Khiching museum. They include images of the Buddha, Arapachana, Manjushri, Vasudhara, Jambhala, Tara, Lokesvara, and Vajrasattva.

The other structures found here are brick structures called Itamundia. The central cell served as a shrine. The lintel has in its center, the figure of the Buddha in bhumi-sparsha-mudra seated on a visva-padma above a Vajra. Within the sanctum was found a life-sized stone image of Buddha (now in Khiching Museum) in the bhumi-sparsha-mudra, on a visva-padma supported by lions, below the Bodhi tree. Square plinths of several votive stupas together with a circular one, all made of bricks, were found in front of the structure.

The remains of the 11th century AD. Sankhurajargarh, a place in the region of Rayabhanja, comprises a small brick sanctuary and a brick oblong mandapa with stone pillars, both now in the last stages of decay.

One of the important centers of Buddhism in the Gupta period was Tamralipti, a modern taluk (district Mindapur), also the principal emporium to which flocked merchants from various parts of the globe for trade. Fa-hian, who resided in this seat for two years in the beginning of the fifth century AD, preparing copies of sutras and drawing pictures of images, found the religion flourishing with 24 monasteries in the country. A terracotta plaque with a relief of the Buddha in the bhumi-sparsha-mudra with the Buddhist creed written in Gupta characters was found in Panna.

Hiuen-Tsang visited Bengal in about AD 638. He writes about four kingdoms:

(1) Pundravardhana (Northern Bengal) with 20 monasteries, and about 3,000 monks of both the Hinayana and Mahayana orders

(2) Samatatac Tippera (Noakhali region of south-eastern Bengal) with more than 30 monasteries, 2,000 monks of the Sthavira sect and an Ashokan stupa near the capital

(3) Tamralipti (south-western part of Bengal) with about 10 monasteries (as against 24 of Fa–hian), more than 1,000 monks and an Ashokan stupa near the capital

(4) Karnasuvarna (northern part of western Bengal) with more than 10 monasteries also 2,000 monks of the Sammitiya sect

In the seventh century AD, among the many centers of Buddhism in eastern India, Harikela earned the reputation of being a great seat of learning. I Tsing, a Chinese pilgrim in his *Memories of Priests* who visited India refers to A-li-ki-lo or O-li-ki-lo, identified with Harikela.

Buddhism reached its zenith under the active patronage of the Parama Sangata Palas. They ruled over four centuries in major parts of Bengal, and saw the growth of a large number of monasteries which became the radiating centers of Buddhist learning.

The prosperity of Buddhism in south-eastern Bengal was uninterrupted, even though the supremacy of the Palas was overthrown here by the Chandras (AD 900–1050), the new rulers being ardent Buddhists themselves. The manuscript in the Cambridge University Library contains paintings that depict the famous Buddhist divinities of this tract, including the two-armed seated Tara of Chandradvipa, the 16-armed seated Chunda of Pattikera, etc. while a manuscript from AD 1071, presumed to be in the library of the Asiatic Society of Bengal, adds another famous image of Samatata, namely, Buddharddhi Bhagavati Tara.

The long rule of the Palas saw the enormous growth of this Vajrayana pantheon. Many sculptures from this category are now in Bangladesh and Indian museums, as well as the Asutosh Museum in Kolkata.

In the beginning of the 13th century, Muhammad Khaliji fled to eastern Bengal, but the majority of the Buddhist centers did not long survive the Muslim conquest.

Buddhist Sites

Nandadirghi Vihara – Jagajjivanpur

Location: Jagajjivanpur 36 km east of Malda town close to Rajshahi district in Bangladesh

To the north-east of the village are a number of mounds, locally known as Dangas and Bhitas. Among the prominent mounds are Tula Bhita or Salai Danga, Akhari Danga, Nim Danga, Mai Bhita or King's mother's Mound, and Nand Garh which was thoroughly destroyed. Apart from these places, several other archaeological sites have also been identified here.

The importance of this site was indicated by a chance discovery of a copperplate charter. On March 13, 1987, a local resident came upon the charter while digging a piece of land at Tula Bhatia. The charter turned out to be an invaluable document revealing the identity of a hitherto unknown ruler from the Pala dynasty who ruled in Eastern India.

Issued from the victorious camp of Kuddala Khataka in the province of Pundravardhena in the seventh regal year (circa AD 854) of Maharajadhiraja Mahendrapala, the son and successor of Devapalsa, the charter mentions the constructions of a monastery (vihara) under the patronage of General Vajradeva at Nandadirghika Udranga for the increase of religious merits of the donor, of the parents of the donor, and all living beings. Vajradeva requested the king to grant him the above mentioned land for *'worship, copying (manuscripts) and such other activities'*. Accordingly, King Mahendrapala granted the required land for eternity.

Jagajjivanpur is immensely rich in terracotta plaques; more than 250 plaques have been found from the Tula Bhita mound alone. Made of fine clay, often with a micaceous compound, the plaques are normally red in colour. The Jagajjivanpur plaques present a broad range of themes – mundane, sacred, and decorative.

Apart from adding a new ruler to the already complex Pala genealogy, the charter provides detailed information about a Buddhist establishment in northern Bengal – probably one of many viharas to which Sandhyakara Nandin would allude at a later date. Inscriptional evidence indicates in categorical terms that the vihara was constructed in the ninth century, an event celebrated by the charter.

Vidyadhari Region in South Bengal

Location: The river Vidyadhari branches off from the river Bhagiratji at Tribeni, about 52 km south of Kolkata and flows down in a north-easterly direction with several branches and also, with some of her tributaries to the Bay of Bengal after traversing a distance of about 120 km.

This vast area was dotted with numerous cities and ports even in the pre-Christian and early Christian eras.

A village to village survey in this region has led to the discovery of 17 sites that yielded remains of Buddhist monuments.

Simulia

The site in Simulia lies within the jurisdiction of PS Gaighata in the district of north Paraganas, and three big mounds have been discovered here – Manglapota, Bhogapota and Sivapota. The unauthorised exposition of the mound of Manglapota has brought to light the ruins of a massive structure, which might be the remains of a Buddhist establishment. Incidentally, the names of some of the neighbouring villages of Simulia end with the affix 'thuba', which distinctly points towards the Buddhist origin of these names.

Ancient Mound Bharatpur, Barddhaman

This site was jointly excavated by the Archaeological Survey of India and the University of Barddhaman (1972-73 and 1973-74) and they have put together information about the findings of Buddhist artefacts dating from the Chalcolithic period to circa AD 12-13 century. During the later period circa AD 800-900 a Buddhist stupa was constructed at the site.

Chandraketugarh

The ancient site of Chandraketugarh near Berachampa is in the district of north 24 Paragansa. Paragansa covers an area of about 3 sq. km of rolling mounds; a garh with a rampart wall, represents an early historical urban settlement, which existed through later years as well.

During successive excavations, a stupendous brick temple complex facing the north with long projections on three sides, a vestibule attached to the main shrine, the remains of two votive stupas and some significant antiquities like a red-mottled sandstone Buddha image, plaques with stories about the Buddha and the *Jataka* tales were discovered which revealed its connections with Buddhism.

Khas Balanda

Situated at a distance of about 10 km south-east of Berachampa in the same district, Khas Balanda is marked with the ruins of an ancient religious establishment, probably belonging to the late Gupta or early Pala period, which was ultimately converted into a mosque, named Lal Masjid. This heavy stone and brick structure has been identified by some scholars of repute with the Buddhist vihara Balanda mentioned in a Nepalese manuscript. Studded with several mounds, this site and some places in the neighbouring villages Dhara and Dhangor have yielded some important antiquities related to a Buddhist establishment, which includes a magnificent standing image of Bodhisattva Manjushri made in black basalt dating to about 11th century AD.

Sitakunda

The village Situkunda, 2 km east of the Baruipur Railway junction has numerous mounds, old ponds, and an ancient underground massive brick structure.

Baishata

Situated on the northern bank of the river Nalua in the district South 24 Parganas, Baishata, the huge twin mounds of Baishata Mathavadi was identified by Renell in his map of deltaic Bengal as

Pagoda in 1978-79. Recent trial digging in these mounds conducted by the State Archaeology Department of West Bengal has exposed a brick stupa foundation, a circumambulatory path around the main structure and other material remains pertaining to a Buddhist settlement.

Dhosa

The remains of a Buddhist monument have been discovered at Dhosa situated on the western bank of river Piyalli, at a distance of about 10 km from Gocharan Railway station.

Lower Gangetic Valley

Fartabad

Fartabad, situated at a distance of 3 km south-west of Garia railway station, has some old ponds and underground structural remains. A horde of sculptures of Buddhist and Brahmanical images were found here. Other small villages around Fartabad area such as Ghoser Chank Kankandighi and Raidighi proved beyond doubt the value of the antiquities at the site. The antiquities found here are portable fine-grained sandstone images of Tara and a similar Hariti made in metal.

Kankandighi

A statue of the Buddha in low-relief, carved in stone, has been discovered at Kankandighi and is now preserved in the Khadi – Chhatrabhog Samgrahasala in South 24 Paraganas. It shows the Buddha seated in Vajraparyankasana on a visvapadma with a lotus-stalk and leaves rising from the pedestal and exhibiting saamadhimudra. The figure is depicted within an arched frame supported by two pillars on both sides.

Devil's Mound and Raja Karuna's Palace, Chiruti, Murshidabad

The mounds locally known as Rakshasidanga and Raka Karuna's Palace (Rajabari Danga) have been excavated by the Archaeological Survey of India and Archaeology Department of University of Kolkata respectively. The discovery of a terracotta seal by the University of Kolkata bearing the legend 'Raktamrittika Mahavihara' has identified the location of the monastery bearing the same name as described in the accounts of Hiuen Tsang who visited the place in the first half of the seventh century AD. A wide area contains vestiges of ancient remains datable to AD 100-1500.

Barakona Devi Mound, Panchthupi, Murshidabad

It is one of the groups of five mounds indicating remains of a stupa as signified by the word 'Panchthupi' (as it is locally known today). The mound, undated, is nearly 70 feet in diameter, the exposed portions of which show bricks of a large size.

Discovery of a Pre-Pala Monastic Complex at Moghalmari, Dantan, West Midnapur

The Department of Archaeology, University of Kolkata, under the direction of Dr. Asok Detta and assisted by other faculty members, PhD students and technical staff resumed the excavation at Moghalmari since February 15, 2007. The excavations have so far revealed the existence of Pre-Pala (possibly seventh-eighth century AD) Buddhist monastic complex (with extensive stucco and/or lime decoration on the eastern part of the mound). These exquisite decorative elements in stucco/ lime are unique in eastern India. Embellishments on the front wall of the temple in particular and the monastic establishment(s) in general, will definitely throw new light not only on the early medieval history of western Midnapur, but also on that of the entire West Bengal. The Buddhist character of the monastery is further supported by the discovery of a stone sculpture representing the Buddha in the well known bhumi-sparsha-mudra pose. The discovery of the Moghalmari monastic complexes is unquestionably comparable to those discovered at Nalanda (south Bihar), Raktamrittika (Chhiruti, Murshidabad) and Nandadirgghika (Jagajjivanpur, Malda).

The earlier excavation in 2003-04 at the same site had revealed the existence of terracotta stupa bases and a clear indication of the existence of a monastic complex. The monastic complex is dated on the basis of a terracotta inscription in Post-Gupta Brahmi characters from the early sixth or seventh centuries AD.

The excavations further reveal a series of cells attached to the outer wall of the monastery in the western part of the mound and the temple complex to the eastern part of the mound. Besides, the excavations have also yielded terracotta lamps, iron nails, as well as a commendable variety of ceramics including red, buff, and different shades of grey wares.

Monasteries in Darjeeling

Bhutia Busty Monastery

The Bhutia Busty monastery is located about 1.5 km from Chowrasta. Founded in 1879, the monastery follows the Vajrayana school of Kaygyud Na Nijingmapa order (Red Hat sect).

The origin of Darjeeling's name is linked to this monastery. In Tibetan, 'Dorjee' means thunderbolt and 'ling' means resting place. Once the monastery was located on the Observatory Hill in the 19th century, before it was shut down by the Nepalese, and was reconstructed on the present site in 1934, according to traditional Tibetan architectural conventions. It now shows a strong Sikkimese influence.

Dali Monastery

Druk Thubten Sangan Choling or Dali Monastery was founded by Kyabje Thuksey Rinpoche, a disciple of Drukchen Tenzin Khenrab Gelek Wangpo, the great monk of Drukpa Kargyud lineage. The sole aim of this monastery is to safeguard the Buddhist religion and Tibetan culture.

Ghoom Monastery

Ghoom monastery, also spelt as Ghum, is the popular name of the Sampten Choling monastery or Yiga Choling monastery located at Ghum at an elevation of 8,000 feet, it is about 8 km from Darjeeling. The Monastery follows the Gelukpa sect of Tibetan Buddhism. The original monastery was built in 1915 and has supported the monastic community over the years.

The Monastery houses a 15 feet high statue of Maitreya Buddha polished in gold embedded with precious stones, and is a major attraction in the monastery. Thangkas adorn the ancient walls of the monastery. The Library has preserved 108 volumes of Khangyur and other religious scriptures.

Ghoom monastery was built in 1875 by Lama Sherab Gyatso and is the largest of the three monasteries in Ghum.

Makdong Monastery

'Makdong' means warding off war. The monastery was so named as it was built at the time of the First World War. The monastery was built to safeguard the social, cultural, and ethnic identity of the Yolmowa community. It was built by Sangay Lama, a highly respected religious leader of the Yolmowa sect.

Zang Dhok Palri Phodang Monastery

Zang Dhok Palri Phodang is located atop Durpin Hill. It was constructed in 1976 by the visiting Dalai Lama. The monastery houses a rare collection of scriptures that were brought into India after the invasion of Tibet in 1959. The gonpa has impressive wall paintings in the prayer room, and a rare three-dimensional mandala.

West Bengal and Sikkim are neighbouring states. You can visit the important monasteries in Sikkim as well, as the main starting point for Darjeeling and Gangtok is one and the same. Convenient, private and state transport is easily available from the main connecting station that is Siliguri, or New Jalpaiguri. Accommodation is available to suit the needs of every tourist.

Before I could start collecting information about Buddhist sites, I never thought of the presence of archaeological Buddhist sites in West Bengal, except for a few monasteries. As per my regular habit, I visited the ASI office of Government of India as well as the Government of West Bengal. During my visit to Kolkata, I also visited the Deputy Registrar of the University of Kolkata as I heard they had some publications I could refer to. I am grateful to Mr. Gautam Sengupta, Director of Archaeology, Museum,

Cultural Affairs Department, Government of West Bengal, who sent information about archaeological sites in West Bengal by courier to my house from as far as Kolkata to Kolhapur in Maharashtra. Mr. Sujit Kumar Barua, Deputy Registrar of University of Kolkata has obliged me by reading and correcting this chapter about the archaeological sites at West Bengal.

General Information

Area: 88, 752

Capital: Kolkata

Boundaries: Orissa, Jharkhand, Bihar, Sikkim

Countries – Nepal, Bhutan, Bangladesh and Bay of Bengal

Chief Language: Bengali

Main Towns: Kolkata, Kharagpur, Medinipur, Asansol, Murshidabad, Siliguri

Air: Kolkata, Bagdogra, Kalaikunda, Panagarh, Malda, Barrackpore, Behala, Balurghat, Coochbehar

Rail: Length – 3,697.25 km; Railway stations – Howrah, Asansol, Sealdah, Kharagpur, New Jalpaiguri

Road: Length – 79,255 km including 1,715 km NH

APPENDIX 1

Sample Itineraries for the Buddhist Sites in India

Itinerary 1

Cities Covered: Patna, Bodhgaya, Rajgir, Nalanda, Patna, Vaishali, Patna, Varanasi, Sarnath, Kushinagar, Lumbini, Kapilvastu, Sravasti, Varanasi

Expected duration – 10 to 12 days

Itinerary 2

Cities Covered: Patna, Bodh Gaya, Rajgir, Nalanda, Patna, Vaishali, Kushinagar, Lumbini, Kapilvastu, Sravasti, Varanasi, Sarnath, Varanasi

Expected duration – 10 to 12 days

Itinerary 3

Cities Covered: Kolkata, Darjeeling, Kalimpong, Gangtok, Bagdogra, Kolkata

Expected duration – 7 to 9 days

Itinerary 4

Cities Covered: Delhi, Patna, Bodh Gaya, Rajgir, Nalanda, Patna, Kolkata, Darjeeling, Gangtok, Bagdogra, Kolkata

Expected duration – 10 to 12 days to see major monasteries

Itinerary 5

Cities Covered: Delhi, Bhubhaneshwar, Dhauli, Udayagiri, Lalitagiri, Ratnagiri, Lungudi and around hill, Radhanagar Fort and Port, Bhubhaneshwar, Kolkata, Darjeeling, Gangtok, Bagdogra, Kolkata

Expected duration – 12 to 15 days

Itinerary 6

Cities Covered: Mumbai, Aurangabad, Bhopal, Agra, Varanasi and then proceed to U.P. and Bihar

Expected duration – 15 to 21 days

Itinerary 7

Cities Covered: Mumbai, Aurangabad and around Aurangabad, Hyderabad and then to Vijaywada, Visakhpatnam and around these cities

Expected duration – 9 to 11 days

Itinerary 8

Cities Covered: Delhi, Jaipur, Agra, Mathura, Delhi and then by air to other states

Expected duration – Up to Delhi 6 to 7 days

Maharashtra and Gujarat can be a good combination as new information about Buddhist sites in Gujarat is emerging.

Andhra Pradesh, Himachal Pradesh, Ladakh, Maharashtra, Sikkim are dotted with many known and unknown sites.

At present, Bihar, Uttar Pradesh, Ladakh and Sikkim are world renowned for Buddhist sites. Tourists also visit a few sites in Andhra Pradesh, Maharashtra and Orissa. But these states are dotted with innumerable places where studies and archaeological excavations are being carried out.

These itineraries are only suggestions. Infrastructural and transport facilities are changing rapidly in India. The Government and Ministry of Tourism is trying hard to promote tourism in India. These days, tourists can travel to any place according to their budget and timeframe.

APPENDIX 2

Vipassana

Vipassana is one of India's most ancient meditation techniques. It was rediscovered 2,500 years ago by Gautama Buddha, and is the essence of what he practised and taught during his 45-year ministry. During the Buddha's time, a large number of people in northern India were freed from the bonds of suffering by practising Vipassana, allowing them to attain great success in all spheres of life. Over time, the technique spread to the neighbouring countries of Burma, Sri Lanka, Thailand, and others, where it had the same ennobling effect.

Five centuries after the Buddha, the noble heritage of Vipassana had disappeared from India. The purity of its teaching was lost as well. In Burma, however, it was preserved by a chain of devoted teachers. From generation to generation, over 2,000 years, this dedicated lineage transmitted the technique in its pristine purity.

In our time, Vipassana has been reintroduced in India, as well as to citizens from more than 80 other countries, by Shri S N Goenka. Goenkaji was authorised to teach Vipassana by the renowned Burmese Vipassana teacher, Sayagyi u Ba Khin. Before he died in 1971, Sayagyi was able to see one of his most cherished dreams realised. He had the strong wish that Vipassana should return to India, the land of its origin, to help it emerge from its manifold problems. From India, he felt sure it would benefit all mankind.

Goenkaji began conducting Vipassana courses in India in 1969, after 10 years, he began to teach in foreign countries as well.

Vipassana courses are held regularly at permanent centers and rented sites in different countries. Vipassana is a path to freedom from all suffering; it eradicates cravings, aversion and ignorance that are responsible for all our miseries. Those who practise it remove, little by little, the root causes of their sufferings and steadily emerge from the darkness of worries to lead happy, healthy, productive lives. There are many examples bearing testimony to this effect.

For further information about Vipassana centers in India contact the main Vipassana Centre in India:

Vipassana International Academy

Dhamma Giri, Igatpuri

Dist. Nasik, Maharashtra, India

Tel. (91) 02553 244076, 244178

Web: www.vridhamma.org

Email: info@vridhamma.org

APPENDIX 3

REFERENCES

Monisha Mukundan, *Ashoka – The Great*, Rupa and Company

Ancient Buddhist Monasteries – India & Nepal, Archaeological Remains, Monuments & Museums, Part I & II, Archaeology Survey of India, New Delhi

Debala Mitra, *Buddhist Monuments*, Kolkata

T.W. Rhys Davids, *Buddhist India*, Motilal Banarsidas Publishers Pvt. Ltd,. New Delhi

Major R.S., *Buddhist Cave Temples of India*, Wauchope

Owen C. Kail, *Buddhist Cave Temples of India*, Taraporevala & Co. Mumbai

Maj. R.S.Wauchope, *Buddhist Cave Temples of India*

Jas Burgess, *Buddhist Cave Temples and Their Inscriptions*, Archaeology Society of India, New Delhi

Sukumar Dutt, *The Teaching of Buddha Society for the Promotion of Buddhism Tokyo-Japan Buddhist Monks & Monasteries of India*

E.J. Thomas, *Buddhist scriptures*, Pilgrims Publishing, Varanasi

A.C. Jain, *Buddha & Buddhist Shrines in India*, Jainco Publications, New Delhi

Buddhist Shrines in India, Ministry of Information & Broadcasting, Govt. of India

Devapriya Valisinha, *Buddhist Shrines in India*, Mahabodhi Society, Sri Lanka

S. Radhakrishhnan, *Gautama: The Buddha*, Hind Kitabs Limited Bombay

Bimal C. Law, *Geography of early Buddhism*, Trubner & Co. London

Romesh C. Dutt, *Civilization in the Buddhist Age BC 320 to AD 500*, Low Price Publication, New Delhi

Essence of Buddhism, Tibet House, New Delhi

Nan Huai-chin, *Basic Buddhism – Exploring Buddhism and Zen*, Jaico Publishing House, New Delhi

H. Hackman, *Buddhism as a Religion*, Low Price Publications, New Delhi

Sister Nivedita, *Footfalls of Indian History*, Advaita Ashram Kolkata

Stella Kremisch, *Holy Places in India*

Dr. B.R. Ambedkar, *The Buddha and His Dhamma*, Buddha Bhoomi Publication

The Buddha & his message, Popular Prakashan, Mumbai

D.D. Kosambi, *The Culture and Civilization of Ancient India in Historical Outline*, Vikas Publishing House Pvt. Ltd., New Delhi

Dr. R.L. Soni, *The Cultural Background of India*, The Institute of Buddhist Culture

Prof. P.V. Bapat, *2500 years of Buddhism*, Publication Division Ministry of Information and Broadcasting

D.C. Ahir, *Gautama Buddha*, Books for all

R.R. Diwakar, *Bhagwan Buddha*, Bhartiya Vidya Bhavan, Mumbai

Sister Nivedita, *Siva and Buddha*, Udbodhan Office Kolkata

Swami Raghunathanda, *Bhagwan Buddha & Our Heritage*, Advaita Ashrama, Kolkata

Editor: P.N. Chopra, *India Early history*, Publication Division, Ministry of Information & Broadcasting

Madan Gopal, *India Through the Ages*, Publication Division, Ministry of Information & Broadcasting

Edited by Vijay Sri, *India is One*, Aurobindo Society, Pondicherry

D.C. Ahir, *Buddhist Shrines in India*, B.R. Paperback New Delhi

Duncan Forbes, *The Buddhist Pilgrimages*, Motilal Banarasidass Publishers, New Delhi

Sukumar Dutta, *Buddhist Monks & Monasteries of India*

Swami Vivekananda, *Buddha & His Message*, Advaita Ashrama Kolkata

Ven. Dr. Dodamgoda Rewatha Thero, *The Lotus Path from Lumbini to Kushinagara*, Varanasi

Encyclopedia of Indian Culture, Ramakrishna Mission

Edited by A. Ghosh, *An Encyclopedia of Archaeology*, Munshiram Manoharlal, New Delhi

Reviews – *Archaeology Survey of India*, New Delhi

ANDHRA PRADESH

B.R. Subrahmanyam, *Buddhist Relic caskets in Andhradesa*, Ananda Buddha Vihara, Secundarabad

K.R. Subramaniam, *Buddhist Remains in Andhra & the history of Andhra between 225 & 610 AD.*

B. Subrahmanyam, *History of Buddhism in Andhra, Buddhist Relic caskets in South India*, Bharatiya Kala Prakashan, New Delhi

Department of Archaeology, *Vajrayana Buddhist Centres in South India, Buddhist Archaeology in Andhra Pradesh*, Govt. of Andhra Pradesh

The Lotus Path, Department of Archaeology; Govt. of Andhra Pradesh

Andhra Sculptures, The Govt. of Andhra Pradesh

Amaravati; Nagarjunkonda, Archaeology Survey of India New Delhi

Brochures & leaflets on Buddhism, Andhra Pradesh Tourism Development Corporation

BIHAR & UTTAR PRADESH

R.B. Lal, *Bodh Gaya,* Department of Publication, Bihar

Glimpses of Gaya & Bodh Gaya, Kushinagara, Ministry of Information, Government of India

J. Vijaya Tunga, *Lumbini to Kushinagara,* Sri Lanka

Dr. Gitu Giri, *Lumbini: The Buddhist World,* Lumbini Academy, Lumbini

Dr. Gopal Sharma, *Nalanda University,* Educational Development Institute, Nalanda

K.C. Amit Singh, *The Buddhist Heritage of Magadha*

Rajgir, Nalanda, Pawapuri, Bodh Gaya guide, Rakhi Prakashan, Gaya

Sarnath, Sravasti, Archaeology Survey of India, New Delhi

Uttar Pradesh A to Z, Uttar Pradesh Tourism development Corporation

GUJARAT

M.S. Moray, *Buddhism in Gujara,* Saraswati Book House, Ahmedabad

Brochures & leaflets on Buddhism, Gujarat Tourism Development Corporation

HIMACHAL PRADESH

B.R. Sharma, *State of Our Union Himachal Pradesh,* Publication Division, Ministry of Information & Broadcasting

The Buddhist Trail in Himachal Pradesh, Good Earth Publication, New Delhi

Himachal Pradesh A to Z, Brochures & leaflets on Buddhism, Himachal Pradesh Tourism Development Corporation

JAMMU & KASHMIR

Lonely Planet, A to Z Jammu & Kashmir

Brochures & leaflets on Buddhism, Jammu & Kashmir Tourism Development Corporation

R.C. Roychoudhary, *Ladakh – The Land & People, History and Culture of Ancient Kashmir*

HARYANA

Save Stupas, Save Buddha, The Buddhist Forum Voice of Dhamma

KARNATAKA

Buddhism in Karnataka

KERALA

Buddhism in Kerala, Vajrayana Buddhist Centres in Kerala & Mysore

MAHARASHTRA

Umendra Verma, *Aurangabad-Daulatabad-Ellora-Ajanta*, Jayna publishing co., New Delhi

M.N. Deshpande, *Buddhism in Maharashtra*

States of Our Own Union – Maharashtra, Publication Division, Ministry of Information and Broadcasting

M.K. Dhavalikar, *Late Hinayana caves of Western India*, Deccan College Postgraduate and Research Institute, Pune

Panhahale Kaji; Ajanta, Archaeology Survey of India New Delhi

Brochures & leaflets on Buddhism, Archaeology Survey of India — Aurangabad Circle, Maharashtra Tourism Development Corporation Gazetteer of Bombay, Thana, Konkan

NORTH INDIAN STATES

Brochures & leaflets on Tourism, North Indian States, Department of Tourism

ORISSA

Thomas Donaldson, *Buddhist Heritage of Orissa, Archaeology of Orissa, Iconography of the Buddhist Sculpture of Orissa*, Abhinav Publications, New Delhi

Dr. Bimalendu Mohanty, *Glimpses of Buddhist Legacy*, Winsom Books India, New Delhi

Debala Mitra, *Lalitgiri, Udayagiri, Ratnagiri*, Archaeology Survey of India, New Delhi

N.K. Sahu, *History of Orissa*, Department of Archaeology, Orissa State

WEST BENGAL

Information supplied by Archaeological Survey of India, Govt. of India & Govt. of West Bengal, Brochures & leaflets on Buddhism, West Bengal Tourism Development Corporation

PUNJAB

Buddhism in North India & Pakistan Brochures, Punjab Tourism Corporation

SIKKIM

Information on all Buddhist monasteries provided by Ecclesiastical Affairs Department, Government of Sikkim

Heritage of Sikkim, Archaeological Survey of India – Kolkata Division

Brochures & leaflets, Tourism Development Corporation of Sikkim

GLOSSARY

Abhidhama: Knowledge of Dhamma, or of Enlightenment

Ahimsa: Not harming a living being

Amitabha: The primary Bodhisattva in the northern Mahayana pantheon

Arhat: An enlightened person, who has extinguished craving and achieved Nirvana

Ashokan Edicts: Edicts engraved on stone and pillars by Ashoka, the great Mauryan king, in which he described rules of morality and how his subjects should live and be ruled.

Atthamahathanani: Eight places of pilgrimage for Buddhists.

Avalokiteswara: The Mahayana Bodhisattva of compassion

Bhikshu/Bhikku: Literally, a beggar, the name by which the Buddha called his followers

Bodhi: Enlightenment, realisation

Bodhisattva: Bodhi – knowledge, sattva – in embryo; one in whom true knowledge developed. A being in the final stage of attaining Buddhahood, who has vowed to help all sentient being to achieve Nirvana

Bodhi Tree: The Pipal tree under which while Gautama was in a state of meditation he attained 'Knowledge' or 'Enlightenment'

Brahmi: The script used for writing inscriptions by the Mauryans. The inscriptions on Ashok's pillars were in Prakrit language, Brahmi script.

Buddha: The Enlightened One

Chaitya: A sacred place; most commonly used as halls of worship

Chakra: Literally, wheel; a recurring motif in Buddhist art; a symbol of Buddha's teachings

Chankama: Pradashinapath, or circumambulatory path

Chham: A dance performed by Buddhist monks wearing masks, which ends with the symbolic destruction of evil

Chhatra: The umbrella on the top of the stupa

Chorten: Tibetan for stupa

Dagoba: Derived from Dhatugarba or Dhatugoba, synonymous with the word Chaitya

Dhamma: Sanskrit Dharma, for Buddhists it refers to the teachings of the Buddha

Dhammapada: Religious books containing the sayings of Buddha

Dhamma yatra: Buddhist pilgrimages

Dhyana: A state of mind achieved through higher meditation

Dukhang: Assembly hall

Dukka: Sufferings. The Buddhist concept that the world is characterised by more unsatisfactory experiences than pleasure

Garbha: The hemispherical dome of a stupa – a womb.

Gelukpa: A sect of Vajrayana Buddhism, also known as yellow hat sect. The Dalai Lama is a member of this sect.

Gompa: Gonpa/ monastery

Gon-khang: Secret chamber where the chief protective deity of Gelukpas, Mahakala Vajrabhairava is enshrined and one can find masks, weapons and shulls that help in performing protective rituals

Hinayana: Literally small vehicle. A term used by the Mahayanists to describe earlier orthodox sects of Buddhism (Theravada school). Their scriptures are written in Pali, an ancient Indian language

Jatakas: The stories of the Buddha's previous lives before he become the Buddha. These tales often have a didactic message, but also serve as entertainment

Kagyupa: A sect of Vajrayana Buddhism, it lays stress on mysticism and direct transmission of esoteric teaching from Master to disciple

Kangyur Text: Collected editions of Buddha's teachings

Lama: A teacher or guru, the term specially refers to incarnate monks regarded as spiritual preceptors. The title Dalai Lama, literally means the Ocean of Wisdom

Lha-khang: The main prayer hall of the monastery

Law of Anicca: Everything is perishable, nothing is permanent

Mahayana: Literally Great Vehicle. One of the two major forms of Buddhism, Mahayana is considered the more liberal and practical. Its scriptures are written in Sanskrit. The school of Buddhism that is predominant in China, Korea, Vietnam and Japan

Mandala: Ritual drawings which represent the cosmos

Mani stones: Stones carved with the sacred chant 'Om Mani Padme Hum', the sacred and powerful mantra of Avalokitesvara

Mantra: Ritual sound, word, or phrase used to evoke certain religious effects

Mara: The personification of evil. The god of death.

Mudra: An attitude. Buddha is depicted in five definite 'attitudes' or 'mudras' the most usual of which are (1) the Dharma-chakra-mudra (turning the wheel of the law) where he is represented sitting on a 'simhasana' with his hands in front of his breast holding the little finger of the left hand between the thumb and forefinger of the right; (2) the Dhyana-mudra (attitude of abstract meditation), where he sits with his legs crossed over each other, with the palms on the feet, turned upwards; (3) the Vajrasana or Bhumi-sparsh-mudra (earth touching attitude), when the left hand is on the upturned soles of the feet, and the right resting over knee, pointing to the earth. These attitudes are liable to slight variation. There are others also – the right hand raised, in Abhaya-mudra; and when resting on his right side with his head to the north in which attitude he is said to have lain at his death.

Nirvana: Nir – without, van – desire. A state of mental bliss without craving or desire. Literally extinction, the ultimate goal of Buddhist characterised as the extinction of both craving and the extinguishing all illusions

Nyingmapa: Founded by Guru Padmasambhava, one of the four major sects of Vajrayana Buddhism

Padmapani: Padma – lotus, pani – hand. The lotus handed. One of the Bodhisattvas found in attendance on the Buddha

Pali: A dialect of Sanskrit. Pali is the language of the older collections of Buddhist scriptures and the scared language of the Theravada Buddhism

Parinirvana: The final extinction from samsara, the cycle of birth, life and death

Pitaka: Literally basket; three Pitakas in Pali which constitute the Buddhist canonical texts. They are the Vinaya, Sutra, and Abhidhama Pitaka

Prajna: Knowledge or wisdom

Pradakshinapatha: Circumambulatory path around the Lhakhang of the gonpa

Punya: Spiritual merit

Sangha: The Buddhist community of monks and nuns

Siddha: Yogic master or spiritual person adept in Tantra

Sutta: Aphoristic scripture; said to be the original teachings of the Buddha

Tara: Female saviour in Mahayana tradition

Tathagata: An epithet used for the Buddha; literally, the thus gone, or the thus come

Theragatha and Therigatha: Literature composed by the bhikkus and bhikkunis

Torana: An arched entrance

Triratna: Three jewels of Buddhism, the Buddha, the Dhamma, and the Sangha

Upasaka: Lay Buddhist follower

Vaijrayana: Literally, the vehicle of the vajra, the great movement in Mahayana Buddhism in Tibet. It is divided into four sects: Nyigmapa, Sakyapa, Gelukpa and Kagyupa in the chronological order of development.

Vassavasa or Varssavasa: A rain retreat for the Sangha

Vinaya Pitaka: Code of Buddhist discipline as set in Pali

Vihara: A cave dwelling for monks.

Yantra: Sacred diagram used for ritual purposes

www.ingramcontent.com/pod-product-compliance
Lightning Source LLC
Chambersburg PA
CBHW060105170426
43198CB00010B/779